OXFORD MEDIEVAL TEXTS

General Editors

C. N. L. BROOKE   D. E. GREENWAY
M. WINTERBOTTOM

MAGNA VITA SANCTI HUGONIS

THE LIFE OF ST HUGH OF LINCOLN

MAGNA VITA SANCTI HUGONIS

THE LIFE OF ST HUGH OF LINCOLN

VOLUME ONE

EDITED BY

THE LATE DECIMA L. DOUIE

Formerly Reader in History, University of Hull

AND

DAVID HUGH FARMER

Reader in History, University of Reading

CLARENDON PRESS · OXFORD

1985

Oxford University Press, Walton Street, Oxford OX2 6DP

London New York Toronto
Delhi Bombay Calcutta Madras Karachi
Kuala Lumpur Singapore Hong Kong Tokyo
Nairobi Dar es Salaam Cape Town
Melbourne Auckland

and associated companies in
Beirut Berlin Ibadan Mexico City Nicosia

Oxford is a trade mark of Oxford University Press

Published in the United States
by Oxford University Press, New York

First published by Thomas Nelson and Sons Ltd 1961
Reprinted with corrections and published by Oxford University Press 1985

British Library Cataloguing in Publication Data
Adam, b.c. 1150, Chaplain of St. Hugh
[Magna vita Sancti Hugonis. English & Latin].
Magna vita Sancti Hugonis = The life of St. Hugh of Lincoln.
—(Oxford medieval texts) 1. Hugh of Lincoln Saint   2. Catholic church—Bishops—Biography
3. Christian saints—Biography
I. Title.   II. Douie, Decima L.   III. Farmer, David Hugh
270.4'092'4   BX4700.H8
ISBN 0-19-822207-6 v.1
ISBN 0-19-822208-4 v.2

Library of Congress Cataloging in Publication Data
Adam, of Eynsham, fl. 1196-1232.
Magna vita Sancti Hugonis = The life of St. Hugh of Lincoln.
(Oxford medieval texts)
Text in English and Latin; introd. in English
Reprint. Originally published: Edinburgh; New York:
Nelson, 1961. With new pref.
Bibliography: p.
Includes index.
1. Hugh, of Avalon, Saint, 1135?-1200.
2. Christian saints—England—Biography.
I. Douie, Decima L. (Decima Langworthy), 1901-1980.   II. Farmer, David Hugh.
III. Title.   IV. Title: Life of St. Hugh of Lincoln.   V. Series.
BX4700.H8A62 1985   282'.092'4 [B]   84-27385
ISBN 0-19-822207-6 (v. 1)
ISBN 0-19-822208-4 (v. 2)

Printed in Great Britain
at the University Press Oxford
by David Stanford
Printer to the University

282.0924
Hugh

CONTENTS

PREFACE

TO THE SECOND IMPRESSION

Since the first impression of this work went out of print, many requests have been made for its republication. This has now become possible owing to the revived interest in St Hugh. Preparations are advanced for the celebration in 1986 of the eighth centenary of his consecration as bishop of Lincoln. Grateful acknowledgement must be made to the Chancellor of Lincoln cathedral, Canon J. S. Nurser, and to the Willoughby Memorial Trust (Lincolnshire) which has made a generous contribution to the costs of printing. Minor errors and misprints have been corrected, while suggestions from reviewers for greater precision in a few passages have been adopted.

During the last twenty years a number of books have been published which shed further light on St Hugh. These include editions of the early Carthusian writings in *Sources Chrétiennes* with English translations by Eric Colledge and James Walsh.[1] Sir Walter Oakeshott has identified the Winchester Bible given to Hugh by Henry II as a manuscript still in the Bodleian Library, Oxford (see I, 86, note). Dr Diana Greenway has published a new edition of the *Fasti* for Lincoln, while Dr D. M. Smith has prepared a volume of St Hugh's Lincoln *Acta*.[2] This eagerly awaited work will add considerably to our knowledge of Hugh as a diocesan bishop, an aspect not fully covered in the present work by Adam of Eynsham.

Meanwhile other books have further illuminated some of Hugh's contemporaries. W. L. Warren's study of *Henry II*

[1] *Lettres des Premiers Chartreux* (ed. par un chartreux, *SC* 88, 1962) ; Guigues II, *Lettre sur la vie contemplative; douze méditations* (ed. E. Colledge et J. Walsh, *SC* 163, 1970) ; English translation by the same editors, *The Ladder of Monks* (London, 1978). Mention should also be made of the series *Analecta Cartusiana* (ed. J. Hogg, Salzburg, 1970-).

[2] J. Le Neve, *Fasti Ecclesiae Anglicanae 1066–1300, III Lincoln*, ed. D. E. Greenway (London, 1977) ; *English Episcopal Acta, Lincoln 1185-1200*, ed. D. M. Smith (British Academy, London, forthcoming).

(London, 1973) and C. R. Cheney's of *Hubert Walter* (London, 1967) reveal further the characters of outstanding rulers who did not always see eye to eye with Hugh. The latter's *Pope Innocent III and England* (Stuttgart 1976) tells us more of the lawsuits in which Hugh acted as judge-delegate of the Holy See. Two scholars who owed benefices to his patronage, Walter Map and Gerald of Wales, are better known than formerly: the former through *De Nugis Curialium* being republished, the latter through new translations of his works on Ireland and Wales. Here Lewis Thorpe has reminded us that the *Journey through Wales* was originally dedicated to Hugh.[3]

The death of my senior colleague and partner in this work, Dr Decima Douie, in 1980 unfortunately deprived this revision of her scholarly help; care has been taken to limit changes in the translation, which was her work, to those we believe she would have approved. Each section of the Introduction is initialled by the author responsible. As in the first impression, so also now, appreciative acknowledgement is made to the staffs of the libraries where we worked, especially the Bodleian Library, Oxford, and Quarr Abbey, and to the General Editors, particularly Sir Roger Mynors, whose unfailing encouragement of an inexperienced textual critic and scholar was decisive in bringing this work to completion.

University of Reading   DAVID HUGH FARMER
4 June 1984

---

[3] Walter Map, *De Nugis Curialium*, ed. M. R. James, revised by C. N. L. Brooke and R. A. B. Mynors, OMT 1983 ; Gerald of Wales, *The History and Topography of Ireland*, ed. J. J. O'Meara (Harmondsworth, 1982), *The Journey through Wales and The Description of Wales*, ed. L. Thorpe (Harmondsworth, 1978), pp. 38, 63. See also Robert Bartlett, *Gerald of Wales* (Oxford 1982).

INTRODUCTION

I

THE AUTHOR AND CONTENTS OF THE MAGNA VITA

St Hugh of Lincoln, the only professed Carthusian monk ever to be a bishop in England, was born about 1140 at Avalon near Grenoble in Imperial Burgundy.[1] He was the third and youngest son of a knight, who retired to the cloister of the Austin Canons at Villarbenoît after the death of his wife, and took Hugh with him, then only eight years old. In due time the latter was professed there as a canon and was placed in charge of a parish when still only a deacon, but at the age of about twenty-five he joined the nearby monastery of the Grande Chartreuse in obedience to a call which seemed irresistible. There, in a solitude which was seldom disturbed, he lived the semi-eremitical monastic life of prayer, reading and work, among beautiful but austere mountain surroundings.

In course of time he was appointed to the office of Procurator, which included the charge of the lay brothers, the guests and the whole temporal administration. His abilities and spiritual worth were made known by a knight of the neighbourhood to king Henry II, who obtained him in about 1179 as prior of Witham, his languishing Carthusian foundation in Somerset, begun a year or two before. So successful was Hugh in this charge and so acceptable to Henry II that the latter secured his election as bishop of Lincoln in 1186. Hugh did all he could to avoid the charge, but once he had accepted

---

[1] ' Vir igitur hic . . . de remotis imperialis Burgundie finibus, haud procul ab Alpibus, originem duxit.' Giraldus, *Vita S. Hugonis*, Dist. I, i, *Opera*, VII, 89. It is sometimes stated that Boniface of Savoy (archbishop of Canterbury 1243-1270) was a Carthusian : in reality he was twice a novice at the Grande Chartreuse but was never professed (cf. Le Couteulx, *Annales Ordinis Cartusiensis* (Montreuil, 1888), IV, 292).

it he proved himself a model bishop who so earned his contemporaries' affection and respect that his death in 1200 was
mourned by all classes as the death of a friend, and his funeral
was one of almost unparalleled magnificence. The chroniclers emphasise his pastoral zeal, his detestation of all
kinds of simony and his persistent struggle for the Church's
independence.

The control of the Church by the Crown and the churchmen's largely successful attempts to escape it have been recently
described as the principal features of English Church life
between Becket and Langton.[1] The government of the Church
by the new canon law, under the strong influence of the Papacy,
was being firmly established, and like any system it depended
for its success largely on those who administered it. Hugh,
as the ruler of one of the largest dioceses and the frequently
chosen judge delegate in important cases, played a prominent
part in this process, but his principal biographer, the Benedictine monk Adam of Eynsham, had little to say about his
activity in this sphere. Instead he gave to posterity a detailed
and vivid portrait of the saint, based on his own close contact
with him as his chaplain for the last three years of his life.
The acknowledged specialists in hagiography say that the
Magna Vita was written so accurately that no one who lived
in those days can be better known to us than Hugh. Its
reliability and fullness of detail are said to be almost unsurpassed
in medieval hagiography.[2]

Its author Adam, who was subprior and much later abbot
of Eynsham, belonged to an Oxford burgher family. His

---

[1] cf. C. R. Cheney, *From Becket to Langton* (1956) *passim*

[2] *Propylaeum ad Acta Sanctorum*, 529 ; cf. H. Thurston, *Butler's Lives of the Saints* (1938) XI, 228, and the same author's *Life of St Hugh of Lincoln* (1898), pp. x-xiii. See also J. F. Dimock, *Magna Vita S. Hugonis Lincolniensis* (R.S. 1864), p. xliv : ' We may look on much of what this volume contains as if it had been penned by Hugh's own hand.' Dimock was the first person to identify the author of the *Magna Vita* as Adam abbot of Eynsham. Previously, as in the abbreviation printed by Migne (P.L. 153, 937-1114), the work was attributed to ' Alexander of Canterbury.' In the MSS the work is entitled *Vita S. Hugonis* ; the appropriate name *Magna Vita* appears to be modern.

father, perhaps to be identified with a certain Edmundus Medicus, owned property there and died in the Holy Land between 1185 and 1190.[1] Willelmus de Oxonia appears in Eynsham charters as the abbot's brother, and another brother Edmund, a young cleric and a visionary, made himself known to Hugh. In 1196, Edmund, then a novice at Eynsham, became unconscious for two days and described to his brother Adam how he had seen the next world and especially Purgatory, where he witnessed the sufferings of many people he had known on earth. This vision was made public with Hugh's approval : its best manuscript is headed : ' Here begins the introduction of brother Adam, prior of Eynsham, to the vision of his brother and spiritual son, the monk Edmund, in the year of Our Lord 1196.' [2]

The bishop of Lincoln had the right of patronage to Eynsham abbey, and its close connection with the bishop made it easy for Hugh to seek a chaplain there. This Anglo-Saxon community of Benedictines, made famous by Aelfric, had been dispersed at the Conquest, but it was refounded by Remigius, first bishop of Lincoln. After being transferred to Stow in Lincolnshire by one bishop and sent back to Eynsham by another, the community settled down to a quiet and relatively uneventful existence. It was never a house of the first rank and numbered about thirty monks in the 13th century. But its situation on the main road to the West and its proximity to the royal hunting-lodge at Woodstock

---

[1] H. E. Salter, *Eynsham Cartulary* (O.H.S. 1907), II, 262, 272. For further information about Adam's family, *ibid.*, I, xv-xxi, II, 257-76.

[2] Edmund appears unnamed in *M.V.*, V, 3. The best MS of the Vision of the Monk of Eynsham is Digby 34, printed in vol. II of the *Eynsham Cartulary*, which alone makes Adam *prior* of Eynsham. Another text is in *Analecta Bollandiana* (1903), XXII 225-319. Another medieval writer, suggested by H. L. D. Ward, *Catalogue of Romances*, II, 512, to be Ralph of Coggeshall, gives as an argument for the vision's authenticity the fact that it was written by ' Dom Adam, subprior of the same monastery, a very grave and religious man . . . at that time chaplain to the lord Hugh, bishop of Lincoln ' (cf. MS Royal (B.M.) 13 D v, f. 45). Extracts of the vision were reproduced by Wendover and Matthew Paris. French and English versions exist, the latter under the misleading title ' The monk of Evesham ' (Arber, 1869 ; Paget, 1909).

and to Oxford brought it many visitors, and at a council held there in 1186 Hugh was elected bishop.[1] Ten years later he successfully vindicated his claim to its patronage after a long lawsuit, and he then stayed there for a week, arranging for the election of the new abbot, Robert of Dover, who was blessed in Lincoln cathedral on 11 November 1197.[2] It was now that Adam became Hugh's chaplain and inseparable companion for the last three years of his life.[3] His duties included the care of the bishop's vestments, jewels and relics, and he was also the bishop's confessor. This office especially enabled him to describe himself as ' pre ceteris episcopo familiarissimus,' and there can be no doubt that he was high in his master's favour, for he was one of the few who accompanied him on his journeys and even on his annual visit to his monastery at Witham.[4] Hugh's brethren there entrusted to Adam the task of writing the life at the suggestion of two former Benedictines in the community, Robert Fitz-Henry who had been prior and Ralph who had been sacrist of the cathedral priory of Winchester.[5]

The Carthusians had been judicious in their choice of a biographer. In spite of his conventional protests to the contrary, Adam's literary skill was quite sufficient for the task ; even more important was the spiritual insight which enabled him to appreciate Hugh and to realise the value of the contemplative life which made him what he was. Adam's accuracy and truthfulness, noticed by many readers, have been often confirmed by contemporary sources. His reverence for his master did not blind him to his apparent defects, and he made no attempt to gloss over the dying bishop's intransigence to his metropolitan, his peppery impatience with his canons or his irritation with his servants, which were in contrast to the

---

[1] *M.V.*, III, 1
[2] *M.V.*, IV, 8
[3] ' A quo tempore, per annos tres et dies quinque . . . die semper et nocte adherens ipsi et ministrans ei.' *M.V.*, II, prologue. Hugh died on 16 November 1200 : three years and five days before brings us to 11 November 1197.
[4] cf. *M.V.*, V, 14, 16 ; IV, 10
[5] *M.V.*, II, 14

perpetual equanimity described by the classic biographies of
St Anthony and St Martin.[1] Neither did he hide Hugh's
unusual accessibility to women, which was rather different from
the example of his own patron St Hugh of Grenoble and the
recommendations of the Carthusian *Consuetudines*.[2] Further
unconventional elements are Hugh's rejection of the example
of St Thomas of Canterbury who accepted fines instead of
penances, and his detachment, or even scepticism, about
supposed miracles.[3] Adam, in short, gives us not a *saint de
vitrail* but the portrait of a living man.

This portrait is avowedly incomplete. Like other bio-
graphers Adam underlined the traits which most appealed to
him while diminishing or omitting the others. As a result we
have an admirable picture of Hugh the monk and the saint,
but we learn little about him as diocesan administrator or
cathedral builder. Few readers would suspect that Hugh had
the reputation of being the most learned religious of his time in
England, or that he had revived the famous Lincoln schools.[4]
Even on Hugh's relations with his parochial clergy Adam is
tantalizingly reticent, and his work as judge delegate of the
pope is scarcely mentioned. But if Adam failed to describe the
full extent of Hugh's greatness, he did appreciate his God-
centred and self-forgetful life, in which contemplation bore
fruit in ardent and tireless charity.

After Hugh's death Adam probably returned to Eynsham.
Like many of the English clergy he went into exile during the
interdict. This may partly account for his unfavourable but

---

[1] *M.V.*, III, 12 ; V, 16

[2] *M.V.*, IV, 9, 12 ; *Consuetudines*, c. xxi (P.L. 153, 681-2)

[3] *M.V.*, IV, 7 ; III, prol. *Miraculum*, it should be noted, had at
this date, a wider and less precise meaning than it later acquired under
Scholastic influence. It was hardly distinct from *mirum*, an extraordinary
event proceeding from unknown causes which was a manifestation of
God's power (cf. *Dictionnaire de Théologie Catholique*, article ' Miracle,' and
A. van Hove, *La Doctrine du Miracle chez St Thomas* (1927), 26-41).

[4] cf. Ralph of Coggeshall, *Chronicon*, 111-2. His testimony agrees well with
that of Giraldus who described Hugh as *litteratissimus*, and credited him
with the feat of being able to complete from memory any sentence of the
Bible begun by another. cf. Gir., VII, 68, 90. For Hugh's welcome by
the students at Paris, cf. *M.V.*, V, 13.

shrewd account of king John. The date when he began the *Magna Vita* is not known, but the last chapter of book II was written after 1206, and part of book V was written in exile in 1212. It seems probable that the work was finished soon after.[1] Adam was elected abbot of Eynsham in the second half of 1213. There had been a vacancy for five years, caused by the death of abbot Robert in 1208 and the exile of Hugh of Wells, bishop of Lincoln (1209-35), who had left the country immediately after his appointment.[2] As abbot of Eynsham ' qui fuit capellanus dicti Hugonis episcopi ' Adam gave evidence in 1219 to the commission appointed by pope Honorius III to enquire into Hugh's life and miracles. He described the cure of the mad sailor and the phenomenon of torches remaining alight round Hugh's coffin on its journey from London to Lincoln. This was in preparation for the canonization of St Hugh which took place in 1220 and was announced by archbishop Langton at Henry III's second coronation.[3]

One event during his abbacy brought Adam into close touch with the town and university of Oxford, where his brother Edmund had been a student long before. Eynsham undertook to contribute 52/- a year to poor students and to give 2d. each to a hundred of them on the feast of St Nicholas. This contribution had been imposed on the town by cardinal Nicholas of Tusculum as a penance for the hanging of some students in a riot in 1209,[4] and it is possible that Eynsham took over this obligation in return for a lump sum of cash, for the monastery was in financial difficulties. In 1209 Eynsham was already in debt to the bishop ; in 1227 they also owed £152 10 0 to David the Jew of Lincoln. In the same year the chapter had decreed that nothing was to be sealed unless first read to them, and it was also alleged that Adam had cut the

---

[1] *M.V.*, V, prol. and 9, where Adam describes his visit to Cheshunt with the abbot of Waltham when they saw the sailor cured by Hugh thirteen years before, i.e. in 1199.

[2] *Eynsham Cartulary*, I, pp. xviii-xix, 171

[3] H. Farmer, ' The Canonization of St Hugh of Lincoln ' in *Lincs. Architectural and Archaeological Society Papers* (1956), 86-117

[4] *Eynsham Cartulary*, II, 163

woods wastefully. In 1229 he was deposed as ' a manifest dilapidator of the goods of the monastery'.[1] This accusation need not be taken too seriously as many monasteries were in financial difficulties at this time and contemporary popes were much concerned with reforming the system and giving the community adequate control. A similar charge had been made against Adam's predecessor Geoffrey (†1196). The interdict and the long vacancy had no doubt increased Eynsham's difficulties, and the example of St Hugh's boundless generosity was not the best possible training for an administrator of a small monastery.

After his deposition Adam's name still appeared as a witness to charters, and in 1233 he was exempted, possibly because of old age, from doing suit in person for the manor of Little Rollright, assigned to him by his monastery during his retirement.[2] This is the last mention of him, and he must have died soon after.

Although Adam's portrait of St Hugh was a vivid and personal one, its author also followed hagiographical convention to a certain extent. It was common form to assert, as Adam did, that one was only writing the truth, that one's work was only a heap of materials for more competent future writers, that it was written in very poor style without the eloquence which would do justice to the subject. The purpose of the work was ' not the ostentation of vain discourse, but the edification of readers who should find in Hugh's life a revelation of God's power and a model for imitation.' [3] To say that these statements were conventional is not to say that they were insincere ; in Adam's case they were true. But the assessment of the value

---

[1] *Annales Monastici* (R.S.), I, 70 ; *Rotuli Hugonis de Welles* (C. and Y.), II, 30 ; cf. *Eynsham Cartulary*, I, pp. xx, 234-5. For the wills of Hugh of Wells see *Historical MSS. Commission*, 10th Report, App. 3 ; Gir., VII, App. G
[2] *Calendar of Patent Rolls*, 1232-1247, 14-16 ; *Eynsham Cartulary*, I, p. xx
[3] *M.V.*, I, prol. ; V, 20

of his Life depends not so much on his frequent assertions that he was writing nothing of which he was not sure, but rather on the quality of his sources and the impression of his own character left by the *Magna Vita* itself.

His sources were few but good. Most important of them was Hugh himself. Like other hagiographies of the best class the *Magna Vita* was based on a close personal knowledge of its subject and it was written relatively soon after his death. Hugh was an excellent raconteur, and Adam's devotion to him, not unlike that of a medieval Boswell, was expressed by recording many authentic facts and sayings which would otherwise have been lost. The Carthusians, especially Bovo, were also helpful and accurate informants about Hugh's monastic life, while the old folk who lived near the Grande Chartreuse told Adam about Hugh's youth during their visit in 1200. Although Adam stated that other written lives were in existence, the only one he certainly used was Giraldus' sketch of Hugh in *De episcopis tergeminis*, a supplement to his *Vita S. Remigii*, written during Hugh's lifetime.[1]

Adam's education, as shown in his works, was of the usual monastic type. He had a detailed knowledge and a ready command of the text of the Bible, which he used for his purposes according to current convention. To us his selection of texts sometimes seems quaint or naïve; at other times it is appropriate enough. In his explanations he made use of the *Glossa Ordinaria*, Peter the Lombard's Gloss on the Psalter and at least one more which has not been identified. His patristic reading included St Jerome, St Gregory, Cassian and Bede. He also cited liturgical texts of all kinds, and several lives of the saints. The most important of these was the life of Hugh's favourite St Martin by Sulpicius Severus, perhaps the most popular hagiographical text of the Middle Ages. He used too the same author's letters about St Martin with Gregory of Tours' account of his miracles, and St Jerome's life of St Paul the first hermit, St Hilary's life of St Honoratus of Arles and Guigo the Car-

---

[1] *M.V.*, I, prol., II, prol. ; III, 6 ; Gir., VII, 73-6

thusian's life of St Hugh of Grenoble.[1] He also referred to such
minor works as the life of St Aicard of Jumièges, the miracles
of St Prejectus, and Gregory of Tours' account of the Seven
Sleepers. His classical citations include Virgil and Ovid,
known perhaps through *florilegia*. Like other hagiographers
who professed themselves ignorant, Adam was not averse to
displaying the extent of his reading, but nearly all his citations
are extremely short.

Adam was rather self-conscious about the limitations of his
monastic education in comparison with that of the curial clerics
who surrounded St Hugh and who took a far greater share in
diocesan affairs than Adam did. This led him into making
apparently unprovoked attacks on the *litterati* for finding his
own writing too rustic,[2] and into writing difficult and elaborate
passages, overcharged with rhetoric, where profusion of
metaphor and citation obscure rather than clarify the meaning.
The most obvious example of this is the prologue to book I.
Ironically the writers whom he tried to imitate wrote much
simpler as well as better Latin, and Adam's best efforts at fine
writing defeated their own end. But these passages are
relatively few, and Adam is more often seen to better advantage.

The choice of material and the scale of the biography were
in accordance with its purpose and Adam's knowledge of his
subject. As it was written by a monk for monks—it was
dedicated to Prior Robert of Witham—it is not surprising that
Hugh's monastic life is described fully and well, and that the
portraits of other monks are among the most vivid in the book.
And as Adam knew Hugh only at the end of his life, it is
understandable that his last years are described in much greater

---

[1] MS 107 of the Lincoln Chapter library, written in large characters
with wide margins in the late twelfth century, contains lives of various
saints, including SS Martin, Honoratus and Hugh of Grenoble, of which
last work it is the only known text of medieval England. In view of St
Hugh's origin in the diocese of Grenoble and his Carthusian esteem both
for Guigo and his patron saint (cf. *M.V.*, IV, 12), and Adam's citations
from this rare life, it seems reasonable to suppose that this MS was connected with St Hugh in some way, and may even have been used by
Adam when he wrote the *Magna Vita*.

[2] *M.V.*, I, 14

detail than his earlier ones. The account of Hugh's episcopate before Adam's arrival is very incomplete, but the thinnest part of the whole work is book I. Here the narrative is conventional, a murder story is introduced to hold the reader's attention, and Hugh himself hardly comes to life until he enters the Grande Chartreuse as a young canon of about twenty-five. There is moreover little indication that Hugh really *grew* in holiness ; perhaps Adam projected something of Hugh's mature perfection into his account of his early years. Here Giraldus complements Adam's picture : he recounts Hugh's skill in taming squirrels and birds at the Grande Chartreuse until forbidden to do so by the prior, and describes how in his early days as a bishop he was ' hot and rigid ', but that afterwards he became mellow and conformed himself to the practice of other bishops.[1]

Book II describes the early history of the Witham Charter-house, and it is especially valuable because all but a fragment of the early Witham chronicle is lost.[2] Adam shows Hugh as a capable and considerate superior to his monks, pressing forward the building activities while making sure that the former inhabitants received adequate compensation, encouraging good candidates but refusing to give a second trial to those who had proved themselves unsuitable, arranging for the copying of books for the library but returning to the monks of Winchester the magnificent Bible, prepared for their own use, which the king had exacted as a present from them. And meanwhile his favour and influence with king Henry had so increased (not-withstanding his frank reproofs) that it was said that there was no one in the whole of his dominions to whom the king would listen more readily.

Hugh's election to the see of Lincoln and his refusals to accept the charge are described from Adam's own point of view, and his account needs to be supplemented from Benedictus

[1] Gir., VII, 77-8, 91-2
[2] This was printed by Dom A. Wilmart in *Analecta Praemonstratensia* (1933), IX, 207 *et seq.*, under the title *Maître Adam chanoine Prémontré devenu chartreux à Witham*. This superseded an inaccurate text in *Bulletin of John Rylands Library* (1932), XVI, 482 *et seq.*

Abbas and the canonization report. In particular one may think that Adam is less than fair to the Lincoln canons, who, having first ventured on a free election of one of their own number, finally went to very great trouble to obtain Hugh as their bishop, who only consented after being told to do so by the prior of the Grande Chartreuse. Adam was also in error in ascribing the election to 1185 instead of 1186 : Hugh's episcopate lasted in reality for fourteen not fifteen years.[1] Soon after his enthronement the famous incident occurred at Woodstock, when Hugh by an impudent jest turned the king's anger into laughter after he had incurred disgrace for excommunicating a royal forester without his permission and then refusing a Lincoln prebend to the king's nominee. The incident is characteristic of one who, convinced of the Church's needs and rights, knew also how to maintain his position without giving offence : he showed that a keen natural sense of humour could be of greater service to the Church's cause than St Thomas Becket's keen natural sense of drama.[2]

Also in this book are to be found the description of Hugh's tame swan at Stow, so often represented in pictures and statues of St Hugh, and a delightful account of his fondness for children and theirs for him. Both of these naturalistic descriptions must be almost unique of their kind in medieval literature.[3]

Books IV and V represent Adam's own memories much more than books I–III. He describes how he had seen Hugh tending the lepers and how horrified he himself was at the sight of them. He also showed how Hugh's love of justice was realised in his conduct of legal cases, when bribes or intimidation

---

[1] The date of 1186 for Hugh's election is given by R. de Diceto, *Ymagines Historiarum*, II, 41 ; Howden II, 308 ; Benedictus Abbas, I, 345 ; Matthew Paris, *Chronica Majora*, II, 325. In his Prologue to Book II Adam said that he came to Hugh's service after his episcopate had lasted for ' twelve years and fifty-three days.' But Adam actually arrived on 11 November 1197 (q.v.), after Hugh had been bishop for *eleven* years. A similar inaccuracy was put in the mouth of Hugh at the Council of Oxford in 1197 where he said that he had been bishop ' fere per tredecim annos ' (*M.V.*, V, 5.)

[2] *M.V.*, III, 9-10

[3] *M.V.*, III, 6-7, 14

were quite powerless to prevent him from performing his duties. The moral courage which enabled him to withstand pressure from the strong and even from the king was matched by a physical courage shown especially in his facing unarmed some armed mobs who tried to kill him, most probably in the anti-Jewish riots.[1] But through all the activities of his episcopate, whether the ordinary ones of confirming, consecrating and ordaining or the more extraordinary ones mentioned above, he remained first and foremost a monk, and the happiest month of every year was the one he spent in his beloved monastery of Witham. Here he lived in all simplicity as a monk of the house who took his turn in the ordinary community duties in choir and whose special delight it was to wash the dishes.[2]

Some of Hugh's teaching on monastic life has been recorded by Adam. Unlike some monastic apologists in ancient and modern times he could not be accused of teaching that it was the only way of salvation. Not only monks, hermits and solitaries, he would say, will attain to the kingdom of God but from everyone it will be required that he has been a true Christian. From each is required charity in the heart, truth on the lips and chastity in the body. Of each of these virtues he gave a conspicuous example, but so little did he think they were exclusive to religious that he taught, with characteristic breadth of sympathy, that married people would obtain the same glory in Heaven as virgins and celibates.[3]

Book V is much the longest of the whole work, and a great deal of it is taken up with St Hugh's various journeys to France and his death and burial. At the beginning of it is described Hugh's own devotion to burying the dead, with a sermon he preached at a funeral, the only one of his to survive. But the principal events in its earlier chapters are Hugh's repeated refusals to yield to the demands of Richard I in matters which

[1] *M.V.*, IV, 4. cf. William of Newburgh, *Historia Rerum Anglicarum*, I, 310 *et seq.*
[2] *M.V.*, IV, 10
[3] *M.V.*, IV, 9

he regarded as violations of the Church's rights. These brought about the greatest crises in Hugh's life. At the Council of Oxford in 1197 he refused to provide knights for overseas service at a critical moment in Richard I's war with the French, on the ground that none of his predecessors had made such a grant and that he would not commit his church to an onerous precedent.[1] In view of his experience with the tribute of a mantle [2] his attitude was understandable, but it is by no means certain that he was correctly informed. His stand was not, as Stubbs thought, a 'constitutional' one, but one for the liberty of his own see. In the event the bishop of Salisbury who had followed his lead made his peace with the king only by paying a large fine, but Hugh travelled to Roche d'Andely to see Richard, and not only succeeded in winning his favour, but also reproved him for his marital infidelity and his acceptance of presents for the nomination of bishops. Richard, like a weak man, placed all the blame on Hubert Walter and gave Hugh some presents which included a fine pike for his dinner. His final comment was : ' If all bishops were like this one, no king would dare to lift up his head against them.' [3]

But soon afterwards Richard tried to obtain that the Lincoln canons should serve abroad in the ' diplomatic service ' at their own expense and his good pleasure. Such an imposition would have fatally compromised a principal achievement of Hugh's episcopate, for he had been most careful in his choice of canons and diocesan officials whose intellectual and moral qualities enabled them to share in his government of the diocese, and he had strongly insisted on the duty of residence. He regarded them, as he said himself, as the apple of his eye.[4] In the event Hugh again went to France to see the king, but Richard was killed shortly before his arrival and Hugh assisted at the funeral instead.[5]

[1] *M.V.*, V, 5
[2] *M.V.*, IV, 7
[3] *M.V.*, V, 6
[4] *M.V.*, III, 12
[5] *M.V.*, V, 10

It was at John's request that Hugh took part in the treaty of Le Goulet ; from there he went to revisit the Grande Chartreuse and the district familiar to him in childhood. He sent messengers to Innocent III asking leave to resign his see and retire to his monastery, but the pope refused : Hugh was too useful a judge delegate to be lost to the service of the Church. Among the many interesting episodes of this journey was a three-day visit to Cluny. Hugh was very impressed with all he found there, and said : ' Truly if I had come here before I fell in love with the Grande Chartreuse, Cluny would have had me as a monk of her own.' This witness to the state of Cluny in 1200 is a useful corrective to the view that it was spiritually decadent by the time of Peter the Venerable and had lost its spiritual vitality to the Cistercians.[1]

Hugh was taken ill on his way back to England. At Canterbury he was worse and was carried most of the way to London in a barge. On his deathbed he gave detailed instructions about his funeral and his cathedral, remaining as shrewd and vigorous as ever to the last. Like a true Carthusian he died on a bed of ashes.

Two discourses recounted here by Adam are presented to us probably in a more developed form than Hugh's actual words. Under obedience to the archbishop of Canterbury, Hugh departed from Carthusian custom by eating a little meat, and Adam introduces here an earlier discourse on monastic abstinence in favour of the mitigations then current in Black Benedictine monasteries. It is true that early in his episcopate Hugh had presided at the settlement of the Sempringham lay-brothers' rebellion when they were granted better food and clothing in return for their peaceful resumption of their way of life ;[2] but it seems most unlikely that one who had eaten abstinence fare all his life should describe it as ' likely to induce insomnia, lethargy and total incapacity for the ordinary

---

[1] *M.V.*, V, 15
[2] cf. M. D. Knowles, ' The Revolt of the Lay brothers of Sempringham' in *English Historical Review* (1935), L, 465-87

exercises of monastic life.' The picture is overdrawn, and Adam rather than Hugh seems responsible.

The prophecy that king Philip of France would destroy the stock of shameless Eleanor ' like an ox which eats grass down to its very roots ' in retribution for her marriage to Henry II— ' already three of their sons have been destroyed and the fourth will have only a short respite '—may well be authentic, but perhaps it all became clearer in Adam's mind thirteen years after the event. It is also interesting to note that Adam did not mention Bouvines in this connection although the simile of the ox would have given him an excellent opening for doing so. It seems likely that the *Magna Vita* was finished before that decisive battle in 1214.

A different problem is set by the somewhat clumsy construction of the last chapters of the work. Hugh's death is described in ch. xvi, which ends with a doxology. Ch. xvii's title contains the words ' Et alia quedam *in modum epilogi* de rebus variis ' etc. This chapter describes the funeral and ends with a longer doxology. It would be reasonable to suppose that the *Magna Vita* originally ended here, especially as ch. xviii again describes Hugh's death and the next two chapters his funeral. Adam's other work, The Vision of the Monk of Eynsham, also has an elaborate doxology at the end of a chapter which is not the last of all. Perhaps Adam revised both his works in retirement and then added these supplementary chapters ; no manuscript of a more primitive redaction has however survived.

As it is, the *Magna Vita* ends with king John declaring the value and usefulness of the monastic life which had trained such a man as Hugh. For once Adam was in agreement with him. John's appreciation took the practical form of remitting the Cistercians' wool-dues and founding for them later the royal abbey of Beaulieu.

Hugh united in his person qualities which might at first sight seem incompatible. Efficient and courageous, he was sometimes so lost in prayer to things around him that his horse needed a leader. Habitually gentle and kind, he could be stern and intransigent ; austere to himself, he was hospitable to others. A student who left almost no writings,[1] he was also a man of vigorous action. Even when he reproved, he won respect and affection. Many will subscribe to Ruskin's opinion that he was ' the most beautiful sacerdotal figure known to me in history.' [2] It is mainly due to Adam that such a judgment can be made.

D. H. F.

II

THE CARTHUSIANS AND WITHAM

When a famous teacher of Rheims named Bruno resigned his canonry to become a hermit, he had no idea that he was to found a religious order. In 1084 he settled with a few companions in a mountain solitude later called the Grande Chartreuse, but within four years he was called to Rome by his former student, now pope Urban II, to serve the Apostolic See, and in 1101 he died as a hermit in Calabria without writing a rule or revisiting the community of the Chartreuse. He was not canonized until 1515.

The way of life he had inaugurated was described by Guibert of Nogent and Peter the Venerable, both Benedictines, in the early twelfth century. Its most striking difference from that of other monasteries was its emphasis on solitude, thus described by Guibert :

' There are thirteen monks who have a convenient cloister in accordance with cenobitic custom, but they do not live *claustraliter* like other monks. Around the cloister each has his own cell where he works and sleeps and eats. On Sundays they

---

[1] The only writings of Hugh's to survive are charters and a few official documents printed in P.L. 153, 1114 *et seq.*, not all of which are authentic. A late scribe of MS Digby 53, f. 66, ascribes to him the following couplet :

Cella vale ! Tu scala Iacob, tu campus agonis,
Dans ventis palea(m) in celo grana reponis.

For Hugh's appreciation of books, see *M.V.*, II, 13 and p. 126, note 1

[2] Ruskin, *Praeterita*, iii, 1

receive (for the whole week) their bread and the vegetables, which are cooked by each one in his own cell . . . They do not go to the church for all the canonical hours but only for some of them . . . They wear hairshirts next to the skin and their other garments are very poor. They live under a prior : the bishop of Grenoble takes the place of abbot and provisor. Although they abase themselves in poverty in many ways they are amassing a rich library, and the less they abound in the supply of material bread, the more diligently do they work for the food which perishes not.' [1]

Peter the Venerable added that they restricted their possessions of land and cattle, that their numbers were fixed at thirteen choir monks and eighteen lay brothers, that they never ate meat and had fish only when it was given to them. On feast days they sung the whole Office in the church and ate two meals in the refectory. [2]

The Carthusian blend of eremitical and cenobitical life was new, although it was composed of traditional elements from the Desert Fathers, St Jerome and Cassian but tempered throughout by the discretion of St Benedict. It owed something also to the example of St Romuald at Camaldoli. The usual monastic occupations of prayer, reading and manual work were pursued in a solitude which was less absolute than that of the monks of Egypt and provided occasion for the frequent exercise of fraternal charity. This form of life would probably not have survived but for Guigo I, fifth prior of the Grande Chartreuse (†1136), who codified the existing customs, which are still the basis of Carthusian observance. These *Consuetudines* were written to secure uniformity in the six Charterhouses founded by Guigo in France ; soon after his death houses were opened in Spain and Denmark. [3]

---

[1] Guibert of Nogent, *De vita sua*, I, 11, P.L. 156, 853 *et seq.*
[2] *De Miraculis*, II, 28. P.L., 189, 944
[3] Guigo was also a notable scholar, who re-edited St Jerome's letters, wrote a life of St Hugh of Grenoble also some *Meditationes* (cf. Dom A. Wilmart, *Le recueil des pensées du B. Guigues*, Paris, 1936). His works are printed in P.L. 153.

When St Hugh joined the Grande Chartreuse as a young canon in c. 1163, the life there was similar, even in detail, to that described by Guibert nearly sixty years before. A few of the fasts had been abandoned, but the poverty was unchanged and the library had increased. Making books, i.e. preparing parchment, copying, correcting and binding, was the Carthusians' staple occupation : in Guigo's phrase they ' preached the word of God with their hands as they could not do so with their lips ' [1] : their medieval library lists are evidence both for their industry and for the breadth of their interests. Their life was spent in search of union with God, through an austere régime which united prayer and work, solitude and obedience, poverty and learning, in a separation from the world which was almost complete. Yet the see of Grenoble was filled by Carthusian bishops from 1132 till 1248, and by 1200 there had been one Carthusian cardinal and thirty-two Carthusian bishops.[2]

The first Carthusian foundation in England was brought about in an unusual way. News of Henry II's quarrel with Becket came to the Grande Chartreuse through a letter written by John of Salisbury when in exile at the Charterhouse of Mont-Dieu. The prior of the Grande Chartreuse sent a letter of remonstrance to Henry, and he was chosen by Alexander III, together with Anthelm a former prior and then bishop of Belley, to be bearers of a letter from him urging Henry to make peace in 1168. After the murder of Becket, Henry was reconciled to the Church (1172), and part of his penance was to make a pilgrimage to the Holy Land. This proved impracticable, and his promise was commuted to one of founding monasteries. Carthusian tradition is witness that Witham was one of these. Henry had already shown favour to the strict Order of Grandmont, and the equally fervent, but better organised Carthusians began their first house in England near Selwood forest

---

[1] *Consuetudines*, xxviii, P.L. 153, 693-4
[2] Thurston, 133

(Somerset) in 1178–9 under Narbert. He was unfitted for the task and soon retired ; another prior was appointed but died almost at once ; other difficulties described by Adam seemed to make failure certain. Witham was only saved by the arrival of St Hugh in late 1179 or early 1180 ; in a few years he transformed it into a flourishing monastery whose fervour soon became known throughout southern England.[1]

Adam's account of Witham's financial difficulties can be completed from the Pipe Roll. Witham first appears there in 1179–80, when £63 6 8 was paid to them. In 1180–1 the sum was only £32 14 0, which would well accord with the crisis described in bk. II, c. vi, and brought to an end when Henry saw St Hugh and Br. Gerard, possibly in October 1181 when he was ' much in Wiltshire '. The payments for 1181–2 were very much more generous : they amounted to £126 7 0 in all, including £80 for building, £20 for food and £10 for seed. After such generosity it is not perhaps surprising that only £40 and 10 marks were received the following year, but in 1183–4 the total was £110. These fluctuations in the annual income could easily cause difficulties in the community, particularly in the earliest years before the building was completed.[2]

[1] Gir., VII, 93. St Hugh was the third prior of Witham, not the first (as stated by A. L. Poole, *From Domesday Book to Magna Carta*, 229). The date of 1179-80 for his arrival was first suggested by Thurston, 90-3, and was accepted by J. Armitage Robinson, M. D. Knowles and others. Robinson believed that the entry in Stapleton, *Magni Rotuli Scaccarii Normanniae*, I, 37, ' In passagio fratrum de Cartosa et Reinaldi clerici regis qui eos duxit in Angliam, xx sol. per breve regis,' refers to St Hugh's journey. Dimock, believing that the resignation of Guigo II took place in 1174, ascribed St Hugh's arrival to that year ; but modern Carthusian authors are certain that Guigo resigned in 1179. See below, II, 3-4 and notes.

[2] *Pipe Roll*, anno 26 Henrici II *et seq.* The total sum given by Henry from 1179-88 amounted to £528, 18s. 5d. and 220 marks, of which £320 and 200 marks were given for building. This should be compared with the £1400 he gave for re-building Waltham Abbey and £880 for Amesbury. cf. A. L. Poole, *loc. cit.* The only completely regular income Witham received from the Exchequer was £12 a year, and this sum only was received in 1184-85. In other years the receipts were considerably increased by *ad hoc* donations, among which grants for building continued until 1187-88, after St Hugh became bishop of Lincoln. The small annual grant of £12 reappears in the sixth year of Richard I.

Progress in the buildings, which comprised an upper and lower house in accordance with primitive Carthusian practice, was matched by an increase of personnel : some of the new recruits were professed canons or Benedictines. The murmurings of an unsuccessful candidate like Alexander of Lewes and the sarcasms of Richard of Devizes addressed to his former prior who persevered there were the only discordant voices in the general chorus of praise for the Carthusians, to which Peter of Blois contributed, and even such hostile critics of the monks as Walter Map, Giraldus and Nigel Wireker.[1]

Whatever criticisms might justly be made of Carthusian life, producing uninteresting or stereotyped characters would not be one of them. The fiery Br. Gerard's outburst to king Henry II, when he accused him to his face of miserly indifference to the fate of his monastery, was remembered by St Hugh with acute discomfort. Br. Einard, the white-haired veteran of many foundations, with his ' deep voice and his eyes in which shone something divine ', was only prevented from making an unauthorised return to the Grande Chartreuse by St Hugh's skilful intervention. And the eloquent Adam of Dryburgh, formerly abbot there, whose transfer from the Premonstratensians had been obtained by St Hugh, allowed him no grounds for complacency by reproving him for what he chose to think was tepidity.[2]

When St Hugh was bishop he still kept control over Witham by delegation of the General Chapter, and he deposed his successor as prior, Albert of Portes, one of the original founders. Quality and fervour were the Cathusian aims at Witham as elsewhere, and theirs never became a way of life accessible to the many like Cistercian life at Clairvaux or Rievaulx. During St Hugh's lifetime the Witham ideal found written expression in the *De Quadripertito Exercitio Cellae* by

---

[1] cf. M. D. Knowles, *Monastic Order in England*, xxxix : ' The critics of the monks (pp. 662-78) ' and *M.V.* II, 10-11 and notes. The present parish church of Witham was the lay brothers' church and it was re-vaulted by St Hugh.

[2] *M.V.*, II, 6 ; IV, 11, 13

Adam of Dryburgh, and after his death the same writer served his community further by his prominent share in the ' conversion ' of Hubert Walter, who, on a visit to Witham, offered the community a chasuble, received the discipline from Adam ' like a child ' and took the community under his special protection. Such was the happy ending to Hubert's former hostility to St Hugh and the Carthusians.[1]

After St Hugh's death Witham continued in its chosen obscurity. The Carthusians seem to have taken no steps to obtain St Hugh's canonization, requested by the English bishops and the Lincoln Chapter in 1219 and granted by Honorius III the following year. In 1227 a Carthusian foundation was made at Hinton, also in Somerset ; Hinton and Witham remained the only Carthusian houses in England for more than a century. The strong desire for the contemplative life in the later Middle Ages led to the foundation of seven more Charterhouses in England : when the Reformation came, the Carthusians showed themselves the most courageous of all the monks.

St Hugh was the first Carthusian saint to be canonized, and his feast was kept on November 17. It obtained a higher rank in the Carthusian calendar as the Middle Ages progressed, until it was raised to the highest of all by the General Chapter of 1339. This decision led to an increasing demand in Charterhouses in different parts of Europe both for manuscripts of his life and for paintings and sculptures which represented him. The most solemn cult of St Hugh was observed in Lincoln cathedral, where his body was translated to a new shrine in the Angel choir in 1280 in the presence of king Edward I and his

---

[1] cf. A. Wilmart, *Maître Adam . . . devenu chartreux à Witham* in *Analecta Praemonstratensia* (1933), IX, 207-32. A new edition of this Witham chronicle fragment is in preparation. The work *De Quadripertito Exercitio Cellae* is in P.L. 153, attributed to Guigo : Adam's other works written as a Carthusian have not survived, except for some sermons still in manuscript.

queen, archbishop Pecham and many other prelates.[1] For the rest of the Middle Ages he remained Lincoln's local saint and also the principal saint of the Carthusian Order.

D. H. F.

III

SAINT HUGH'S EPISCOPATE

Giraldus Cambrensis' two lives of St Hugh, the first written during the author's residence at Lincoln between 1196 and 1199, and the second and longer one in the early part of the thirteenth century, are an admirable supplement to Adam's biography.[2] The Welsh scholar and churchman was attracted by those aspects of Hugh's personality and work which his monk-chaplain ignored. Of particular interest is his account of the famous theological school at Lincoln which was the cause of his going there when the renewal of the war between Richard I and Philip II prevented him from studying in Paris. A former Paris master already known to him, William de Montibus, so called because he had lectured in the schools on Mont-Ste-Geneviève, was chancellor at Lincoln from 1191 till 1213 and made it, with the possible exception of Oxford, the most renowned of the English schools. His surviving works include two collections of sermons, which have been described as ' helps to young theologians ' and show that he was a practical rather than a speculative theologian, without much originality but able to give the average parish priest a good theological grounding, which was probably St Hugh's intention in inviting him to Lincoln. When William showed surprise that, when the

---

[1] For the translation of St Hugh see Gir. VII, 219 et seq. MS Bibl. Royale (Brussels) 8946 contains a transcript of a covering letter sent by the Lincoln chapter to the Grande Chartreuse to accompany the gift of a phial of oil which had flowed from his tomb in 1445

[2] Giraldus Cambrensis, Opera Omnia, VII, 39-42, 67-147. Both lives were presented to archbishop Langton in 1214.

bishop kissed lepers, his kiss, unlike that of St Martin, had no healing properties, Hugh made the beautiful answer: ' Martin by kissing the leper cleansed his body, but the leper's kiss cleanses my soul.' Another of the Lincoln theologians was John of Cornwall, a pupil of both Thierry of Chartres and Peter Lombard. It is possible that the humorous anecdote, related by Giraldus, of the parish priest who misconstrued *in diebus illis* as *in die Busillis* and was thus convinced of the existence of a king called Busillis, an error which gave the master an opportunity of expatiating on the ignorance of the clergy, took place at Lincoln, and not at Oxford where John was lecturing at the turn of the century. Hugh, who was not above making jokes about the illiteracy of the clergy, would have enjoyed this howler. Giraldus' respect for Master John is shown by his recommending him to the pope in 1198 for the bishopric of St David's because of his knowledge of Welsh. John was a canonist as well as a theologian ; he and another canon of Lincoln, Robert of Melun, acted as St Hugh's judges delegate in an appeal case between the canons of Osney and a certain John of Hambledon, in which they had the assistance of some of the Oxford masters. Although there is no evidence of the bishop's patronage of the nascent University, the two most distinguished canonists on the Lincoln chapter, Simon of Southwell and John of Tynemouth were both masters there, and the former also taught at Paris. The latter assisted Hugh's judges delegate in a tithe case at Oxford in 1188 between the monks of Evesham and the canons of Bicester. Simon was Hubert Walter's official and vicar-general, and both he and John were members of the archbishop's household and that of bishop Puiset of Durham, as was also William of Blois and three other Lincoln *magistri* Henry, Stephen and Richard of Lindsey. William, who was bishop of Lincoln from 1203 till 1206, is probably the same person as the master William who was sub-dean 1192-7 and precentor 1197–1203. He was often employed by Innocent III as a judge delegate, as also was Roger of Rolleston, one of the two *familiares* of archbishop Baldwin sent by him to Hugh when he asked for skilled assistance in his legal and administrative work.[1] The eminent theologians and lawyers at Lincoln must have more than revived its mid-twelfth century fame as a centre of learning which had even attracted Icelandic scholars. The school, however, declined after William de Montibus' death, although there was a brief revival during the chancellorship of his most distinguished pupil, Richard le Grant or Wetherset, Langton's short-lived successor at Canterbury in 1224. No tradition connects the greatest English thirteenth century scholar Robert Grosseteste with the school at Lincoln, but at least he obtained his first promotion from St Hugh.

Hugh was perhaps too modest about his legal knowledge, and contact with the Lincoln lawyers and his own studies caused him, in spite of his distaste for such work, to be much in demand as a judge delegate, and the ability with which he dealt with difficult points of Canon Law amazed even highly trained canonists. The only case described by Adam in detail is one of little interest (his protection of the interests of two poor orphans whom a wealthy Londoner, Jordan de Turri, tried unscrupulously to defraud), but Hugh also acted in this capacity in some of the most complicated and important contemporary law suits including that of archbishops Baldwin and Hubert Walter over the foundation of a collegiate church at Hackington near Canterbury, and later at Lambeth. His part in the final award is mentioned by Adam, and also his counsel to Baldwin to abandon a plan which, however admirable in itself, was embittering his relations with his chapter and would involve him in heavy expenses only to end in humiliation and defeat.[2] This was probably given in the initial stages of the dispute, in which Hugh also acted as judge delegate in a matter connected

---

[1] Gir. *De Rebus a se gestis*, III, 3 : *Gemma Ecclesiastica*, Dist. I, 48, Dist. II, 18, 35. *Opera* II, 129, 133, 250, 304 : *Vita Sti Hugonis*, Dist. I, viii, 107-8. Cf. H. Mackinnon, 'William de Montibus, a medieval teacher' in *Essays in Medieval History presented to Bertie Wilkinson* (Toronto, 1969), 32-45 ; S. Kuttner and E. Rathbone, 'Anglo-Norman Canonists of the twelfth century,' *Traditio* (1951), VII, 281-358.

[2] *M.V.*, III, 12 ; V, 13

with the case, the archbishop's refusal to restore to the monks the churches of Eastry and Monkton given by his predecessor to the almonry.   He and his fellow judges, the abbots of Faversham and Boxley, were to make a preliminary investigation and report to the Curia on the claims of both parties, and pending a decision on these execute the papal mandate ordering their restoration to the monks.   It is doubtful where St Hugh's sympathies really lay, for although the monks plainly regarded him as a supporter, on one occasion he angrily rebuked them for their insubordination, and exhorted them to prostrate themselves at the feet of the archbishop to ask for his forgiveness.[1] Hugh also acted as judge delegate in the acrimonious lawsuits between Geoffrey Plantagenet of York and his chapter, and between the former and bishop Puiset of Durham.   He seems to have had some liking and respect for Henry II's formidable bastard, in spite of his violent and overbearing temperament, since on one occasion when the canons pressed for the execution of a papal sentence of interdict and suspension on the archbishop, who had not appeared at the Curia within the period prescribed by the judges delegate, he replied that he would rather be suspended himself than suspend Geoffrey.   This was in 1195.   After Richard I's death the archbishop and his chapter agreed to submit their differences to Hugh's arbitration and that of the dean of Lincoln and a certain master Columba, but their temporary reconciliation a year later was the work of other arbitrators, who, once they had exchanged the kiss of peace, left them to make their own settlement.[2]   In 1198 after the death of Hugh de Nonant, bishop of Coventry and Lichfield, who had converted the monastic chapter at the former place into a secular one, Hugh, together with Hubert Walter and the famous abbot Samson of St Edmundsbury was

[1] *Epistolae Cantuarienses*, 283.   On the Canterbury case the main sources are this work and Gervase of Canterbury, *Opera Historica*, I, 332-594, *passim*.   Stubbs' introduction to the *Epistolae Cantuarienses* is the best general account of the case.

[2] Howden, *Chronica*, III, 168-88, 305-16 *passim* ;   IV. pp. xxxix-lxxvii, 98-9 and *passim*.   G. V. Scammell, *Hugh de Puiset* (1956), 69-70, 235

commissioned by pope Celestine III to restore the expelled monks.[1] Unfortunately, except for the final award in the Canterbury case, no records have survived, and the chroniclers give no details as to the proceedings.

Hugh's temperament as well as his high birth caused him to adapt himself more easily to his position than the other monk bishop, Baldwin of Canterbury. Giraldus Cambrensis who knew both of them well describes the former as Democritus and the latter as Diogenes, and compares Hugh's frankness, cheerfulness and witty conversation with the archbishop's melancholy, taciturnity and desire to avoid company. His quick temper was preferable to Baldwin's habitual mildness which concealed a mixture of obstinacy and pliancy, and the traditions of a great magnate made him insistent that his household should be well dressed. He also provided his guests with the usual courtly entertainments, such as minstrelsy and even acting, and in spite of his personal austerity kept a good table, frequently exhorting his companions to eat and drink well in order to serve God better and more devotedly. Courtesy and common sense caused him slightly to modify his Carthusian diet, and, although he still ate no meat, he drank a little wine to keep up his strength and put his guests at their ease. His cloistral training did not prevent him from entertaining pious matrons and widows at his table, and blessing them with particular devotion as members of the sex to which the Mother of God had belonged.

According to Giraldus both Hugh and Baldwin were learned men, but the former was by far the better scholar. He also wholeheartedly approved of his promotion of men of virtue and intellectual eminence to canonries at Lincoln. Hugh's strong feeling that Church preferment should be reserved for those who served the altar, which at the beginning of his episcopate almost caused a breach with Henry II, at first made his relations with the distinguished civil servants among his fifty-

[1] Howden, IV, 35-6 ; Walter of Coventry, *Memorials*, 120-1 ; Ralph of Coggeshall, *Chronicon*, 80 ; *The Chronicle of Jocelin of Brakelond* (ed. H. E. Butler), 94-5, and Note R, 155-6 ; M. D. Knowles, *The Monastic Order in England* (1941), 322-4

six canons somewhat difficult. The dean, Richard Fitz-Neal, afterwards treasurer and bishop of London, the author of the *Dialogus de Scaccario* and a lost historical work the *Tricolumnis*, had been a candidate for the bishopric at the time of Hugh's election. Another official with literary gifts was Walter Map, archdeacon of Oxford, whose *De Nugis Curialium* contains a scathing attack on the religious orders with the exception of the Carthusians for whom he had nothing but praise. Unlike Fitz-Neal and some of the other officials of the Lincoln chapter Walter was unsuccessful in obtaining a bishopric. One of the others, William de Ste Mère Eglise, afterwards bishop of London, must have been a good canonist, judging from his frequent employment by Innocent III as a judge delegate.[1] The strained relations upon which Giraldus comments did not last long : Hugh's rueful admission of his peppery temper at chapter meetings was accompanied by a confession of his affection for his canons and of gratitude for their recognition of it. When Hugh during Richard I's confiscation of the temporalities of the bishopric of Lincoln sought the protection of the Exchequer officials for the property of his church during his own absence abroad for a personal interview with the king, Richard Fitz-Neal, having persuaded him to sit down, joked with him about his now being one of the barons of the Exchequer, though Hugh does not seem to have relished the jest. When he met Walter Map at Angers on his journey, the latter tried vainly to dissuade him from proceeding further because of the disturbed state of the country and the fierceness of the king's anger against him. The Angevin court was one of the chief political, literary and artistic centres of Europe, and these men, in addition to their efficient and conscientious performance of their secular duties must have been excellent company for a man of Hugh's varied interests.

[1] Gir. VII, 40, 41, 68, 106-7 ; *M.V.*, III, 9, 10, 11, 12, 13, V, 9, 10 Savaric, archdeacon of Northampton, bishop of Bath and Wells (1192-1205), John of Coutances, bishop of Worcester (1196-8), Godfrey de Luci, bishop of Winchester (1189-1204), William de Ste Mère Eglise, bishop of London (1199-1221), William of Blois, bishop of Lincoln (1203-6).

An incident which occurred at the beginning of his episcopate united Hugh and his chapter in the defence of the rights
of their church. On his way to Lincoln for his enthronement
the monks of St Albans refused him permission to celebrate
Mass in their church, in order to safeguard their cherished
exemption privilege. After consulting his canons Hugh
excommunicated them and placed their churches in his diocese
under an interdict, with the result that the community, faced
with the inconvenience of being unable to buy and sell or
obtain food and lodging in a vast area adjacent to their
monastery, soon sought his pardon. His refusal of the customary fee of a palfrey to the archdeacon of Canterbury for
enthroning him, and his later freeing of his church from the
annual tribute of a mantle to the king, although dictated by
his horror of simony, benefited his chapter as well as himself,
as did also his recovery of Eynsham and the other lost churches
and judicial rights of his see after long and tiresome litigation
in the king's court.[1]

His confirmation of his predecessor's charter exempting the
canons' churches and prebends from all external jurisdiction,
including that of the archdeacons and his own official, and
his own privilege authorizing the chapter to excommunicate
all detainers of its lands and violators of its rights showed
his concern for its position as an independent ecclesiastical
corporation, subject only to his own authority. His gift of
the church of Wellingore in Lincolnshire to the common
fund, and his confirmation of the appropriation to it of the
churches of Orston, Edwinstowe and Scredington and half of
the church of Glentham may have been with a view to
encouraging residence by increasing the income of the residen-
tiaries. Each canon whether resident or non-resident was forced
to pay his vicar an adequate stipend on pain of deprivation.

---

[1] *M.V.*, III, 6, 12, IV, 7, 8; Giraldus, *Speculum Ecclesiae*, Dist. II 30.
Opera, IV, 94-5; VII, 40-1. For Richard's charter remitting the tribute
of a mantle and confirming the judicial rights of the church at Lincoln,
cf. *Registrum Antiquissimum* (Lincoln Record Society, 1931), I, N.N., 197,
199, pp. 122, 124-5.

A sense of spiritual solidarity amongst the whole body was developed by the revival of a daily Mass for benefactors living and dead, and the recitation of the psalter daily on their behalf, the psalms being divided amongst the canons, the first group being allotted to the bishop.[1] The prestige of the Lincoln chapter, largely as the result of Hugh's policy, led the newly formed chapter of Moray to apply to it in 1213 for a copy of its statutes, a request which led to the compilation of the first written version of the customs of an English cathedral. As Hugh certainly occasionally presided over his chapter it is probable that he made some contribution to its constitution. Giraldus Cambrensis' warm testimony to his virtues, written after some years' residence at Lincoln, shows how completely Hugh had won the affection and veneration of his canons during the first ten years of his episcopate. ' His remarkable holiness, integrity, virtue and uprightness made him conspicuous among the churchmen of our day as one peculiarly endowed with the grace of God. In almost every way he sets an example for others to imitate. If his end resembles his beginning, Lincoln will have had no greater bishop since blessed Remigius.'[2]

The site of the cathedral on the brow of the hill at Lincoln was symbolic, for it was indeed the religious centre of the diocese. The clergy trained in its school came there annually with some of their parishioners to present their offerings to the mother church and take part in the great Pentecostal procession. The splendour of the offices, particularly the nocturnal ones, was greatly enhanced by the almost double provision of candles, due to the revenues assigned by Hugh to the treasury for the purpose. It was his intention to bequeath to the altar of the

---

[1] *ibid.*, N.N. 289, 294, pp. 252, 255-6 ; III, N.N. 977-89, 999, 1002, 1037, pp. 315-22, 330-1, 364 ; VII, N.N. 2099-2100, pp. 129-30. cf. K. Major, ' The Finances of the dean and chapter of Lincoln from the twelfth century to the fourteenth, a preliminary survey,' in *Journal of Ecclesiastical History*, 1954, V, 149-67, and H. Bradshaw and C. Wordsworth, *Statutes of Lincoln Cathedral* (1897), II, 300-7
[2] Gir., VII, 42

Blessed Virgin his precious ring which contained certain of the relics of which he was such an assiduous collector. On his last visit to the Grande Chartreuse, however, he gave it to the community there with the other relics he had collected on his travels. Fortunately Adam, who had been its custodian, was there to remind him of his previous bequest, and after his master's death took the ring to Lincoln in its golden case studded with precious gems. This gift would have added to the reputation of the church as a place of peculiar sanctity and attracted pilgrims there even if St Hugh's own shrine and the miracles wrought there had not made it temporarily at least a second Canterbury. (See *M.V.*, V, 14, 19.)

Hugh's greatest memorial at Lincoln is the choir of his cathedral which had been practically destroyed by the great earthquake of Palm Sunday, 1185. All that now remains of the Norman cathedral of Remigius and Alexander the Magnificent is the West Front, though from Adam's description of Hugh's funeral the nave (which however was rebuilt between 1225 and 1233, possibly to bring it into harmony with the new choir) was left intact. Immediately after the earthquake, Hugh's predecessor Walter of Coutances, although already archbishop of Rouen, founded the famous Works Fraternity, the names of whose members may be recorded in the Great Bible at Lincoln. These received an indulgence of forty days, and thirty-three weekly Masses were celebrated in the cathedral on their behalf as well as a certain number each year in the religious houses of which the bishop was patron. The additional indulgence of eighty days issued by Hugh, and those granted by his fellow bishops, enabled the rebuilding to be begun in 1192. The bishop himself took an active part in the work by carrying a hod with stones and cement. One of the miracles recorded in the canonization process is the cure of a cripple who received permission from the master mason to wear it round his neck, and after a few days discarded one of his sticks and then the other. He then used the hod to assist the masons as Hugh had done. The latter's continuous interest in the work is shown by his deathbed request to his master mason or clerk of the works, Geoffrey de Noiers, that the chapel of St John the Baptist where he intended to be buried should be ready for consecration by the bishop of Rochester when the king and magnates came to Lincoln in November. This was either the one furthest from the choir in the north-eastern transept, or the one immediately behind the high altar, which in Carthusian churches is generally dedicated to the Baptist.[1] During the excavations of 1886 a stone coffin enclosing one of lead was found here, which was possibly the original one from which Hugh's body was removed at the time of its translation to the shrine in the Angel Choir. Whichever chapel it was, it is clear that the rebuilding followed the usual medieval plan of beginning with the choir.

The fullest contemporary description of the work at Lincoln is that given by Henry of Avranches in the metrical life of St Hugh, probably composed about 1220. By this time the rebuilding had proceeded as far as the crossing between the nave and the choir, since he names and describes the two great windows of the western transepts, the bishop's eye and the dean's eye, the latter of which still retains its original tracery and some of the glass, including the little panel representing St Hugh's funeral. This, however, was the work of William of Blois, but Hugh is generally supposed to have been responsible for the eastern transepts and the two chapels on each side of the choir of the eastern limb of the western ones. His own presbytery was destroyed when the east end was extended during the second half of the thirteenth century by the erection of the present presbytery and the Angel choir to provide a fitting site for his shrine. Much of the actual structure of the two transepts and the choir between them was probably badly damaged when the new central tower crashed in 1237, so that it is conjectural how much of Hugh's work survives. The actual date of the vaulting is also a matter of controversy, but it is generally assumed that the sexpartite vaulting of choir and transepts belongs to the early thirteenth century, but the

---

[1] *M.V.*, V, 16, 20 ; Gir., VII, 178, 217-18

unusual quinquepartite vaulting of the aisles is earlier. The theory, however, that the beautiful double arcade of the choir ambulatory, with its alternate columnettes of white stone and Purbeck marble with their loose leaf capitals, was added after the fall of the tower has now been generally abandoned. If the little figures on the spandrels as well as the arcading itself can be ascribed to Hugh, which seems likely, they are the earliest examples of Gothic sculpture in England.

The excavations of 1886 laid bare the ground plan of Hugh's choir, with its chevet surrounded by a three-sided ambulatory, and the polygonal apsidal chapel beyond, with two side chapels separated from it by two circles too small for chapels and too large for staircase turrets. Although similar eastern terminations are to be found in France, the corona at Canterbury has been suggested as a possible model. Other structural features borrowed from the choir of William of Sens and William of Kent, completed about fifteen years earlier, are the plans of the triforium and clerestory, including the little arches above the course of the latter, and the quinquepartite and sexpartite vaulting, although the long rib is peculiar to Lincoln. Even the piers seem to be derived from those in the presbytery at Canterbury. The decorative character of the work and the lavish use of Purbeck marble are, however, new, although it had been used sparingly at Canterbury, Colchester and Iffley and in the church of the lay brothers at Witham (now the parish church), which was probably completed about 1180. It also occurs in the choir of Old Clee church, consecrated by St Hugh in 1192, as do also the clustered capitals, which are also found at St Giles, Oxford which he consecrated in 1200. At any rate, in spite of Hugh's Burgundian origin and the French name of the master mason, who may have belonged to a family of de Noiers domiciled in the diocese since the Conquest, the work at Lincoln is essentially English. Its effect on contemporaries is shewn by Giraldus Cambrensis' comments on the beauty and novelty of the architecture, particularly the effect of the strong contrasts of light and shade produced by the use of white stone and Purbeck marble, and by its influence on Beverley, Salisbury and the chapel of the nine altars at Durham.

Nothing remains of the episcopal palace mentioned by Giraldus in his first biography, or of Hugh's other buildings.[1] His cathedral is thus his only, as well as his best, memorial, and the harmony of the design, the combination of strength and delicacy, of size and grandeur with the exquisite execution of the smallest detail, and the striking contrasts of light and shade recall the mixture of austerity and courage, fiery temper and iron determination, gentleness and courtesy which made the Burgundian bishop one of the most popular of English saints.

In his biography Adam confesses that Hugh's energy in the performance of his episcopal duties was often a tax on the strength of his attendants. Unlike his fellow bishops he was exceedingly conscientious in holding confirmations and, out of reverence for the sacrament and fear that the children to whom he was devoted might be injured or frightened by the horses, always dismounted for the ceremony. Two good stories told by Giraldus Cambrensis humanise this conventional picture of the ideal bishop. On one occasion Hugh, being annoyed by the late arrival of an elderly peasant, who appeared just as he had mounted and was about to ride away, made the blow which formed part of the ritual exceptionally hard. He was even more severe with a father who wanted to change his son's name from John to something more high-sounding, for he imposed a year's fasting on bread and water every Friday and Lenten fare each Wednesday, on the ground that it was both foolish and impious to wish to alter a name meaning ' God's grace '. Adam gives many examples of his zeal for the burial of the dead, and declares that neither court ceremonies nor political business were allowed to interfere with this charitable duty. When he was abroad at the time of Richard I's death personal danger owing to the disturbed state of the country

---

[1] *Gir.*, VII, 40, 97 ; *M.V.*, III, 13

never prevented his reverent and punctual celebration of mass and recitation of the offices. His extreme conscientiousness made the appointment of priests to the livings in his gift a perpetual torment, and his horror of simony caused him to forbid his archdeacons and officials to impose pecuniary penances, in spite of the example of St Thomas Becket which was cited in support of the practice. (See *M.V.*, IV, 7; V, 1, 2.)

Although exceedingly hospitable, the atmosphere of Hugh's household except on important occasions must have been almost monastic, as Adam tells us that it was his habit to have the Bible and theological works read aloud at meals. He was, however, easily accessible, for his biographer's brother, in spite of being a stranger, was able to see him privately and relate his vision. His custom of making regular visits to his different manors and of gathering the local clergy round him on these occasions was possibly the nucleus of the visitatorial system of his successors, and, together with his frequent visits to court and to royal and ecclesiastical councils, must have made him a familiar and venerated figure in his vast diocese. His absorption in prayer during his journeys, and his inability to speak or understand the Midland dialect, did not prevent the people from flocking to receive his blessing, and many of the miracles recorded in the canonization process occurred when he was on his travels. Adam also describes his charity and concern for lepers, and his readiness to help all unfortunate people, even if it involved him in difficulties with the royal officials. His popularity with the Lincoln Jews, displayed so strikingly at his funeral, was certainly well-deserved, since, during the anti-Jewish riots at the beginning of Richard I's reign, he had risked his own life to protect them. His generosity to his own tenants whatever their status appears in his refusal of a heriot from a poor widow, on the ground that she ought not to lose her ox as well as her husband, and his remission of the relief of 100s. due from a knight's fee. His generosity, charity and hospitality made him a poor man, and only the contribution of his clergy towards the 3,000 marks demanded by Richard I as commutation for the annual tribute of a mantle prevented his temporary retirement to Witham until he could save the sum required. Their readiness to make pecuniary sacrifices to keep their bishop in their midst must be almost unprecedented in the history of the medieval church.

His charm, courtesy and affability were combined with great sternness to sinners and violators of ecclesiastical discipline and the liberties of the Church, even when such offenders enjoyed the protection of powerful persons like the justiciar-archbishop. Adam's account of the terrible fate of those who defied his malediction reads like a medieval version of 'Struwelpeter'. Most of the stories are commonplaces of medieval hagiography, but if any of them were current during Hugh's lifetime it is not surprising that the royal officials ordered by Richard I to confiscate the temporalities of Lincoln dreaded the bishop's anathema almost more than the king's anger. (See *M.V.*, III, 13; IV, 3, 7; V, 7, 20.)

Hugh certainly held visitations and synods, though not perhaps so regularly as the later legislation of the Fourth Lateran Council of 1215 prescribed. The famous incident of his removal of the body of Henry II's mistress Fair Rosamund from its tomb before the high altar at Godstow is expressly stated to have taken place during a visitation of the religious houses of his diocese, and certain statutes issued at a synod survive. These make the usual attempt to enforce the wearing of clerical dress, and forbid the charging of fees in ecclesiastical courts, unjust excommunications and suspensions by archdeacons and their officials, the imposition of payments for a number of masses as penances on the laity, and the performance of any priestly function unless proof was given that the celebrant was in holy orders. The development of the chantry system and the beginning of the thirteenth century jurisdictional conflict between the ecclesiastical and secular courts are shown in the decrees forbidding vicars choral to accept fees for chantries and religious houses for anniversary masses and trentals, and ordering the clergy not to sue each other before lay tribunals. A regular citation system already existed, as Adam gives Hugh's refusal to allow his clerks to use the common form ' meminimus nos te alias citasse ' if he did not actually remember citing the offender, as an example of his scrupulous truthfulness. His conscientiousness in the performance of his episcopal duties, and the size of his diocese, made it amazing that he managed to spend a month or more at Witham every year, although this return to a life of prayer and contemplation may have given him the refreshment, strength and concentration needed for his exacting and unremitting labours. These, however, were not unrewarded, for the scenes which took place when his body was taken from London to Lincoln for burial show how completely he had won the love and veneration of both clergy and laity.[1]

Hugh's interests and activities were not completely confined to ecclesiastical matters. One of the best known incidents in Adam's biography is his opposition at the Council of Oxford in December 1197 to the proposals made on the king's behalf by Hubert Walter, who was presiding over the assembly in his capacity as justiciar, for the creation of a long-standing army. The traditional forty days military service, or scutages on each knight's-fee of the tenant-in-chief's *servitia debita* had become hopelessly inadequate owing to the almost continuous war, the higher standard of training and equipment, the development of new methods of warfare, the fall in the value of money and the consequent rise in the wages of hired knights. Already the Crown had resorted to the practice of calling out only a fraction of the service due, and of exacting fines greatly in excess of the scutages on each of their fees from those who did not serve. This new system naturally caused widespread discontent, which was increased by the long-drawn-out war and

[1] *M.V.*, III, 13, 14; IV, 1-7, 9-14; V, 2, 3, 5, 7-9, 19-20; Gir., VII, 9, 41-2, 94-7, 102-7; Benedictus Abbas, I, 357, II, 231-2

the liability to serve in parts of the Angevin territories where the Anglo-Norman baronage had no lands to defend, especially as they had to contend with the unwillingness of their own vassals, who had no estates outside England, to serve abroad. The year after the Council of Oxford, abbot Samson of St Edmundsbury found it impossible to raise even the tenth part of his *servitium debitum* demanded by the king, since his vassals, whilst admitting their liability to scutage, declared that they owed no corporal service outside England. Having with some difficulty obtained the king's permission to hire the four knights required, he paid them their wages for forty days, and learning from friends at court that the campaign was likely to last longer, he paid an additional £100 to Richard I to be quit of any further obligations.

The St Edmundsbury incident partly explains Hugh's resistance to the scheme laid before the assembled magnates at Oxford, which was that they as a body should provide and maintain a force of three hundred knights to serve for a year, or give the king the money to hire them at the rate of three shillings a day. The bishop of London, who as dean of the province of Canterbury was first asked to give his opinion, agreed ; but when it came to Hugh's turn he refused, giving as his reason that when first he became bishop of Lincoln he had taken pains to ascertain the rights, privileges and obligations of his church and had discovered that it owed no service abroad. He would return to the Grande Chartreuse and resume his former eremitical life rather than consent to impose a new burden upon his see, which would give his successors cause to quote against him the text ' Our fathers have eaten wild grapes and the teeth of the children are set on edge '. Finally he rebuked the archbishop for sponsoring a scheme which should have troubled his conscience and would sully his reputation. His lips trembling with indignation, the latter then asked Herbert, bishop of Salisbury what help he was prepared to give the king, who replied that he could only make the same answer as the bishop of Lincoln. The archbishop, having vented his wrath on Hugh, dissolved the meeting and reported to Richard I that the resistance of the two bishops had caused the rejection of the scheme. The king immediately ordered the confiscation of the temporalities, and the bishop of Salisbury paid for his boldness by a heavy fine. Hugh's personal encounter with the king at Roche d'Andely, where he won Richard's admiration for his boldness in bearding him and administering a playful shaking, saved him from the consequences of his opposition.

Richard's action in confiscating the temporalities of Lincoln and Salisbury was not that of an angry tyrant, since it was the normal penalty for refusal to fulfil feudal obligations, and Hugh was mistaken in believing that his church owed no military service abroad. The long vacancy at Lincoln before his election and the crown's policy of accepting scutage from the ecclesiastical tenants in chief, whilst at the same time never abandoning its claim to corporal service, are the probable explanation of his misapprehension. The new system of fining had been applied to them as well as to their secular counterparts and in April 1196 the king's instructions that his lay tenants in chief should serve with seven knights or less were coupled with a demand that his ecclesiastical ones should provide a sufficient number of knights to win his favour. Although historians have discounted Giraldus Cambrensis' declaration that at Oxford Hugh was acting as the accredited spokesman of his fellow clergy, it is certain that he was expressing the general discontent of the whole body of tenants in chief at a new and heavy financial burden. This would explain the justiciar's indignation and subsequent abandonment of the scheme for a long-service army. The question of military service abroad was a crucial issue in the Magna Carta crisis, and the clergy refused to admit their obligation to pay scutage for the continental campaigns during the early parts of Henry III's reign, deliberately describing their financial contributions towards them as *dona* or *auxilia*. Hugh's resistance at Oxford is thus the first public expression of the feeling amongst the tenants in chief, which was to be an important factor both in the loss of the Angevin dominions and the first successful baronial revolt against the monarchy.[1]

By confining himself to Hugh's encounters with Henry II and Richard I, Adam gives a one-sided picture of his part in secular politics. Like his episcopal colleagues he naturally attended such ceremonies as coronations and the national councils. The chroniclers mention his presence at the council of Geddington of February 1188, where arrangements were made for Henry II's projected Crusade, on which occasion he took the cross, but for some reason was prevented from fulfilling his vow. He was also present at the second council at the same place in September 1189 and at the one held at Pipewell a few days before to provide for the government of the country during Richard I's absence in Syria. In the December of the same year he and Geoffrey Plantagenet, archbishop elect of York, were given the commission to escort the king of the Scots to Canterbury to do homage, a circumstance which would account for William the Lion's affection for Hugh, and the latter's liking for his fellow envoy which made him unwilling to suspend him. John's insistence on his presence at the negotiations at Le Goulet was due to his being sent by Henry II with the archbishops of Canterbury and Rouen and the bishop of Coventry on an embassy to Philip II in the summer of 1188. Their efforts to secure peace were unsuccessful however, as was also the interview between the two kings at La Ferté Bernard, at which Hugh was also present. Shortly after this he returned to England.[2]

Longchamp's arrest and imprisonment of Geoffrey Plantagenet at Dover on his return to England in September 1191

[1] *M.V.*, III, 9; V, 5, 7; Gir., VII, 103-4; *Chronicle of Jocelin of Brakelond* (ed. H. E. Butler), 85-7; Howden, *Chronica*, IV, 40. On the Council of Oxford, cf. J. H. Round, *Feudal England* (1895), 528-38, and H. M. Chew, *The Ecclesiastical Tenants in Chief and Knight Service* (1932), 38-45

[2] *M.V.*, V, 19; Gir., VII, 102, Benedictus Abbas, II, 40, 66, 79, 84-5, 97; Howden, II, 343, III, 8, 15, 305-6, IV, 90; Gervase of Canterbury, *Opera Historica*, I, 410, 432-3; William of Newburgh, I, 310; *Itinerarium Regis Ricardi*, 5-9

caused Hugh to have a share in the last stages of the crisis which culminated in the deposition of the unpopular Poitevin justiciar. Being at Oxford, which owing to the disturbed state of the country had become the centre of the administration, he solemnly excommunicated Longchamp's brother-in-law the Constable of Dover, his wife and the other perpetrators of the sacrilegious act. He accompanied John and William the Marshal and the other members of the Council of State to Reading, and after the decision had been taken to summon the justiciar to stand his trial at the bridge of Loddon he was one of the bishops sent to him with a safe-conduct. Later when London, owing to the promise of a commune, had opened its gates to the opposition and Longchamp had taken refuge in the Tower, Hugh went there on October 9 with the bishops of Winchester and Coventry to negotiate with the ex-justiciar, whom according to Giraldus Cambrensis they found in a state of complete collapse. This, however, did not prevent him from behaving with considerable spirit, for, whilst accepting his replacement as justiciar by the archbishop of Rouen in accordance with the king's commission, he refused either to resign the chancellorship or surrender the royal castles in his custody, since his mistrust of John would make the last the act of a traitor. Finally, however, Longchamp agreed that his brother and brother-in-law should act as hostages for his appearance the following day at a meeting in the fields to the east of the Tower, where it was decided that he should remain chancellor and retain the castles of Hereford, Canterbury and Dover, but must leave England. From abroad he got the pope, whose legate he was, to intervene on his behalf. Letters were sent to the English bishops, excommunicating the archbishop of Rouen and Longchamp's other opponents with the exception of John. These were sent to Hugh with instructions to assemble his fellow bishops and publish them in their presence. Hugh also received instructions to sequestrate the possessions of the archdeacon of Oxford, John of Coutances, a relative of the archbishop of Rouen. In spite of his respect for papal authority there is no record that he ever carried out these orders.[1]

The second seizure of the temporalities of Lincoln just before Richard I's death, owing to Hugh's resistance to his demand that twelve of the richest canons of Lincoln should be sent abroad on diplomatic missions at their own expense, led him with some misgivings to adopt the policy which had proved successful before to go and see the king. The news of Richard's death reached him near Angers on the eve of Palm Sunday, and in spite of warnings of the danger owing to the disturbed state of the region he insisted on going to Fontevrault to assist at the funeral, visiting queen Berengaria on the way in order to console her in her bereavement. According to Hugh any other course of action would have been base and ungrateful, since whenever they were together Richard had always shewn him the greatest kindness and respect. His occasional acts of injustice had been due to the deliberate misrepresentations of malicious persons. A conversation between Hugh and Giraldus Cambrensis on the subject of Hubert Walter would certainly have been entertaining. After the funeral he met John, who had now been accepted as his brother's successor, at Chinon, and was given a cordial welcome. The king dismounted to embrace him and begged him to remain with him till his return to England for his coronation. Hugh only consented to stay for a few days, but this enabled Adam to give a graphic description of John's behaviour immediately after his accession. The king had been accepted with considerable reluctance and so was anxious to win over public opinion, particularly in the original Angevin lands where there was a considerable party in favour of Arthur. His courtesy and graciousness to beggars seems however to have been considerably overdone, and even with Hugh he could not hide his natural

---

[1] Gir., *Vita Galfridi archiepiscopi*, II, i-x, *Opera*, IV, 388-404, 410-431 ; Benedictus Abbas, II, 210-25 ; William of Newburgh, I, 333, 341-5 ; Howden, III, 138-47, 152-4 ; R. de Diceto, *Ymagines Historiarum*, II, 90-100 ; Richard of Devizes, *De Rebus Gestis Ricardi primi*, 411-9 ; Gervase of Canterbury, I, 504-7

levity and lack of religious feeling. Examples of this are his childish display of the amulet on which he alleged the luck of his family depended and his petulance when the bishop pointed out to him the kings amongst the damned in the representation of the Last Judgment over the main portail of the church at Fontevrault. Worse still, on Easter Sunday he played with the ten gold pieces presented to him to offer at the Mass, as if reluctant to part with them, until Hugh, who was one of the celebrants, angrily bade him put them down and go away. Also during the bishop's long sermon on the conduct and destinies of good and bad rulers, which was listened to with reverent attention by the rest of the congregation, he sent three times to ask him to end it and proceed with the Mass, as he wanted his dinner. The next Sunday at Rouen, when he was invested with the lance of the duchy of Normandy, hearing the laughter and applause of his former associates, he turned round to smile at them and let it fall to the ground, an incident which after the loss of the Angevin possessions was interpreted as an omen. He communicated neither on Easter Sunday nor at his coronation on Ascension Day, and his attendants declared that he had never done so since reaching years of discretion.

When Hugh was at Paris he was visited by Louis of France and Arthur of Brittany, who received Hugh's admonitions to live in friendship with his uncle whose vassal he had become by the recent peace with great anger and disdain, whilst his companion listened to the bishop with respectful attention. Hugh at Louis' request went with him to see his young bride Blanche of Castille, who was suffering from a recent bereavement and also possibly from homesickness, and he left her greatly cheered. His last meeting with John was on his deathbed, where he hardly replied to the king's lavish protestations of sympathy and concern, but merely asked him to respect his will and commended the church of Lincoln to his protection.[1] His later prophecies of the evils which would shortly come upon the English church and of the divine vengeance on all the sons

[1] *M.V.*, V, 7, 10-13, 16

of Henry II's adulterous marriage may well be conventional hagiology, since the last prediction was a commonplace of the writers of the time.

Hugh's political activities were quite compatible with his strong disapproval of ecclesiastics, taking part in secular administration and his distaste for the work of a judge delegate. He believed that as bishop he was bound to defend the property, rights and privileges of his church, of other people and of ecclesiastical communities, by excommunication and other spiritual censures, even if this involved a conflict with the secular authorities. The promotion of peace between Christian princes was even more important as it involved not only their own spiritual welfare but also that of their subjects, and it was the duty of a Christian bishop to admonish and rebuke them. His courage, strong convictions and the general respect felt for him gave him an influence in secular affairs which even Richard I and his archbishop found formidable and, on occasion, decisive.

D. L. D.

IV

MANUSCRIPTS AND PREVIOUS EDITIONS OF THE MAGNA VITA

The extant MSS of the *Magna Vita* fall naturally into three classes.

1. THE OLDEST FORM OF TEXT

It is generally agreed that MS Digby 165 [1] of the Bodleian Library at Oxford (B) best preserves Adam's work in its

---

[1] MS Digby 165 contains 135 leaves, pricked before ruling, and measuring $10\frac{1}{4}''$ by $7\frac{1}{4}''$. The writing space is $6\frac{7}{10}''$ by $4\frac{1}{8}''$; there are 29 lines per page. Chapter headings are written in red, and there are floriated capitals in red and blue. A tiny contemporary hand wrote summaries of chapter-contents in a few words in the margin and there are some untidy scribbles on several leaves. The *Magna Vita* is the only work it contains except for some tables referring to theological works, written in a late hand on the *verso* of the last two leaves.

original form. This beautifully written book with exceptionally wide margins belongs to the second half of the 13th century. The first quire is missing : this contained the Prologue, ch. I–VI and part of ch. VII of book I. With these all indication of provenance has gone except a late inscription on the last page of all : *Liber* (?) *magistri Roberti de La . . . .* Frequent marginal notes of *lege* and *noli legere*, presumably for public reading, seem to indicate a monastic (Carthusian ?) origin. This MS reproduces a text with strong idiosyncracies and awkwardness of style and vocabulary which suggest that they are the author's own. This feature makes it our most faithful MS in spite of the scribe's repeated tendency to omit individual words. Other errors are not numerous.

2. THE LONG ABBREVIATION

In his preface the abbreviator describes his purpose as ' removing those wordy elaborations which the aforesaid brother (Adam) introduced for elegance and edification, and also those digressions which concern not St Hugh's life but others'.' This text reproduces very faithfully about two thirds of the whole work ; although it omits whole paragraphs and even chapters, its quality is so good that it is valuable evidence for those parts of the text which it contains. Nothing new was added except an occasional word to join the separated parts of the unabridged text. About three quarters of the passages chosen for retention correspond with the *Lege* indications in B. The most faithful member of this group is a MS which belonged to the former London Charterhouse (o) and is still there : its text is closely related to B, although it was not written until the fifteenth century. This MS also contains abbreviated sermons of Adam of Dryburgh, the fragment of the Witham chronicle, and several patristic sermons. Another MS of this abbreviation is now MS 483 in the Toulouse Municipal library it is in very bad condition. A third MS of this class was in the possession of Lord Brownlow until it was sold at Sotheby's on

April 15, 1929; all efforts to trace it have failed. Its variants
in the Prologue and ch. I–VII of bk. I were fortunately collated
by Dimock and printed as an Appendix to vol. VII of the works
of Giraldus Cambrensis. Most of these readings agree with
those of the London Charterhouse MS.

3. CONTINENTAL VULGATE TEXTS

None of these is older than the fifteenth century. They are
generally unabridged, but aim at providing a smoother text
of the *Magna Vita*, together with interpolations and additions
from the Canonization Report in the same volume. Adam's
unusual words are sometimes deliberately altered or an
explanatory gloss added to them, his syntax is corrected,
enclitics are added or altered, and citations from Scripture
harmonized with the received text. These alterations often
make these MSS of slight value as evidence for the original
text except as a check on scribal errors ; but they provide
interesting evidence of the transformations which the life of a
saint could undergo. MSS of this class are fairly numerous :

c = Paris, Bibl. Nat. MS Latin 5575. An incomplete copy of
    unknown provenance. Contains bks. I–III except the last
    page, and the list of chapters for bk. IV. Probably the
    earliest survivor of this class, but it has many scribal errors.
    Written in the fifteenth century.

t = Trier Stadtbibliothek 163/1212. Came from St Alban's
    Charterhouse near Trier. Written in a fair German hand
    of the middle of the fifteenth century.

d = Brussels Bibl. Reg. Codex 298–306 (2133) from Sint Martens
    Lierde in the diocese of Cambrai. About the same date as
    the preceding and might have been copied from it. Omits
    portions of bk. V.

u = Utrecht University 396, from the Charterhouse of Utrecht.
    Written in 1476 by a monk of the house, William Simons-
    zoon of Amsterdam.

w = British Museum MS Add. 38007. Written in 1511 by a

Carthusian of St Barbara's at Cologne, who copied the text from a MS of the Charterhouse of Wesel.

v = a sixteenth century transcript by Peter de Wal, a Brussels Carthusian chronicler.

The last five of this series form a Rheno-Flemish sub-recension of the text. A transcript of this kind was prepared for the seventeenth century Bollandists (from an inaccurate copy of w) by Dom Servatius d'Oers of the Enghien Charterhouse in 1671, and another of the same date from Gaillon is in the municipal library at Louviers.

Various very short abbreviations of the *Magna Vita* are in existence : John of Tynemouth's (printed in C. Horstmann, *Nova Legenda Angliae*, Oxford 1901) is the best. A Metz MS 651 (m), written c. 1400 at the Charterhouse of Rettel, is of about the same length and provides occasional support to c : it includes additions from the *Legenda*. Yet a third abbreviation is to be found in Basel MS A. VI. 36. A longer abridgement, made in 1500–1 by Werner Rolewinck, a Cologne Carthusian, was printed by Surius there in his *Vitae Sanctorum* in 1575. Another one, a very free rendering in dialogue form by Peter Dorlandus, prior of the Diest Charterhouse, was printed by Petreius also at Cologne in 1608 (*Chronicon Cartusiense*, lib. III, pp. 69–133). Neither of these is a faithful reproduction of Adam's text, and each contains additions from the *Legenda*.

It is interesting to note that the first *printed* texts of St Hugh's life, enumerated above, were also the least accurate. A considerable advance was made when Pezius printed a text of the Long Abbreviation in volume X of his *Bibliotheca Ascaetica* (Ratisbon, 1733). This reproduced a MS of the Charterhouse of Gaming in the diocese of Passau as edited by Leopold Widemann. It was reprinted in vol. 153 of Migne's *Patrologia Latina*.

The first complete text of the *Magna Vita* was edited for the Rolls Series by Rev. J. F. Dimock in 1864. This was a very creditable performance, and its text was based on B, c and Pezius. B is generally well collated, but the friend to whom c was entrusted was notably less successful. Dimock did not know of the existence of any other MSS.

In 1890 the Carthusians printed the text of Peter de Wal's transcript, as edited more than two centuries earlier by Dom le Vasseur. Variants were added from Dimock and Pezius, but it made no claim to be a critical text. (*Ephemerides Carthusienses*, vol. II, Montreuil).

For the present edition B, o, c, d, and t have been collated, and also the printed texts of Pezius (p) and le Vasseur (v). Readings of the Long Abbreviation are represented by the symbol Q, and those of the Rheno-Flemish sub-recension by the symbol X. c has been collated separately. The reader will see at once how the two classes of text generally developed independently.

As it would have been beyond the scope of this edition to record each variant of every MS, the most characteristic ones have been chosen. Insignificant ones such as *-que* for *et*, *ergo* for *igitur*, *sanctus Hugo episcopus* for *episcopus* and *ille* occur very frequently in the Continental texts and they are not recorded. Spelling mistakes such as *Ierolomis* for *Ierosolimis*, *milititiam* for *militiam* etc. have been disregarded even when they occur in B. But this Bodleian MS is the foundation of the present edition and its readings have frequently been preferred to the unanimous or almost unanimous readings of the other texts. For the prologue and chapters 1-6 (and part of 7) of book I, which are wanting in B, the text printed below is based on the Long Abbreviation (o), where it exists ; where it does not, preference has often been given to c. B's antiquity and its quality are such that it will probably always be the basis of the text of the *Magna Vita* : it was written within about 30 years of

Adam's death, and may well be a copy of his original.[1]

As the *Magna Vita* was written by an English monk for an English monastery, it is not surprising that the best MSS are of English origin, but it seems not to have been often copied in medieval England. Bishop Richard Gravesend of London had a copy,[2] and there was more than one at Lincoln. A fifteenth century inventory of the shrine there has the entry : ' Item a booke of seint Hugh life cheyned ', and a fragmentary Certificate of Ornaments (1565–6) mentions ' two bokes of the liffe of saint Hughe '. Leland described a ' Historia de vita et gestis sancti Hugonis lincoln. episcopi ' which is certainly the *Magna Vita* and should probably be identified with the lost *Vita S. Hugonis* of the fifteenth century Chapter library catalogue. It would be reasonable to suppose that most of the English Charterhouses had a copy of the complete text or the Long Abbreviation, but there is no mention of either in the fifteenth century catalogue of the Grande Chartreuse. But in the seventeenth century, as Dom le Couteulx testifies, copies were to be found *passim* in Charterhouses on the Continent, which then numbered about 160. The popularity of the work was both late and Continental, but the older English MSS are still the best witnesses to Adam's original text. The printing of the text by Dimock in 1864 led to a well-deserved revival of interest in St Hugh, which is still increasing.

D. H. F.

---

[1] An interpolation on the last line of f. 80 r, believed by Dimock (*Magna Vita S. Hugonis*, R.S., pp. ix and 250) to prove this MS to be no more than a copy of a copy, is in reality a device of the scribe to conceal an error made in ruling the lines, which left him with one extra line to fill.

[2] cf. J. R. H. Moorman, *The English Church in the 13th Century*, pp. 182-3.

ABBREVIATIONS

M.V.	*Magna Vita Sancti Hugonis* (references are to books and chapters)
Gir.	Giraldi Cambrensis Opera (R.S.), 7 volumes
R.S.	Rolls Series
P.L.	Migne, *Patrologia Latina*, Paris 1879
C.S.E.L.	*Corpus Scriptorum Ecclesiasticorum Latinorum*, Vienna 1866
T.R.H.S.	*Transactions of the Royal Historical Society*
E.H.D.	*English Historical Documents*, (ed. D. C. Douglas) London 1953
O.H.S.	Oxford Historical Society
C. and Y.	Canterbury and York Society
Le Couteulx	C. le Couteulx, *Annales Ordinis Cartusiensis*, Montreuil 1888-91, 8 volumes
Witham Chronicle	A. Wilmart, 'Maître Adam, chanoine Prémontré devenu Chartreux à Witham,' *Analecta Praemonstratensia*, IX (1933), 207-37
Canonization Report	H. Farmer, 'The Canonization of St Hugh of Lincoln'. *Lincs. Architectural and Archaeological Society Papers*, 1956, 86-117
Thurston	H. Thurston, *The Life of St Hugh of Lincoln*, London 1898
+	adds
om	omits

Note : Scripture references are to the Vulgate and Douay Version ; liturgical references, unless otherwise stated, are to the *Missale Romanum* and the *Breviarium Monasticum O.S.B.*

LATIN TEXT
and
ENGLISH TRANSLATION

MAGNA VITA SANCTI HUGONIS

LIBER PRIMVS

Prologus

Dominis et amicis in Christo carissimis, R.[1] priori et qui cum eo sunt sanctis Withamensibus monachis, seruorum suorum minimus, frater A. uite que nunc est et future gaudia.[a]

Silentium michi, patres dilectissimi et domini in Christo plurimum reuerendi, si nichil aliud nisi quod puer essem imperaret, non nimis [b] indebite uel ad balbutiendum impelleretis, qui loqui nesciret, seruulum uestre sanctitatis. Esset quoque [c] mecum ignorantia mea, quam suis uiribus maiora temptantem [d] excusaret aut [e] etiam commendaret supplex obedientia.[f] Nunc autem et sensibus paruulum et sermone imperitum, et quod maxime michi lugendum est, puritatis minus conscium, non quibusque [g] auditoribus set senioribus, in omnibus premissis quibus ego egenus et pauper nimis sum prediuitibus loqui iubetis. Iubetis, inquam, nec a iubendo flecti adquiescitis, quatinus non nudis loquendo uerbis perfunctorie transeuntibus, immo tenacibus scribendo litteris [h] ex hiis que de uiro beatissimo Hugone Lincolniensi presule uidi, audiui et certius cognoui, ad subsidium memorie aliqua scedulis [j] tradam.

---

[a] *This sentence in* Qv *only*
[b] minus X
[c] + utinam Xc
[d] maiora attemptaret.   Excusaret X
[e] enim sic me c ; aut / seu Xc
[f] suppliciter obedientem X
[g] quibuscumque oX
[h] + scilicet Xc
[j] scedis Q, cedulis X

THE LIFE OF ST HUGH OF LINCOLN

BOOK ONE

PROLOGUE

To his lords and most dear friends prior R[obert][1] and the holy community at Witham, brother A[dam], the least of their servants sends this with his prayers for their welfare in this present life and that of the world to come.

Dear fathers and venerable lords in Christ, if nothing constrained me to silence but the fact that I am a child, if you in your holiness were demanding childish prattle from a servant who has not yet learned to talk, this would not be too improper. Even my ignorance would tell in my favour ; for in attempting a theme far beyond my capacity, I should win forgiveness and even merit for my humble obedience. As it is, although I am a child in understanding and completely without eloquence, and, even more serious, very conscious of my lack of virtue, nevertheless you command me to speak, and to speak not to any ordinary audience but to my elders and betters, who are rich in the very qualities I lack. You ordered me, I say, and would take no refusal, to ensure their survival I should report certain particulars concerning that most saintly man Hugh, bishop of Lincoln, from amongst those incidents, the truth of which I could vouch for, from the testimony of my own eyes, or from trustworthy evidence, and this not merely in words which are soon forgotten, but in writing as a permanent memorial.

---

[1] Probably Robert of Caveford (= Keyford, in Frome), an Englishman and seventh prior of Witham who succeeded another Robert, formerly procurator, mentioned below V, xvi. Robert of Caveford was prior when Adam of Dryburgh died, c. 1212. cf. Witham Chronicle § 19.

Instantiam beneplaciti seu rationem arbitrii uestri iudicare non est meum. Est autem debiti, est et desiderii mei, super facultatem et preter estimationem uirium mearum, uobis per omnia obedientem me *a* inueniri. Sit *b* autem, sicut et *c* esse debet, dignatio uestre benignitatis,*d* carbonem Ysaie purificando,[2] sermonem scientie erudiendo,[3] suppliciter a liberalissimo communique Domino impetrare orando, ' qui dat omnibus affluenter et non improperat.'[1]   Audiui quidem ad Iheremiam factum uerbum Domini, ' Ad omnia que mittam te ibis, et uniuersa que mandauero tibi loqueris.'[4]   Ipsius et de uobis istam legi sententiam : ' Qui uos audit me audit, et qui uos spernit me spernit.'[5] Tantam plane in uobis non spernere, tantam potius audire preopto in uobis loquentis et habitantis maiestatem ; nec causari quo minus uos audiam necessarium iudico, sanctitatis Iheremie me tam expertem quam *e* et in utero et post uterum miserum, immo et miserrimum peccatorem. Expedit enim quo plus sanctitatis exsortem, eo amplius subiectionis illius emulatorem inueniri. Vos autem, si placet, in scribendis per me que superna pietas dignabitur inspirare, non meam imperitiam set uestram potius audiri cognoscentes iussionem et legi,*f* hec ipsa qualiacumque fuerint sic accipite, discutite, uerbisque uel sententiis sic elimata et castigata, quibus uisum fuerit communicanda prebete, tamquam proprium uestrum sentientes esse quicquid in hiis plus minusue studio lectoris uidebitur prodesse.

---

a om X
b Scit X
c om X
d dignationis uestre benignitas X, benignitatis o
e quoniam c ; om X
f om o

It is not for me to question your urgent request or the reason for your decision. It is my bounden duty as well as my desire that you should find me obedient in everything, even in matters beyond my judgment of my capacity and powers. Your charity must condescend to intercede on my behalf with the most bounteous Lord of all men who gives to everyone abundantly and does not reproach them [1] that he may send Isaiah's living coal to cleanse me [2] and the word of wisdom for my instruction.[3] I have heard what the Lord said to Jeremiah, 'You will go everywhere that I send you and will speak everything that I command you.' [4] I have read and applied to you his words, ' Who hears you, hears me and who rejects you rejects me.' [5] Verily, I desire exceedingly not to reject you but rather to obey Him who speaks through you and dwells in you, nor do I think it right to plead as my excuse for not listening to you the fact that I am completely devoid of the holiness of Jeremiah, and am from the womb and ever after a pitiful, yea a most pitiful sinner. It behoves those most removed from his holiness to be the readier to imitate his obedience. May it please you to overlook my defects as a writer, since whatever God may inspire me to set down has only been undertaken by me at your request. Receive it, such as it is, in this spirit, go over it, cut out and prune the words and even the matter and pass it on to be read by those you may think fit, realizing that anything in it which may to any degree profit the devout reader, is really your property, since you inspired it.

[1] Jas. 1:5
[2] cf. Isa. 6:6-7
[3] cf. I Cor. 12:8
[4] Jer. 1:7
[5] Luke 10:16

Nosse quoque lectorem,[a] sicut et uos meminisse
decet,[b] quia non seriatim et integre uitam scribere uiri
huius beati, fundatoris et institutoris uestri,[c] communis
patroni nostri suscepi, cum muneri tanto imparem me
et penitus insufficientem nullus ignoret. Iure uero
credendum, non modo ab uno aliquo suorum tot
doctissimorum filiorum, immo et a pluribus, hoc iam
sublimiter attemptatum, feliciterque prout homini possi-
bile fuit, licet id certius non approbemus, esse consummatum. Quis enim, ut uere condignum erat,
uniuersa que de tanto uiro salubriter innotescerent,
scribendo explicaret? Quis, ut etiam experta loquar,
non dico scriberet aut referret, set Hugoni dum in terris
ageret adherens, Hugonem uidens et audiens, Hugonis
occulta et manifesta quantum homini fas erat agnoscens,
que in Hugone miranda fuerunt [d] et imitanda [e] digne
comprehenderet? Quis, ut paucis utar, uite illius et
morum sinceritatem, set suauitatem, set sanctitatem, set
singularem in tot gratie spiritualis [f] karismatibus emi-
nentiam quantalibet mentis perspicacia complecti
potuisset?

Et quidem in carne illo adhuc agente set meritis
celum optinente, non modica set nec pauca de hiis
quosdam me longe doctiores scripsisse agnoui, ex quibus
aliqua inspexi; quod [g] etiam pro excusatione mea
pretendebam uobis, cum a mea pueritia [h] hunc scribendi
laborem impendi Hugoni, ut dicebatis, meo impensius
exegistis. Quo quam maxime sermone de supplici
uestro triumphastis, et in morem [i] Helisei fluctiuagos
humilitatis mee estus, tamquam Iordanicos uortices,

[a] lector X	[b] debet X, debetis v
[c] nostri X	[d] fuerint cv
[e] + quis X	[f] spiritualibus Xc
[g] que cd	[h] imperitia Xc
[i] mortem Q	

Both you and my readers should remember and understand that I do not intend to write a full biography in chronological order of this saintly man, your founder and instructor and our common patron. Everyone would agree that I am unequal to and incapable of such a task. It must be common knowledge that not one but several of his more learned disciples have not only attempted, but successfully achieved this, as far as human talent can do so. I do not wholeheartedly admire their work, for to write a full and satisfactory life of such a man is impossible. I speak from experience. Who is there among Hugh's disciples during his earthly life, who saw and heard him and shared as much of his public and private life as was permissible, who could, I will not say write and recount but even understand and take example from his wonderful character and deeds? Who, in short, can claim to know completely a man of such utter integrity and candour, of such charm and holiness, and of such remarkable and outstanding moral and intellectual eminence?

I am well aware that even during his earthly pilgrimage when his virtues had already made him a citizen of Heaven, many persons far more competent than myself wrote in some detail about him, and I have even perused some of their works. I brought this forward as an excuse to you, when you so urgently insisted that I, in spite of my inexperience, should undertake the task of composing a written memorial to my master Hugh, as you called him. This one word in your petition triumphed over my hesitations and consciousness of my insufficiency. Like Elisha you have made a path for your feet through the foaming waters of Jordan. The name of Hugh acted like a charm on the misgivings due to my sense of my lack of literary skill,

pedibus uestris peruios reddidistis, quando decliuem
uerecundie mee inscitiam [a] Hugonis mei nomen tetigit,
ut tunc Helie pallium aquas illas patefecit,[1] cessi
protinus ; et ex gestis beati uiri, ac si de pulcherrimo
ligno quodam paradisi uel paucula me poma decerp-
turum, si Dominus facultatem [b] suppeditare dignaretur,
promisi. Que tandem isto qualicumque libello inserta,
ut solent fructus pretiosi calatho uiliori [c] nonnumquam
includi, uestre iam quanta possum ex deuotione trans-
mitto sanctitati, dulciter si placet suscipienda, dulcius
amplectenda set dulcissime delibanda. Ne uero aliter
pro mittentis aut continentis uitio aut uilitate eueniat,
missum et contentum facile ut spero optinebit.

Bene ualeat et [d] uigeat in omni pietate et sanctitate,
ac pro nobis iugiter intercedat uniuersitas sanctissimi
cetus uestri, domini mei et patres merito semper
uenerandi.

[a] inscientiam X
[b] om c, *with* promisi *after* decepturum
[c] uiliore o
[d] om o

and like the mantle of Elijah opened a way through the river.[1] I immediately consented, and have promised that if the Lord will deign to bestow on me the power, I will select and relate some of the deeds of that blessed man. These few apples plucked as it were from the finest tree in Paradise, and set down in this poor little book (since it is customary for excellent fruit to be packed in a basket of little value), I send to your reverences with the utmost affection. May it please you to receive it with favour, to find it still more to your taste when you have handled it, and even more delightful when you have thoroughly digested it. The sender and the package may have their failings and defects, but the contents, I trust, will amply atone for them.

Farewell, my lords, and ever revered fathers. May all your holy community flourish and increase in sanctity and devotion. I commend myself to their prayers and yours.

[1] cf. 4 Kings 2:8-15

CAPITVLVM I

Qualiter Hugo, genitricis solatio destitutus et regularium collegio clericorum una cum genitore sociatus, iugum Domini ab adholescentia portauerit ; et propria ipsius relatio de institutione sua.[a]

Illustris sobolis clarissimi genitores ea ratione splendidius iustiusque exornant insignium [b] titulos liberorum, si a quibus ducitur linea generose propaginis, ab ipsis materia uirtutis et incentiuum [c] ducatur probitatis. Eo quippe omisso, stemata, ut quidam [d] ait, quid faciunt ? Quid enim confert generosum quemlibet in huius mundi lucem prodiisse et in mundo degenerem uixisse, cum satius sit natalibus quam moribus extitisse obscurum et nasci quam fieri non preclarum ? In uno conditionis necessitas excusatur ; in reliquo peruersitas conditionis reprobatur.[e] Suos itaque genitores simul et germanos uiri sanguine clari set clarissimi sanctitate, Hugonis antistitis preconia iure insignia collustrant dum ab illis sancte institutionis prelibauit exordium, ab istis strenue actionis percepit adminiculum. Verum ista procedens sermo manifestius locis absoluet oportunis.

Et genitricis quidem solatio, cum prime [f] necdum etatis metas excessisset,[g] orbatus est, collegioque regularium clericorum una cum genitore [h] breui postmodum sociatus. Erat ferme [j] octennis cum militie spiritualis subiit tyrocinia. Boni quippe parentis salubriter pro eo inuigilante [k] sollertia, prius docetur militare Deo[1] quam

[a] + puerili c	[b] signum tituli X
[c] incrementum X	[d] ille c, quis v
[e] X *ömit this sentence*	[f] om o
[g] attigisset X	[h] + in X
[j] fere X	[k] inuigilauit X

Chapter I

How Hugh, being deprived of a mother's care, was admitted with his father to a house of regular canons, and bore the yoke of the Lord from his youth onwards. His own account of his early training.

Illustrious and noble parents rightly enhance the renown of their famous children, if high birth is itself a spur to virtue and honour. It has been said that unless it has this effect, of what value is illustrious lineage? How does it profit a man to be nobly born, if he act dishonourably? It is better to come of low and humble stock, than to be base and mean in disposition. Necessity causes the first condition to be condoned, whereas perversion makes the second blameworthy. The far-famed reputation of bishop Hugh, a man of distinguished birth, but even more distinguished by reason of his sanctity, rightly brought glory to his parents and brethren. He, in his turn, received from them the rudiments of a Christian education and the first stimulus to courage and valour. We will treat of this less ambiguously in the right place.

Being deprived of a mother's care when still a young child, he was shortly afterwards admitted with his father into a community of canons regular. He was barely eight years old when he was enrolled in the monastic army. The solicitous care of his worthy father wisely ordained that he should learn to fight for God[1] before he acquired the art of living in the world. Even in his childhood no time was wasted in naughtiness, much less

[1] cf. 2 Tim. 2:4

addisceret uiuere mundo. Nam et ipsa eius tenerioris quoque rudimenta etatis non otio, multominus uero lasciuie cessere perdenda. Elementaria litterarum non hoc sibi uendicauerant gignasia, ubi labor et dolor, ex ipsarum amara prodeuntes radice, exultationem parturiebant ei et multam requiem, quandoque satiando *a* earum dulcissima fructus suauitate. Ita uero in Christi tyrone, homo natus ad laborem [1] laboribus mox natus exercetur, ut auis aptior ad uolandum in eodem citius redderetur. Ita non modo ab adholescentia, immo et ab infantia, iugum Domini portare consuescens, celerius canos sensus attigit, quo fieret ydoneus solitarius sedere et leuare se supra se.[2] Sic demum infantile corpusculum flagella pedagogi attrectant, sic discipline compedes motus in eo pueriles cohercent ut et *b* uirtutibus uitia preteriret, et tota uita eius presens, a sui ortu usque ad occasum, unum esset et iuge martirium.

Nam et ab illius ore ueridico que sequuntur pluries accepimus. Vt enim fuit reuerenda grauitate affabilis et cum sanctitate singulari accedentibus ad se, secumque uiuentibus dulcissimus et communis, familiariter sepius cum suis agens talia de seipso simpliciter referebat. ' Reuera,' aiebat, ' ego mundi huius gaudia numquam attigi, iocos numquam didici, numquam sciui.' *c* Consequenter prime institutionis sue seu educationis in hunc modum ordinem retexebat. ' Pater,' inquit, ' meus, cum pueriles ingressus annos elementa iam prima litterarum percepissem, patrimonium liberis suis in funiculo distributionis [3] partitus est. Portionem uero, que inter fratres minimum me contingebat, regularium clericorum collegio contulit. Nec diu moratus, omnia que mundi

a satiandus X
b om Xc
c sitiui cm

in sin. He learned his early lessons in no harsh school and these were to him a source of pleasure and delight rather than of toil and suffering.

Man is born to labour,[1] and so even from his birth Christ's disciple was trained to labour, so that like a bird he should fly more readily and rapidly through constant training. Being accustomed to bear the yoke of the Lord from his youth, nay rather from his childhood he soon attained the maturity required for solitude and contemplation.[2] The rod of the master afflicted his childish frame, and the fetters of discipline restrained his boyish inclinations, vice gave place to virtue and all his earthly life from its beginning to its ending was one of penance and submission.

The incidents which follow are true since we heard them many times from his own lips. Although grave and dignified and of a singular holiness he was accessible to all who came to him, and on friendly and intimate terms with his household. When talking confidentially with his servants he would often speak candidly of himself as follows : ' Truly,' he would say, ' I never tasted the joys of this world. I never knew or learnt how to play.' Then he would describe his early training and upbringing in this way, ' My father, when I, having just reached boyhood, was learning to read, divided his patrimony by lot amongst his children.[3] He gave the portion which fell to me, the youngest brother, to a college of regular canons. Almost immediately, he abandoned the world to enter the army of Christ. and

---

[1] Job 5:7
[2] Lam. 3:27, 28
[3] cf. Ps. 77:54

sunt funditus abiciens, Christi militiam subiturus, tyro
in castris celestibus, in mundanis iam emeritus, repente
efficitur.   Nec enim emeritorum immunitas sibi potuit
esse amori, que, etsi fatigatis militia indulget quietem,
set defunctos a miseria non absoluit etiam post mortalis
uite expletum laborem.   Vite igitur regularis, cuius iam
olim gesserat *a* mentem, suscepit *b* uestem ;   et quod
sibi concessum non fuisse *c* medullitus gemebat, in ipso
mundi ingressu de mundo egredi, que mundi sunt
nescientem facile persuadens, me pariter secum spiritualis
militie consortem asciuit.

' Est ecclesia in territorio Gratianopolitano, canonice
professionis clericos fouens, numero quoad minus
septem. Spectat quoque cum suis incolis locus ipse ad
matricem et cathedralem Gratianopolitanam ecclesiam,
que ipsa eiusdem professionis nobili pollet examine.
Hanc semper affectu coluit speciali *d* genitor meus, que
et suis castellis ac terris situ confinis erat ; et ipse, ut
filius deuotus, maioris ecclesie gratiam in filie ipsius
reuerentia *e* se complecti gaudebat.   Inter canonicos
illius loci senior quidam religione celeberrimus, scientia
quoque spectabilior ceteris habebatur.   Huic nobilium
liberi certatim a parentibus tradebantur, secularibus
simul et ecclesiasticis litteris imbuendi, necnon et ethicis
informandi disciplinis.*f*   Hic michi sacras litteras inter
ipsa rudimenta summopere ingerens, blandimentis quibus
posset et monitis teneros annos meos *g* ad solidioris
spiritualisque amorem doctrine accendere nitebatur.
A ludendi uero iocandique uanitate uaria mentis mee

---

a gessit Xc
b suscipiens uestem Q ; suscepit habitum X
c fuisset Xc
d *om* o
e reuerentiam Xc
f X *omit this sentence*
g teneros animos ad Xc

this veteran in earthly warfare became at once a recruit
in the heavenly forces.   The peace of retirement had
no attraction for him, since whilst giving repose to
war-worn warriors, it gave no assurance of salvation to
the dead when they had completed their earthly labours.
Having long been at heart a canon regular, he now
assumed their habit and since he regretted that the
privilege of abandoning the world had not been accorded
to him at the beginning of his life, he easily persuaded me,
who had no experience of it, to become his companion in
the army of God.

   ' There is in the diocese of Grenoble a church for at
least seven canons, which belongs to the cathedral of
Grenoble, a famous and numerous house of the same
way of life.   For this church my father always had a
special affection, because his lands and castles were
in the neighbourhood and his filial piety caused him
to rejoice that in showing reverence to the daughter
house he was in effect honouring the mother church.
The nobles competed to commit their children to the
care of one of the senior canons of this place, a man
famed for his piety, and more learned than the others, in
order that they might be instructed in sacred and profane
letters and in virtuous living.   Along with my other early
studies he took great care to give me a knowledge of the
scriptures, and strove with all the allurements and
exhortations possible to kindle in me in spite of my youth
a love for the more solid and spiritual doctrine.   By
various devices he overcame my inclination towards
play and idle diversions, and turned it to profitable
pursuits of every kind.   Frequently, when my young
companions were at their usual sports, he would rebuke
me mildly and with paternal kindness, saying, " My
dear son, do not be infected by the foolish and aimless

intentionem arte suspendens, honestis implicabat cuiusque *a* rei exercitiis. Coeuis autem et sodalibus pueris
frequenter ex more ludentibus, michi talia leniter
instillabat paterne dulcedinis hortamenta : " Non te,"
inquit, " dulcissime *b* fili, stolida illiciat uagaque leuitas
sociorum. Sine illos, sorti tue istorum studia minus
conueniunt." Addebatque : " Hugonette, Hugonette,
ego te Christo nutrio, iocari non est tuum "."

CAPITVLVM II

Quantum in discenda Dei uoluntate fuerit sollicitus,
et in diuinis officiis sollers et deuotus.*c*

Huius itaque uiri saluberrima institutione, docente
eum interius Spiritus Sancti unctione, proficiebat in dies
puer gratiosus, Deo carus et hominibus. Repletus, supra
quam facile dici posset, spiritu sapientie et intellectus,[1]
gustans uero magisque ac magis hauriens dulcedinem
celestis doctrine, auidius inhiabat uberibus matris
ecclesie. Erat ei ex toto uoluntas in lege Domini in qua
meditabatur die ac nocte.[2] Curabat sollicitius in omni
humilitate et puritate utriusque cathizete, hominis
uidelicet rigantis exterius et Dei interius incrementum
dantis,[3] monitis et nutibus docibilem *d* se et submissum
exhibere. Currebat ut alter Samuel ad quod eum
inuitabat suus, illo quondam caligante, meliorque et
humilior Hely, et cum eodem, uocanti in aure cordis eum
Domino alacriter *e* aiebat, ' Loquere, Domine, quia
audit seruus tuus.' [4]

---

a cuiuscumque Xoc   *b* dilectissime cp   *c* prouidus c
d docilem c   *e* om cd   [1] cf. Isa. 11:2
[2] cf. Ps. 1:2   [3] cf. 1 Cor. 3:6   [4] 1 Kings, 3:9

levity of your comrades." He would add, "Little Hugh, little Hugh, I am educating you for Christ, play is not for you." '

Chapter II

How he sought diligently to discover the will of God, and was assiduous and devout at the divine Office.

Through the admirable training of this man and through the grace of the Holy Spirit teaching him internally, the child of grace grew in virtue daily and was dear to God and man. Words cannot easily describe how much he was filled with the spirit of wisdom and understanding.[1] The more he tasted and imbibed the sweet draughts of heavenly doctrine, the more he greedily sucked at the breasts of mother Church. His whole purpose was to obey the commandments of God on which he meditated day and night.[2] In all humility and simplicity he attended diligently to both masters, to the human one who watered the exterior and to God who gave the interior increase,[3] meekly and submissively receiving their counsels and instructions. Like another Samuel he hastened eagerly to whatever his former preceptor, a better and more humble Eli, suggested to him, and hearing the voice of God speaking in his heart, he answered with alacrity, ' Speak Lord, for thy servant heareth.' [4]

Certabat in eius animo cum studio sciendi desiderium adimplendi uoluntatem Domini.[a] Nouerat quidem, sicut maius esse hanc [b] facere quam scire, ita prius esse hanc scire quam facere. Sciebat id quod inferius horum est utilitate, primum esse proficiendi ordine et temporis ratione. Nitebatur omnem Domini sui uoluntatem plenius [c] nosse, ne forte ignorantem Dominus ignoraret.[1] Cauebat sollicitius ne uel per errorem omittendo agenda, uel admittendo cauenda, ad inimicitias Domini quandoque erumperet, et inter fideles seruos quos pius Dominus amicos suos apellat[2] censeri non posset, cuius animus eo minus custodiret quo periculosius ignoraret. Ad utrumque igitur uelox, ad utrumque sollers, et ignorare que Dei sunt ut erroris seminarium et delinquendi fomitem deuitabat, et agnita non implere, quod multarum plagarum sciret lucrosum, ut extremam perniciem fugiebat. Verissime illud beati Iob ei congruere fidenter dixerim, quia ' semper ut tumentes super se fluctus timuit Dominum ', id quod sequitur altius pensans ' sciens,' inquit, ' quod non parceres delinquenti.'[3]

Iam uero pubertatis tempore adholescentiam [d] mediis in eo annis dirimente, quantum discretionis et scientie,[e] quantum uirtutis et gratie fons ei infuderit quem sitiebat uite, nullus de facili posset stilus euoluere. Plantatus siquidem ab ipsis, ut ita dicam, ortus sui primordiis, tamquam generosus quidam ligni uite surculus, secus salutarium decursus aquarum miserat profunde humilitatis radices deorsum ut faceret fructum sursum, quem etiam in tempore suo cunctis daret habitantibus secum.[4] Sic plane adholescens pius mulcebat primo cunctos sibi

---

[a] Dei X   [b] hanc . . . hanc/habeat . . . habet X
[c] om X   [d] adholescentie tm
[e] et scientie/om X

His mind was equally alert to know and fulfil the will of God. He had learned that although doing is better than knowing, knowledge should precede action, and that the lesser of the two in merit was the first to be pursued in order of time. He endeavoured conscientiously to ascertain the Lord's will, lest perchance he should not know one who knew Him not.[1] He feared exceedingly lest he should incur the wrath of God either by inadvertently leaving undone what he ought to have done, or by doing what he ought not to have done, and thus could not be numbered amongst those faithful servants whom the merciful Lord called his friends,[2] if his soul became ever less watchful as the danger of ignorance increased. Therefore he was careful and eager to avoid both ignorance of the things of God, which is the seed of error, and the result of sin and failure to accomplish God's known will, which he conceived to be the source of many troubles and even of eternal damnation. I can say with truth that the text in blessed Job exactly fitted him, ' When the swelling waves broke over him, he always feared the Lord,' and he was mindful of an earlier one ' Knowing, that he will not spare the sinner.'[3]

When he reached adolescence no pen could easily write of the abundance of wisdom and understanding, and of virtue and grace with which the fountain of life he thirsted for had endowed him. Planted by these, so to speak, from such beginnings he grew like a noble sapling of the tree of life, beside the streams of living water, which, deeply rooted in humility, bore fruit above ground, which in due season he would give to his companions.[4] Thus the saintly youth first drew

---

[1] cf. 1 Cor. 14:38
[2] John 15:14
[3] Job 31:23, 9:28
[4] cf. Ps. 1:3 ; 4 Kings 19:30

multiplicibus gratiarum quibus exuberabat donis, que procedente post tempore longe lateque diffudit. Scintillans namque Spiritus Sancti in pectore eius igniculus, uiciniores quosque suis primo accendit flammis, qui in uastum subinde incendium conualescens, splendoris sui et caloris beneficia in remotiores circumquaque gratius dilatauit.

Videre erat dona gratie et dotes nature quemdam in eius prerogatiua sibi assumpsisse conflictum, ut uix discerneres quenam earum partes in eo ageret potiores. Set uincebat naturam gratia, dum bona indoles accipiebat gratiam pro gratia, superantem, preuentricem, subsecutiuam.

Vigebat ingenii acumine magno, quo uelocius queque *ᵃ* uellet addisceret. Memorie uastissimis gaudebat apothecis, ubi que didicisset nulla obliuione perdenda reconderet.*ᵇ* Hec tamen naturalia nullius fuissent momenti, nisi gratie appositio et preclara que discerentur suggereret, et cumulatius que *ᶜ* suggessisset propagando *ᵈ* augeret.

Feruebant in pectore eius meditationum examina beatarum ; fragrabant celestium odoramenta gaudiorum. Assurgebat ardor desiderii rorantis a supernis mellite dulcedinis, et inter huiusmodi epulas felix anima cantabat sibi : ' Si uix stillam tenuissimam sermonum eius accepimus, quis poterit tonitruum magnitudinis eius sustinere ? ' *ᵉ,*[1]

Cepit interea diuinis adeo sedulus adesse *ᶠ* officiis, ita quoque sollicitus fratrum inseruire obsequiis, ut utro-

---

ᵃ quecumque Xc
ᵇ reponeret Xc
ᶜ + suxisset uel Q
ᵈ propaganda Xc
ᵉ accepimus . . . sustinere / audierimus . . . intueri v (and *Vulgate*)
ᶠ esse Xc

them all to him by the manifold gifts and graces in which he abounded, which in process of time he spread far and wide. The fire of the Holy Spirit sparkling in him, first inflamed his neighbours and then, becoming a vast conflagration, diffused the benefits of its light and heat to the more distant regions.

Nature and grace so contended in him that you could scarcely decide which was the more dominant. Grace prevailed over nature, whilst his natural goodness was the foundation for the grace which subdued it, preceded it and followed it.

The natural acuteness of his mind enabled him to learn quickly whatever he wished, and his richly stored memory prevented him forgetting anything he had learned. Nevertheless these gifts of nature would have been unprofitable if grace had not dictated what he should learn and abundantly increased and developed what he had acquired.

Assiduous meditation on sacred things inflamed his heart and made it fragrant with the sweet odour of heavenly joys. Fervent and sweet desires were kindled in him from on high, and amid such fare the happy soul chanted to itself, ' If we should receive scarcely one syllable of his utterances, the thunder of his power who can endure ? ' [1]

He was so zealous in his attendance at the divine office, and so desirous to be of service to his fellow canons that both duties completely absorbed him. He never forgot, nor could any occupation rob him of this eagerness to remember to give without intermission and neglect due time and place to God, and to his neighbours what

[1] Job 26:14

bique nichil minus quam se totum impenderet. Nichil
umquam obliuio, nil *a* queuis poterat occupatio sedulitati
ipsius furari, quin Deo que Dei erant et que proximorum
proximis inpretermisse et inoffense prout sibi competebat,
pro tempore et loco reddere meminisset. Nec tantum
deputata sibi *b* explere satagebat officia, set omnia
tamquam specialiter a se credebat exigi que, teste conscientia, pro cuiusque *c* utilitate aut refrigerio a se
possent exhiberi.

Denique cum talia de eo coram eo iam episcopo, qui
eum tunc temporis nouerant fratres aliquotiens, me
quoque presente, referrent, ipse aiebat, ' Vtique,
posteaquam Cartusiam adiui, nescio si uel semel michi
aliquando surrepsit morantia in officio aliquo quod
implere deberem.' Dicitur autem uulgo morantia inter
monachos cum legendi, cantandi uel seruiendi munus
sibi assignatum omittit quis, unde moram patitur functio
regularis. Dicebat uero non quidem iactanter set constanter ista de se. Cum enim *d* in dedicationibus
ecclesiarum, in celebrationibus ordinum, uel quan-
documque in *e* diurnis nocturnisue officiis per incuriam
ministrorum, cantorum seu lectorum aliqua tardatio
emergebat, talem suorum castigare cupiens negligentiam,
hoc eis de seipso habende in diuinis officiis exemplum
diligentie intimabat.*f*

In eo autem hec perseuerauit usque in finem diligentia, cunctis agnoscentibus miranda facilius *g* quam
imitanda. Numquam presens tumultuantis frequentie
importunitas, numquam transacte uel presentis cuiuscumque disceptationis implicitas, aut alius qualiscumque

---

a uel cd   *b* *om* Xc
c cuiuscumque Xo   *d* *om* o
e + diuinis X   *f* innuebat diligentie X
g potius X

was due to each of them. He strove to discharge not only
the duties entrusted to him, but everything which his
conscience told him was incumbent upon him for the
profit or relief of anyone.

During his episcopate I heard the brothers who had
known him then relate such things about him several
times in his presence. He replied, ' Verily, after I went
to Chartreuse I cannot remember any occasion on
which I delayed carrying out any duty I had to perform.'
The term ' delay ' is generally used in monastic circles if
anyone neglects the reading, chanting or work allotted
to him, because this causes a hitch in the monastic
routine. He said this about himself calmly and not
boastfully. When any unpunctuality occurred at the
consecration of churches, or at ordinations, or during
the day or night offices as the result of the carelessness of
the assistants, singers, or readers, he rebuked their
negligence by citing himself to them as an example of
exactitude at the divine office.

All are aware that this exactitude which was easier
to admire than to imitate lasted to the end of his life.
Neither the distracting presence of many people, nor
complicated legal business either terminated or pending,
could prevent him from being both internally and
externally ready at the right time and moment to
celebrate mass or to perform any other episcopal
function.

casus undecumque emergens ei potuit surrepere quin
corde semper et labiis paratum et promptum haberet
quicquid tempore [a] et hora tam in altaris quam in
alterius officii ministerii esset prosequendum.

Capitvlvm III

Commendatio morum patris eius.   Et de quodam
negotiatore Hugonis narratio.   Et quod idem paterne
senectuti, iussu prioris sui, deuotus [b] seruierit.

Vt autem cepte narrationis ordinem seriatim prosequamur, Hugone iam adulto pater eius senectutis
extreme crebris cepit urgeri incommodis.   Tantam [c]
uero idem in utraque, prius scilicet in mundana ac
deinceps in spirituali optinuerat militia uirtutis palmam,
ut nichil suis gratius haberetur commilitonibus quam ei
in omnibus gratum deferre contubernium.   Fuerat enim
modestie singularis, moribus suauis et honestus, comitate
strenuus, benignitate acceptissimus.   De quo licet in
rem [d] quam intendimus uideamur in digressionis preiuditium aliquatenus uenire, quiddam relatu mirum,
quod ipsum sepius referre non pigebat Hugonem iam
episcopum, iam leuia nec audientem libenter nec
proferentem, non absurdum putamus [e] inserere lectioni.
Manebat in quodam patris ipsius fundo negotiator
quidam, quem et ipse tunc puer bene nouerat, qui merces
a peregrinis delatas regionibus uicinis uenumdare consueuerat.   De remotis partibus suos post interposita
morarum spatia repetens lares, dominum suum adire

---

[a] tempus o   [b] deuote c
[c] tandem c   [d] a re X
[e] sit c

CHAPTER III

A eulogy on the character of his father, and Hugh's story of a certain merchant. How at the command of his prior, he waited upon his father with filial devotion in his old age.

To resume our narrative. Hugh was just grown up when his father began to be weighed down with the infirmities of old age. He had won the palm of virtue in both warfares, first in the world and later in the cloister, and his fellow warriors desired nothing better than always to have his companionship. He was a man of singular modesty, gentle and yet dignified, whose unusual graciousness and kindliness made him generally beloved. Although it is somewhat of a digression, it does not seem beside the point to insert here a certain remarkable anecdote, which Hugh, who never readily either heard or spoke of trifles, was fond of telling about him when he himself was already a bishop.

A certain merchant lived on one of his father's farms who used to sell to his neighbours goods brought from foreign lands. He had known the man well in his boyhood, for when he returned home after an interval solebat, munusculis, ut erat facetus et liberalis, ipsum plerumque honorans exoticis,[a] et pro suorum cautela, quos in sui absentia clementer fouebat, debitas ei gratiarum rependens actiones.

Contigit uero, instigante humani generis inimico, ut aliquando mercatorem post moras regressum ad propria, coniux ipsius sociato sibi adulteri cuiusdam cum quo mechari consueuerat nefando auxilio, crudeliter iugulatum in agello uicino glebis noualium defossum obrueret. Innotescit interea domino redisse uirum, elapsisque diebus aliquot, cum se more solito eius minime presentaret conspectui, mirabatur super hoc dominus et domestici eius similiter mirabantur. Vicini quoque et conuicanei illius mirum ducebant quod post primum reditus sui diem inter eos non comparuisset. Volens igitur dominus quidnam accidisset ei plenius nosse, multis eum concomitantibus uenit per semetipsum ad domum uiri. Cui occurrens infida mulier, blande salutans eum, cepit de uiri sui adeo repentino discessu conqueri, qui iam diu dominum karissimum et sibi in multis beneficum non uidisset. ' Nobiscum ', inquit, ' uix una cum post longas absentie sue moras nocte quieuisset, mane facto recessit, nec certum nobis est quando domum reuertatur.' Interea uero canis domesticus plausibus ululatibus mixtis mirisque gestibus domino qui aduenerat uel alludens uel conquerens, tam ipsum quam omnes qui aderant in admirationem agebat. Recedentem demum non deserit canis dominum, set ipsum comitatus, ipsi obambulans, nunc quasi amplexurus erigitur in eum, nunc solo prostratus terramque unguibus scalpens, questibus et ululatibus uacat. Milites qui hec uidebant stupentes quandoque subsistebant ; at tunc

---

[a] + id est peregrinis X

abroad he was accustomed, being of an open-handed and generous disposition, to come to his lord with gifts from his travels, in order to thank him for his kindness and protection of his family during his absence.

Once when this merchant returned home after some time, his wife in conjunction with her wicked paramour, being inspired by the evil one, barbarously strangled him and buried him in the corner of a neighbouring field under the clods of some newly ploughed land. Having heard of his return his lord and his servants, after some days had passed, were amazed that he did not come to see him as was his custom. His neighbours also were surprised when the first day after his arrival he did not appear amongst them. Desirous of ascertaining what had happened his lord, accompanied by a number of persons, visited the man's home. The faithless wife met him and greeted him suavely, lamenting the sudden departure of her husband since he had not been able to see his lord, for whom he had long entertained a peculiar affection by reason of his many kindnesses towards him. ' After so long an absence,' she said, ' he only remained for one night with me, leaving at dawn, nor do I know when he will return.' In the meantime, the house dog was barking and howling, and alternately fawned on the lord and cowered against him, so that both he and his companions were astonished at his strange behaviour. When at last he departed, it would not leave him, but accompanied him, now running round him, now jumping up on him, now lying down and scratching the ground with its paws, and howling and yelping. When the knights perceived this, they stood still in amazement. Then the mastiff, seeing that they had halted, went straight to the ditch where the corpse of

molossus, dum illos expectare cerneret, cursum tendebat
uersus aggerem quo tegebatur cadauer occisi. Cumque
canem iam putarent abscedentem nec ulterius rediturum
subsequi dominum postposuisse, ad propria ut ceperat
tendentem cursu ille insequitur uelocissimo ; statimque
ut prius gestu uoceque lamentabili ipsum quasi inter-
pellans, non ante destitit quam eum quibus potuit
nutibus motum, ad locum obruti funeris preuius ipse
perduxit. Veniensque ad sulcum qui scrobem *a* sepulti
cadaueris callide celabat, ut quasi aratro *b* tantum
crederetur inuersus, eruderare dentibus et unguibus
congestos cespites instantius festinabat. Apponunt
tandem et uiri astantes manus ; fodiunt, demumque
cadauer inuentum extrahunt, inspiciunt, agnoscunt ;
mechumque super maleficio discutientes, rei citius
seriem addiscunt. Hec nos de hiis scripsisse lectori non
sit onerosum, que tanto pontifici, multis et magnis
plerumque uiris presentibus, referre non uidebatur
superfluum. Verum ad cepta iam sermo recurret.*c*

Igitur Hugoni qui fratribus uniuersis deuotione
uiribus totis deseruiebat filiali, prioris sui mandato
iniungitur speciali quatinus suo precipue et peculiarius,
in quibus opus haberet, seruiret genitori. ' Nichil enim ',*d*
ait, ' michi aut ceteris fratribus prestabis gratius quam si
uiro adeo spectabili nichil uotiui *e* denegaueris obsequii.
Te uero inter fratres nullus deuotior, set humilitate
pronior, set officiositate nemo te promptior inuenitur,
cui a nobis adeo grati cura negotii demandetur.'
Excipit libens, libentiusque exequitur adholescens pius
patris iussa *f* spiritualis erga necessitates carnalis immo

---

a + id est foueam X   *b* antro Xc
c c omits this sentence   *d* qm X
e notum o ; noti m ; uoti t   *f* iussu Xc

the slain man was hidden. They believed that the dog
had given up following their lord and had gone away
home and would not return again. It, however, ran
quickly after him and with the same gestures and howling
as before, as if beseeching him, until by the best means it
could it had made him come to the burial place. Coming to the furrow which skilfully concealed the grave of
the dead body, for it might have been made by the
plough, it hastily removed the heap of turf with its teeth
and paws. The men present took a hand, they dug
and finally found and exhumed the body. Upon
examination they recognized it, and having questioned the adulterer about the crime soon learned
what had occurred. This story should not bore the
reader, as the great bishop himself did not think it
amiss to relate it often when many important personages
were present.

To resume our narrative again. His prior gave
special instructions to Hugh who served all the canons
with filial devotion to the utmost of his capacity that
he would make his father his peculiar and particular
care. ' Nothing,' he said, ' would give greater pleasure
to me and the other brothers than that you should
devote yourself entirely to the service of so distinguished
a man. None of the brethren is as devoted as yourself,
or as ready to perform the most menial duties, nor is
there anyone to whom the task would be so acceptable.'
The holy youth gladly accepted and even more gladly
obeyed the order of his spiritual father to minister to
the needs of one who was both his earthly father
and his spiritual parent, rejoicing rather that he had
reared him up for and offered him to God, than
that he had before this begotten him in the physical
sense.

et spiritualis *a* quoque parentis,*b* per quem se potius gaudebat fuisse Deo genitum et oblatum quam mundo antea procreatum.

Videres iam eum, qui in singulorum obsequiis fratrum gratiam sibi uberiorem conciliauerat uniuersorum, in eo quam maxime uniuersis placere, quod in paternis necessitatibus studia uinceret singulorum. Quod namque uiro strenuissimo exhiberi uniuersi et singuli preoptarent, solus ille pro cunctis implebat. Hunc igitur, ut ipse sepius gratulando referebat, de cetero quamdiu superuixit, ducebat, portabat, uestibus et calciamentis tegebat, nudabat, lauabat, extergebat, lectum ei sternebat,*c* cibos languenti parabat, paratis debilem ipse cibabat. Hec et hiis similia dulcius ei sapiebant cum ea faciebat quam saperent mella comedenti aut quelibet pigmenta uehementer sitienti. Accipiebat *d* millies ad singula hec benedictiones ab ore patris et has corde auido sitienter hauriebat. Sciebat namque quia ' benedictiones patrum confirmant domos filiorum.' Nimirum ' benedictiones omnium gentium daturus illi Dominus', preueniebat ' eum in benedictionibus dulcedinis', 1 dulcem, amabilem et benedicibilem illum exhibendo uniuersis.

---

a carnales immo et spirituales c
b + curam X
c ei sternebat / consternebat X
d Accipiens cd

You must know that although he had won the affection of the whole community by his readiness to serve each member of it, they were all even more pleased that he should show even greater devotion in ministering to the needs of his own father. He performed on behalf of them all the services which the whole community would have liked to have given to this venerable man. He used often to relate with great pleasure how for the rest of his father's life, he used to lead him and carry him about, dress him and undress him, wash him, dry him and make his bed, and, when he grew feebler and weaker, prepare his food and even feed him. These duties had for him a taste sweeter than honey, or spiced wine for a thirsty man. His father blessed him a thousand times, and each time his heart greedily and thirstily drank in the words of benediction, for he knew that ' a father's blessing brings prosperity to his sons.' For ' the Lord was to give him great blessings from all the peoples ' [1] and was to go before him with the blessing of goodness, by winning for him the affection, favour and praise of everyone.

---

[1] Ecclus. 3:11, 44:25 ; Ps. 20:4

Capitvlvm IV

Quod leuita ordinatus mox predicationis studio
inseruierit.

Annum uero etatis iam ingressus nonum decimum,
petente omni cetu fratrum, per uenerabilem Gratianopolitanum antistitem gradum coactus et^a inuitus
ascendit leuiticum. Erat iam illi sensus pro canis, et
uita immaculata pro etate senectutis.[b][1] Vnde non
immerito muneri et honori tanto cunctorum hunc
sententia et ydoneum censebat et dignum. Indutus
uero sanctitatis amictum, tunicam polimitam et stola
iocunditatis redimitus, candidus ipse et rubicundus facie
quidem et ueste set multo eminentius spiritu et mente,
lotis inter innocentes manibus, circuibat altare Dei cum
summa reuerentia et deuotione.[2] Pronuntiabat euangelium angelica uoce, diuinis obseruiens misteriis [c] cum
metu et feruentissima [d] compunctione.

Cepit etiam mox sancte predicationis studio plebem
informare, ad amorem celestis patrie torpentium corda
instantius excitare. Peccantes publice coram omnibus
arguebat,[3] prorsus cunctis [e] quibus poterat scientiam
salutis quam uberius fuerat assecutus, in commune
dabat. Venter eius musto gemine dilectionis cum spiritu
scientie et pietatis ad summum usque repletus eructabat
ex hoc in illud.[4] Coarctabat eum spiritus uteri sui,[f]
comedebat eum zelus domus Domini uidentem messem

---

[a] Xc *omit these two words*
[c] ministeriis cd
[e] *om* cd
[1] cf. Wis. 4:8-9

[b] etate senectutis / senectute X
[d] + mentis c
[f] eius cd
[2] cf. Gen. 37:3 ; Cant. 5:10 ; Ps. 25:6

CHAPTER IV

How as soon as he was ordained deacon he undertook the work of preaching.

When he was already nineteen, at the request of the
whole community the venerable bishop of Grenoble
raised him to the diaconate, much against his will. His
wisdom and purity of life were greater qualifications
than grey hairs and old age,[1] for which reasons all were
rightly of the opinion that he was worthy of this honour
and responsibility. Clad in the cloak and many-
coloured tunic of sanctity, and girt with the stole of
gladness, white and ruddy both in countenance and
vesture, he was yet more so in mind and spirit. Washing
his hands in innocency, he served at the altar of God
with much reverence and devotion.[2] He read the gospel
with the voice of an angel, and performed the holy rites
with fear and the deepest emotion.

He soon began to give the people religious instruction
by means of sermons, and to arouse in their lukewarm
hearts a fervent love of the heavenly kingdom. He
rebuked sinners publicly in the presence of the whole
congregation,[3] and imparted to all he could the knowledge necessary for salvation, which he himself possessed
in such great measure. His heart was filled to overflowing with the wine of a double love and with the
spirit of wisdom and holiness, both of which gushed forth
from him.[4] The spirit within him constrained him, and
the zeal of the house of the Lord consumed him, for he
saw that the harvest was abundant, but the reapers none

---

[3] 1 Tim. 5:20   [4] cf. Isa. 11:2 ; Ps. 143:13

multam set operarios nullos aut paucissimos.[1] Vnde
cum uerecundia quidem et tremore fluenta putei sui,
iubente prelato, petente populo, in plateis diuidens,[2]
sentiebat ipse dum diuideret, sentiebat et populus dum
biberet aquam cisterne sue, quam pre timore quasi
gelidam cepisset propinare, accedente inter ministrandum
fiducia, feruoris uinei effectu calescere, tamque ministrum
quam bibentes salubriter debriare. Complebatur in
fideli pigmentorum spiritualium pincerna, quod ait
Scriptura : ' Qui inebriat et ipse inebriabitur.' [3] Taliter
quoque potati in uoce psalmi undique clamabant :
' Calix tuus inebrians quam preclarus est.' [4] Bene-
dicebant uero uerum Ioseph, qui in ore sacci fratris sui
minoris posuerat cifum suum.[5]

[1] cf. Job 32:18 ; Ps. 68:10 ; Matt. 9:37
[2] Prov. 5:15-16
[3] Prov. 11:25
[4] Ps. 22:5
[5] cf. Gen. 44:2

or very few.[1] Wherefore, at the command of his superior and at the prayer of the people, bashfully and fearfully he gave them in the public places water from his well.[2] His fervour grew as he proceeded, as did also that of his audience, when they drank of the waters of his cistern which seemed almost cold at first because of his nervousness, but his confidence growing as he talked, it became a strong wine, which warmed and indeed intoxicated both cup-bearer and drinkers. The text of the Scriptures, ' He who giveth to drink shall himself be inebriated ' [3] was fulfilled in this provider of spiritual wine, and all those who had drunk it exclaimed in the words of the Psalm ' Thy cup which inebriates how glorious it is ! ' [4] They blessed the true Joseph, who had placed his cup at the top of the sack of his younger brother.[5]

Capitvlvm V

Qualiter cellam sancti Maximi iure prioris administrauerit.

Gaudebant uniuersi in uerbis gratie que procedebant de ore eius,[1] set pre ceteris prior suus, uir religiosus et pius qui eum educauerat, qui etiam ut animam suam eum diligebat. Hic corde letissimo alumpnum suum cum sublimitate uite sublimari cernens *a* uerbo glorie,*b* contendit etiam ipse ad altiora eum attollere. Vicinam igitur cellulam quam uocant Sanctum Maximum, eo quod eius loci basilica sancto est *c* Maximo, regentium nobili patrono, consecrata, ei committit regendam. Quam ille, rebus quidem necessariis pene uacuam, quia recusare obedientiam obedientie addictum legibus fas non erat, suscepit, bonisque in breui ubertim impleuit. Loci sane ipsius possessiuncule uix unico ad honestam uidebantur habitatori sustentationem cum familia parua sufficere. Verum Hugo sciens 'melius duos simul esse quam unum,' noluit esse solus, ne sibi quandoque dici potuisset : ' Ve soli, quia si ceciderit non habet subleuantem.'[2] Sciens quoque iuxta uiri doctissimi sententiam, sicut iunioris iocundiorem ita cohabitationem senioris *d* esse tutiorem, presbiterum concanonicum annis et moribus grauem in socium accepit. Agelli curam et uinearum rusticis timoratis commendans, ipse *e* lectioni et orationi uacabat. Iactans quoque in Domino cogitatum, et sollicitus que Dei sunt quomodo placeret Deo, nichil de crastino neque de hodierno multum sollicitus[3],

---

a uidens c   *b* gratie X   *c* + proxima X
d senis X   *e* + uero cd

Chapter V

How he ruled the cell of St Maximus as prior.

All rejoiced at the words of grace which proceeded from his lips,[1] but most of all his prior, the good and holy man who had been his master and loved him as his own soul. With a glad heart he saw that his pupil had been set apart by the Holy Ghost as one of God's chosen ones, and strove to raise him even higher. He therefore committed to his rule the neighbouring cell called St Maximus because its church was dedicated to that saint, the patron of rulers. This he accepted, since it was wrong for one under the law of obedience not to obey, although its endowments scarcely provided even necessities, but in a short time he made it flourishing and prosperous. Although its small estates barely sufficed for the adequate maintenance of one canon and a small household, Hugh understanding ' that two men together were better than one ', did not wish to be alone, lest it should be said of him ' Woe to the solitary, since if he should fall, he has none to raise him up.' [2] Accepting the judgment of a certain sage that the companionship of the young is pleasanter, but that of those advanced in years safer, he chose as his fellow another canon, a priest of mature age and behaviour. He committed the sheep and vineyards to the care of certain God-fearing peasants and devoted himself to prayer and study. Casting his care upon God and concerned only about the things of God and how he should please him, and caring nothing about the morrow or even the same day[3], he sang con-

---

[1] cf. Luke 4:22   [2] Eccles. 4:9-10
[3] cf. Ps. 54:23 ; 1 Cor. 7:32 ; Matt. 6:34

psallebat cum fiducia : 'Propter nomen tuum Domine
dux michi eris et enutries me.'[1]   Vnde et Dominus sui
suorumque qui secum erant, propter eius fidem benigne
sollicitus, omnem gratiam habundare faciebat in eis.
Ipsi quoque habundantes exemplo iunioris [a] in omne
opus bonum, sobrie, pie et iuste uiuebant,[2] egenis
alimoniam subministrantes,[b] diuitibus honorificentiam
exhibentes.   Factumque est ut in breui locus rerum
incole morum [c] stipendiis ditati, celebrem opinionis bone
circumquaque famam optinerent ; sacre uero exhorta-
tionis studio non solum ecclesiole sue parochianos,
uerum etiam confluentes undique turbas [d] ad audiendum
uerbum Dei instantius edocebat,[e] monens unumquemque
pro status sui conditione irreprehensibilem se catholice
traditionis et pie per omnia conuersationis sectatorem
exhibere.

Capitvlvm VI

Qualiter illud euangelium ' Si peccauerit in te frater
tuus ' et cetera erga parochianum suum super adulterio
infamatum adimpleuerit.

Erat autem inter creditas cure sue ouiculas ouis
quedam morbida,[f] erratica, lupinis morsibus ultro se
ingerens.   Crimine siquidem adulterii quidam ex
parochianis [g] suis pertinacius laborabat.   Verum quid
cure, quid sollicitudinis, quid instantie huic impenderit

[a] habundanter exemplis pueri iunioris X
[b] . . . uiuentes, egenis alimoniam subministrabant X
[c] loci incole rerum et morum X
[d] + populorum X   [e] edoceret c
[f] + et X   [g] parochialibus X

fidently ' For thy name's sake, O Lord, thou wilt be my leader and wilt nourish me.' [1]   Whence the Lord, on account of his faith in his mercy, took charge of him and his companions and provided bountifully for them. These, taking example from their young superior abounded in good works, and living temperately, piously and justly,[2] assisted the poor with their alms and treated the rich with deference.   Thus, in a short time the church was endowed with goods and the people with virtue, and both acquired fame and a high reputation in the neighbourhood.   By his zealous and eloquent preaching he instructed not only the parishioners of the tiny church but also the crowds who flocked from all sides to hear the word of God, exhorting each of them whatever his rank to be a good and loyal Catholic and to lead a devout Christian life.

Chapter VI

How, in his treatment of an adulterous parishioner he followed the precept in the gospel ' If thy brother sin against thee.'

In the flock committed to his care there was one diseased and wandering sheep which exposed itself deliberately to the wolf's attacks. This was a parishioner who was a hardened adulterer. The earnest endeavours of the devoted disciple of the good shepherd to reform him can best be described in his own words. It happened on one occasion that a number of scholars were with him

---

[1] Ps. 30:4
[2] 2 Cor. 9:8 ; Tit. 2:12

Pastoris Boni sequipeda bonus, eiusdem potius uerbis absoluere dignum duximus. Nam uice quadam, plurimis consedentibus uiris litteratis, contigit, ipso presente et cum eisdem familiariter pluraque *a* conferente, a quibusdam canonici *b* necnon et ciuilis iuris peritis questionem illam de euangelio proponi qua Dominus Petro dicit : ' Si peccauerit in te frater tuus, corripe illum inter te et ipsum solum.' [1] De hiis uero que sequuntur, scilicet de adhibendis secum duobus uel tribus testibus seu de forma dicendi ecclesie peccatum fratris, aliis sic, aliis uero sic diffinientibus set in eamdem assertionem minime accedentibus,*c* episcopus deinde quid sibi uidebatur protulit, suamque sententiam exempli huius prosecutione astruxit.*d*

' Dum,' inquit, ' adholescentulus quondam michi credite parrochie regimen ipse quidam dyaconus administrarem, simplici quodam sacerdote quod sui erat officii in sacramentorum siue officiorum ecclesiaticorum celebrationibus uel collationibus exequente, notam, immo et quod deterius est, noxam adulterii quemdam e parochianis meis contigit incurrisse.*e* Compertam ego famam mali egre satis tuli, rem diligentissime inquisiui ; inuentam et agnitam, cooperante Domini nostri gratia, hoc progressu *f* emendaui. Conueni uirum inter me et ipsum solum, dixi que pro negotio et loco dicenda putaui. Ille econtra reatum suum pertinaciter inficiari,*g* irasci, et quatinus ausum mentis *h* suggerebat ceca obduratio, etiam comminari michi et conuitiari. Abs-

---

a presente et complura familiariter conferente X
b canonicis X
c + Hugo tunc episcopus quando hec questio uentilabatur X
d astrinxit X
e incurrere X
f + temporis X
g + cepit et X
h ausui mentis X

holding an informal discussion on many topics. Certain experts in canon and civil law began to discuss the words of our Lord to Peter, ' If thy brother sin against thee, rebuke him when thou and he are alone together.' [1] Opinions were divided about the interpretation of the rest of the passage concerning the presence of two or three witnesses and the way of denouncing the sin of his brother to the church. As no agreement was reached the bishop finally gave his interpretation which he justified by relating the incident which follows.

' I was still,' he said, ' only a young deacon when a parish was committed to my charge, a certain simple priest being responsible only for the administration of the sacraments and the celebration of the divine office. One of my parishioners was defamed for, and worse still, guilty of adultery. When I heard the rumour I was exceedingly shocked, I made careful investigations, and having ascertained the truth, with the assistance of God's grace, I took the following steps to punish it. I summoned the man to a private interview, and said what I thought the matter and the place demanded. He, for his part, obstinately denied his guilt, then grew angry, and began to threaten and abuse me in such terms as the blind obduracy of his hardened heart suggested to him. At last, he withdrew leaving me sad, as for the time being he had shown himself unrepentant.

[1] Matt. 18:15

cedens demum tam me tristem reliquit quam se in-
corrigibilem ad tempus ostendit.

‘ Precepti uero huius euangelici memor, duobus
primum et post tribus testibus qui rem eque nouerant
mecum adhibitis, hominem corripui, correctionem *a*
suasi, ueniam correcto mediante satisfactione *b* repromisi.
Distulit ille correctionem polliceri ; nec criminis uero
nec suspicionis materiam sustinuit aboleri. Tandem *c*
eius reatum iam omnibus manifestum, media in ecclesia
quadam die sollempni palam coargui,*d* immanitatem
flagitii cunctis audientibus denotaui, tradendum eum
Sathane in interitum carnis [1] si non citius resipiscat *e*
terribiliter denuntiaui. Hiis ille et territus uehementer
et confusus, in medium prosiliuit, peccato suo non sine
gemitu et imbre lacrimarum renuntians, penitentiam
egit, ueniam correctus et reconciliatus accepit.’

Hec uir sanctus de hiis, que presenti hystorie iccirco
inserenda putauimus, quatinus ex hiis manifestius pateat
lectori quid sollicitudinis et zeli, quid discretionis et
studii circa salutem animarum uir Deo plenus *f* ab ineunte habuerit etate et exhibuerit, ut non inmerito super
multa Domini sui bona, in modico repertus fidelissimus,
tempore demum oportuno uideatur constitutus.[2]

---

a correptionem . . . correptus c
b ueniam correctione mediante s
c Tamen o ; Cum . . . reatus manifestus esset X
d argui Xc
e ocius resipiscatur X
f uir Dei plenius c

' Mindful of this precept, I took with me first two and then three witnesses who had known about the matter, and rebuked the man, combining reproof and persuasion and promising him absolution if he repented and did penance. He refused to promise to amend, and would not hear of abandoning his sinful and scandalous way of life. His guilt being universally known, I rebuked him publicly in church on a feast day, bringing home to the whole congregation the heinousness of his sin, and made the terrible pronouncement that he was to be delivered over to Satan for the destruction of his body [1] unless he speedily repented. This made him thoroughly frightened and ashamed, so much so that he came forth and in the sight of all confessed his sin with groans and with floods of tears. He did penance and after correction received absolution.'

Such were the words of the saint, which we thought should be set down in this work, since they make known to the reader the zeal and diligence, tact and wisdom in the care of souls which the man of God possessed even in his youth. Thus, the Lord having found him faithful in small matters in due time and not undeservedly set him over much of his property.[2]

[1] 1 Cor. 5:5
[2] cf. Matt. 25:21

CAPITVLVM VII

Quod cum priore suo Cartusiam inuiserit et uisam dilexerit.

Verum, ut dicit Sancta *a* Scriptura, 'cum consummauerit homo, tunc incipiet.'[1] Iam Hugonem pro modo sue *b* professionis ac supra modum sue etatis perfecte consummatum, in uirtutum apice omnibus conclamantibus, ipse nec initium quidem perfectionis uel digne conuersationis se attigisse putabat.[2] Comperta uero sancta et sublimi opinione Cartusiensium monachorum,*c* inexplebili cordis desiderio eorum anhelabat informari exemplo. At primo quidem dissimulata huius desiderii uehementia, optinere studuit ut simul cum priore suo iam superius memorato illorum mereretur aspectu et affatu *d* potiri. Quo facto, tantus mox in eius pectore spiritualis illius conuersationis amor succensus est, ut nullatenus incendii eius flammam intra se posset cohibere. Experiebatur *e* enim, iam feliciter ardens, infeliciter ardentis uerum eloquium dicentis,[3] 'Quanto plus tegitur, tanto magis estuat ignis.' *f*

Intuebatur uero, et intuendo *g* mirabatur locum, ipso quoque situ nubes pene supergressum celisque contiguum, ab omni penitus terrenorum inquietudine semotum. Considerabat tantam ibi oportunitatem uacandi soli Deo, cui *h* negotio hic precipue uidebatur adminiculari prediues librorum habundantia, legendi facultas copiosa, orandi quies inconcussa. Et quidem

---

a *om* X   *b* + conuersationis seu X
c + cum X   *d* affectu Q
e Experitur ct
f Quoque magis tegitur, tectus magis estuat ignis oX
g intuens X   *h* + quoque X

CHAPTER VII

How, when he visited Chartreuse with his prior, he loved it at first sight.

But, as holy Scripture says ' When a man hath done then he beginneth '.[1]   Hugh, in the opinion of all had already attained to the height of perfection aspired to by his order, and far in advance of his years, although he himself judged that he had never reached even the beginning of the way of perfection and godly living.[2]   He already knew the reputation for extreme sanctity enjoyed by the monks of Chartreuse and wished with all his heart for the inspiration of their example.   Carefully concealing his immense longing, he arranged matters so that he could with his prior, whom I have already mentioned above, see and speak with them.   After this had happened, his heart was almost immediately inflamed with so great a love of their holy way of life, that he could hardly keep his passion to himself.   In the happiness of his love, he understood the truth of the words of one who had loved unhappily, ' The hidden fire burns the more fiercely, the more it is hidden.' [3]

He gazed with awe at this place, situated almost in the clouds, with nothing between it and the sky, and so far removed from the turmoil of the world.   He realized the great opportunity it offered of living alone with God, for which aim the rich collection of books would greatly help the long hours of reading and the unbroken silence for prayer.   The whole place seemed to be planned

---

[1] Ecclus. 18:6
[2] cf. *Rule of St Benedict*, c. lxxiii (*ad initium*)
[3] Ovid, *Metamorphoses* 4:64

quoad loci dispositionem hec ita se habere dignoscuntur. At in loci habitatoribus attendebat carnis mortificationem, mentis serenitatem, spiritus libertatem, hylaritatem frontis, puritatem sermonis. Instituta eorum solitudinem non singularitatem commendabant. Segregabant mansiones set mentes sociabant. Vnusquisque habitabat secum, nec habebat nec *a* agebat aliquid suum. Omnes *b* seorsum, et communiter quisque degebat. Seorsum manebat unusquisque ne impedimentum experiretur ab aliquo ; communiter degebat ne fraterno priuaretur solatio. Hec et huiusmodi notata ibidem ac etiam obedientie secura *c* munitio, que multos sepe solitarios *d* destituit et extreme perniciei exponit, Hugoni placebant, Hugonem rapiebant, ipsumque tamquam extra se repente effectum sibi funditus uendicabant.

Erat in illo cetu sanctorum senior quidam, magni quondam in seculo nominis, tunc quoque in sancto proposito celeberrime opinionis. Huic Hugo secretius pectoris sui estus aperiens, nec tam consilium an faceret quam quonam pacto quam citius quod optabat perficeret, cum gemitu et fletu ab eo inquirens, longe aliud quam sperabat responsum accepit. Intuens namque uir prudens *e* adholescentem, ut aspectus renuntiabat, qualitate delicatum et etate tenellum, sciens etiam ipsum natalibus clarum, nec moribus eius credebat posse rigorem illius ordinis congruere nec uiribus conuenire. Hunc igitur sic terrifica responsione quasi a tali presumptione compescens aut constantiam potius animi

---

a aut X
b + manebant X
c ac precipue obediens et secura X   B *begins here*
d + hanc non sequentes X
e predictus X

just for this. He observed the physical austerities of the inhabitants, their untroubled spirit, their freedom of mind, their cheerful countenances and the simplicity of their words. Their rule encouraged solitude, not isolation. They had separate cells but their hearts were united. Each of them lived apart, but had nothing of his own, and did not live for himself. They combined solitude with community life. They lived alone lest any should find his fellows an obstacle to him, they lived as a community so that none of them should be deprived of brotherly help. He noticed these things there and also the security caused by obedience, of which many hermits are frequently deprived and so are exposed to great peril. Hugh was delighted and attracted by all this, in fact it carried him away and completely captivated him.

Among that band of holy men there was a certain elderly monk, who had had a great name while in the world, and now had a high reputation for sanctity in the community. Hugh secretly opened his heart to him, asking him with groans and tears for counsel, not as to what he ought to do, but as to how he could most quickly obtain his desire, but received a very different answer from the one he hoped for. After a careful examination of the young man, whose appearance proclaimed his breeding and youth, the prudent monk, knowing him to be of noble birth, believed that he had neither the training nor the strength to endure the austerity of the order. Therefore, either to rebuke his presumption or to test his constancy, he gave this crushing answer, ' My son, how can you dare even to consider this? The men whom you see inhabiting these rocks are harder than the stones themselves, and have compassion neither on themselves nor on those who dwell with them. The very

eius explorare nitens, inquit, ' Istud, o filiole, quomodo
uel *a* cogitare presumis ?   Homines quos rupes incolere
cernis presentes, saxis omnibus duriores sunt, nec sui
sciunt nec aliorum secum habitantium misereri.   Locus
iste horridus ipso uisu *b* est, ordo usu grauissimus ; ipsius
cilicii asperior amictus cutem et carnes *c* desuper ossibus
uiuo tibi abraderet ;   discipline rigor teneritudinem
istam, quam in te intueor, penitus exossaret.'

Hic uero Christi tyro et Martini beatissimi familiaris
cultor et deuotus imitator, illato terrore constantior,
Laurentii secum inuictissimi eloquium tacito uersabat
in pectore, qui, prolato ante se omni tormentorum
genere, terrere eum cupientibus ait, ' Has ego epulas
semper optaui.' [1]   Vt enim caminus iniectis exilit aquis
et flammarum in sublime comas extollit, sic sanctorum
ignescens desiderium, cum obuiant aduersa, fortius
conualescit.

Capitvlvm VIII

Vt promissum suum, ad instantiam prioris sui fidei
interpositione firmatum, infregerit et monachus Cartusiensis effectus sit.   Et de huiusmodi transgressione fidei
sententia eiusdem.

Senem itaque memoratum tamquam uotis suis
crudelius aduersantem declinans, aliis quibusdam e
fratribus hos cordis sui estus confestim pandit.   Nec
morantur illi cum ingenti fauore et instanti exhortatione
persistendi in salubri *d* proposito, suum ei et assensum

---

a *om* B ; quomodo uel qualiter X
b aspectu Xc
c carnem Xc
d stabili Xc

aspect of the place is frightening, but our way of life is even harder. The roughness of the hair shirt which you would wear would cut through skin and flesh to your very bones. The sensitiveness which I perceive in you would cause you to break down completely under the austerities of our way of life.'

This terrible picture only made the follower of Christ and devoted disciple and imitator of the most blessed Martin more determined, and he pondered in silence over the words of the invincible martyr Lawrence, who, when those who wished to terrify him, displayed all the instruments of torture, said ' This is the banquet I have always desired.' [1] As a fire burns more fiercely and the flames rise to a greater height if water is poured on to it, so the desires of the saints become more intense and grow stronger when they encounter obstacles.

CHAPTER VIII

How he broke the promise and oath taken under pressure from his prior and became a monk at Chartreuse. His own view of his breach of faith.

Leaving the old man, who had so crushingly rebuffed him, he immediately opened his heart to some of the other monks. They did not put him off, but exhorted him earnestly to persist in his pious purpose, promising him their assistance and consent. Hugh could not conceal his joy, but begged them on no account to

---

[1] cf. *S. Laurentii Passio* (Mombritius, *Sanctuarium*, II, 93) : ' Omne genus hoc tormentorum in corpore tuo uectabitur.' Beatus Laurentius dixit : ' Infelix has epulas semper desideravi.'

impertiri et auxilium polliceri. Tum Hugo gaudio
gestiens infinito hec priori suo celanda summopere
deprecatur. Euangelice nimirum institutionis sedulus
emulator inuentum meminit thesaurum abscondi
oportere,[1] donec *a* omissis potius omnibus que habuisset
quam uenditis, emere illum mereretur et securius
possidere. Verumptamen licet dissimulatione multa
quod moliebatur tegere niteretur, effugere tamen sus-
picionem sollertis nequiuit pastoris nimio eum amore
zelantis. Vnde ad propria eis sub festinatione regressis,
sic lacrimis ora suffusus senior illum affatur :

' O,' inquit, ' fili karissime, scio, utique scio quia in
grande malum meum et irreparabile ecclesie mee
dampnum, te Cartusiam adduxi. Te sibi Cartusia totum
rapuit, te possidet. Nos interim te corporetenus uix
tenemus, set anima tua nobiscum non est. Set nec istud,
uereor, diu erit ; nam spiritum ab ineunte secutus etate,
carnem nullius ducens, illius procul dubio impetu non
istius ductus, nobis in breui es abducendus. Proh dolor !
Lumen oculorum meorum sic subito extinguitur, baculus
senectutis mee,[2] cum eo iam solito plus indigeam,
nutabundo preripitur. Set numquid dulcedo mellis
mei sic derepente uertetur *b* in absinthium et gloria
mea, qua de filio sapiente tantum gloriabatur pater, ita
redigetur in nichilum ? Miserere, fili, miserere potius
patris tui, nec tante strenuitatis tue solatiis canos meos
iam busto proximos destituendo, innate tibi pietatis et
compassionis cancellos transcendas. Quod si materna
uiscera ecclesie que *c* te Deo genuit, si fraterna *d* dulcedo
piorum, que te suauiter fouit, non funditus reuocant

a + tam Q
b uertetur / reuertetur B[1]
c de B
d paterna Q

inform his prior, for being a zealous follower of the precepts of the gospel he remembered that the treasure he had discovered should remain hidden, until having abandoned but not sold, all that he had, he was able to buy it and keep it safe.[1] Nevertheless, in spite of his efforts at concealment, his observant superior, who loved him so much already, was aware of it, and after a hurried journey home, the old man, with a face bathed in tears, addressed him thus.

' Dearest son, I know only too well that to take you to Chartreuse was disastrous both for myself and my church. Chartreuse has bewitched you, and you now belong to it. We may indeed possess your body at present, but your heart is no longer here. I fear you will not remain long, since from your youth you have followed your higher nature, paying no attention to earthly affections, and under its inspiration you will soon desert us. I grieve that the light of my eyes is thus to be so soon extinguished, and the staff with which I supported my tottering footsteps in my old age,[2] is to be removed from me when I most needed it. Will not my honey thus be quickly converted into gall, and a father's pride in so promising a son be brought to nothing ? Have pity, my son, on your father, and do not do violence to your natural feelings and affections by depriving his grey hairs of the support of your vigorous youth when he is already approaching the grave. If the maternal affection of the church which bore thee for God, and the fraternal love of the holy men, who fostered you so tenderly, cannot permanently divert your soul from its pursuit of greater perfection, at least

---

[1] Matt. 13:44
[2] cf. Tob. 10:4

animum ad perfectiora estuantis,[a] saltem in hoc paterne
condescendas [b] senectuti, ne adhuc spirantem deseras,
qui amodo in te solo debuit [c] respirare.'

Inter hec et huiusmodi iam utriusque spiritum luctus
absorbuit cum, resumpto uix flatu, senex etiam hec
locutus est : ' Spero,' inquit, ' spero de ingenita sibi
bonitate confisus dilectissimi filii mei, quia exaudiuit me.
Iuret ergo michi in nomine Domini Dei sui [d] filius meus
quod patre derelicto Cartusiensibus, dum aduiuam,
minime sociabitur. Alioquin suspicionis telum quo
uiscera spiritus mei atrociter transfixit timor nullatenus
auelletur.'

Deus bone ! Quid inter hec mentis, quid animi
seruo tuo fuit, quantus in corde eius gemine dilectionis
conflictus seuiebat ! O mira res, o et [e] perplexitas mira !
Vtrobique tempestas et utrimque serenitas,[f] hinc et inde
et ad naufragium et ad portum impellunt fluctuantem.
Si uocanti ad perfectiora non obediat Deo, deseritur una
caritas ; si potestati contradicat ordinate a Deo, leditur
gemina caritas. Vna deseritur que Dei est ; gemina non
impletur que et Dei et proximi est. O angustie undique !
Set pre nimia, quod dictu mirum est,[g] latitudine. Quid
tamen faciet sic dilatatus et sic angustiatus ? Dicere inter
hec poteras,[h] o anima dilatata, o et anima angustiata :
quid eligam [j] ignoro.[1] Verumptamen dico ego quia
quodlibet horum elegeris, siue prestiteris siue renueris
prestare quod posceris, uita non mors tibi est.

Verum quid egeris, quem exitum inueneris, qualiter
infugeris [k] manus importunas iam uideamus. Solitus
utique et assuetus obedire prepositis et subiacere eis,

[a] estuantem Xc   [b] condescende Xc
[c] desinit Xc   [d] Domini sui Dei B
[e] om c   [f] seueritas B
[g] + caritatis X   [h] poterat cp ; quid poteras X
[j] eligas X   [k] effugeris Q ; effugias Xc
[1] Gloss on Dan. 13:22 from Responsory *Angustiae*

give way to your father in his old age, and do not leave me whilst I still live, for I cannot live without you.'

These words made both absolutely disconsolate. Then, having paused to take breath, the old man continued, ' My confidence in your natural kindheartedness, dearest son, makes me hope that you will not refuse me. Swear to me, in the name of God, that whilst I live, you will never leave me and join the Carthusians. Otherwise, the dart of fear and misgiving, which has so deeply pierced my heart, can never be removed.'

Merciful Heavens ! What a terrible conflict between two loves raged in the heart of thy servant at this appeal ! What a horrible and awful dilemma it was ! The storm tossed the waverer hither and thither, now to shipwreck and now to a peaceful anchorage. If he did not obey God calling him to a more perfect way, he broke one command of love, if he disobeyed the superior set over him by God, he broke both. If the one concerning God were disregarded, both of them concerning God and our neighbour would be violated. Narrow straits indeed on both sides, but due, strange to say, to the very width of his love. What should he do when he was thus made wide and narrow both at once ? In such a pass, O enlarged and constricted soul, you could indeed say : I know not what to choose.[1] At least I can tell you that whichever you decide, either to promise or to refuse to promise what is asked of you, will bring you life and not death.

Let us now see what you did, what way out you found and how you escaped from the restraining hand. You had been accustomed to be obedient and submissive to your superior and could not gainsay or refuse him, and so you agreed to his demand and satisfied him by taking the oath he required of you, committing the outcome

nescius contradicere, ignorans nolle adquiescere, das manum exigenti et precipienti fide corporaliter prestita satisfacis, exitum de cetero tui negotii diuino prorsus arbitrio committis. Meministi matrem luminis Virginem salutis humane puerperam, uoto uirginitatis illibato, in nuptias consensisse, Dei tamen sapientia mirabiliter dispensante, nullum inde uoti preiuditium, immo et magnum *a* integritatis presidium et fecunditatis solatium adquisisse. Nec dissimile quiddam *b* sane presumebas et sperabas tibi a puritatis tue inspectore, a teste conscientie et intentionis tue iudice Deo omnipotente. Set neque in longum pius *c* Deus te defraudauit *d* a spe tua. Nam paulo post, cum hesitares aliquamdiu et quid ageres ignorares, cum et dispendia spiritualis uite cotidie sustineres et contra fidem datam uenire potius abhorreres, infudit subito cordi tuo superna clementia uerissime et lucidissime radium discretionis, inspirans tibi et certificans te plenissime sacramentum non esse obseruandum inconsideratius extortum *e* contra utilitatem anime aut in detrimentum uere salutis. Sciens igitur et exultans quod reuera ista loqueretur in te Dominus Deus, audiens eum et exaudiens, disposita domo tibi credita, nullo sciente quia nullo insidiante nec tale aliquid suspicante, clam discessisti, Cartusiam adisti,*f* cum gaudio exceptus in multa ibidem gratia perstitisti.*g*

Inquisitus sane multotiens a puero tuo utrum ullum aliquando, ut assolet, scrupulum hec fidei transgressio tibi peperisset, michi semper istud idem respondebas : ' Numquam certe inde scrupulum set potius mentis *h* iubilum sensi, cum factum memini unde profectum tantum cepi.' [1]

a magne X	*b* quidem Xc
c om X	*d* fraudauit Xc
e exortum B	*f* aduenisti Xc
g profecisti Xc	*h* iugiter X

of the business to the will of God. You remembered
that the Virgin-mother of the Light and Saviour of
mankind, her vow of virginity unimpaired, consented
to marriage, yet, by the miraculous disposition of God's
wisdom, remained inviolate and gained a protection for
her chastity and the grace of motherhood ; and you
ventured to hope that God Almighty, the omniscient
examiner and judge of your conscience and purpose
would assist you in a similar manner. The most high
God did not long withold your desire from you. Shortly
afterwards, when you were still undecided, and uncertain
what to do, having to endure daily the damage to your
spiritual life, and yet shrinking from breaking your oath,
the heavenly mercy suddenly illumined your heart with
a clear and true ray of wisdom, giving you complete
conviction that an oath thoughtlessly exacted from you
which endangered your soul and your eternal welfare
should not be kept. Therefore realizing that it was the
voice of God speaking within you, you rejoiced and
obeyed, and having provided for the cell committed to
your charge, without any opposition, since no-one knew
or suspected anything, you secretly left it. When you
came to Chartreuse, you received a warm welcome, and
remained there, being bountifully endowed with grace.

Your servant frequently asked you whether sometimes, as might be expected, your broken oath caused
you the least misgiving, and you always replied ' I
never felt the least misgiving but rather heartfelt joy
whenever I remembered an act so profitable to myself.'[1]

---

[1] For the legitimacy of St Hugh's breaking this promise see Le Couteulx,
II, 244-5 and Thurston, 41-44.

CAPITVLVM IX

Quod nouam ingresso militiam hostis antiquus
nouos temptationum congressus intulerit,[a] set tuitio
Saluatoris ei nusquam defuit.

Hic uero si iam uniuersa que seruus Dei egit, que
pertulit, que meruit, que percepit, quantum poscerat
utilitas multorum si temptemus euoluere, et uires
succumbent nec uiuendi spatia sufficient [b] et ad reliqua
eius gesta prosequenda ora penitus obmutescent. Set
transeamus et ista cursim, nec reticentes omnia nec
singula recensentes, queque uero dicenda paucis pro
posse absoluentes. In primis uero illud pretereundum
non uidetur quod de primordiis suis crebro familiariter
nobis ipse referebat :

'Mox,' inquit, 'ut infra celle limen pedem misi,[c]
exsurgentem noue temptationis motum in corde meo [d]
sensi. Nec uniformis temptatio illa fuit ; immo nouam
ingresso militiam omnia temptator innouauit antique
sue malitie instrumenta ; precipue, quasi balistam
robustissimam et eo, ut sperabat, insuperabilem, quo
michi inseparabilem tetendit, immo accendit contra me
stimulum carnis mee. Die et nocte non discedebat [e]
a me, imminens michi et perurgens me, angelus Sathane
colaphizans me.[1] Quid ad hec ego, Ihesu bone ?
Immo quid bonitas tua ad hec, faciens [f] bonitatem cum
seruo tuo ? Ego quidem genibus terram, gemitibus
celum, pectus pugnis, genas lacrimis rigaui, tutudi,
pulsaui, cecidi. Set hec omnia et alia innumera, quasi

---

[a] insultus iniecerit X	[b] sufficerent X
[c] posui X	[d] nouum in corde meo motum X
[e] discebat B	[f] + fecisti X

Chapter IX

How on his first entry into his new order, the old
enemy assailed him with a multitude of new temptations,
but the assistance of our Saviour never failed him.

To describe sufficiently fully for the profit of my
readers all the deeds and sufferings of the servant of God
in this place, and his advancement in the spiritual life
is beyond my capacity. Such a task would, moreover,
take the rest of my life, so that it would be absolutely
impossible to write about the remainder of his career.
I must therefore go through it rapidly, neither omitting
nor relating everything, and telling what has to be told
in the fewest possible words. What he told me frequently
in intimate conversation about the beginnings of his
religious life is too important for omission.

' As soon,' he said, ' as I crossed the threshold of my
cell I felt the stirrings of a new temptation in my heart.
It was not always the same one. Rather did the tempter
direct all the ancient weapons of his infernal armoury
against a new recruit to this holy warfare, and in particular, as if from a very powerful crossbow, he shot bolts
which, he hoped, I could not resist, since they were part
of myself. I mean that he aroused my carnal lusts.
Day and night the angel of Satan never left me, but
continually incited me, assailed me and buffeted me.[1]
What did I do then, O blessed Jesus, or rather what did
you in your goodness and mercy towards your servant
do ? I, indeed, fell upon my knees, besieged Heaven
with my groans, struck my breast with my hands, and

[1] 2 Cor. 12:7

aera *a* uerberans [1] feci, quousque et tu, qui non dormis nec
dormitas qui custodis Israel, o Samaritane benedicte,[2]
manum apposuisti. Tu custos de nocte, ut manum
apponebas uix semiuiuo, uix, ut putabam, relinquendo a
latronibus,[3] hinc inde repente irrepentibus et dire
irrumpentibus omne malum subito dissipabas.

'Tunc uidens cordis aream arefactam carnisque
fornacem fatiscentem, cedentibus inde fluxis cogitation-
ibus, hinc ignitis motibus, mirabar quis fuerim, quis
subito effectus essem. Talibus erga me, immo intra *b*
me alternantibus uices, obliuiscebar persepe mei, memor
tui de terra Iordanis.[4] Inde quasi de duobus unde *c*
nomen et originem is fluuius ducit, duplicabam *d* con-
fessionem humiliationis mee et glorificationis tue ;
misericordias tuas tibi cantans, et iniustitias meas
aduersum me pronuntians, sentiebam quia tu remittebas
impietatem peccati mei.[5] Manente enim me in Hermon
et monte modico, dum detestarem *e* et anathematizarem
omne lubricum turpitudinis obscene, humilians me et
post ferale incendium puluerem me et cinerem sentiens
esse, mox benefaciebas cum seruo tuo, reuelans oculos
meos ut considerarem mirabilia de lege tua.[6]

'Dabas quoque fatigato et defecto uel modice interdum prelibare manna illud absconditum.[7] Illud *f* uero
tantillum quod hinc merui pregustare, tale erat et tam
immensum ut facile contempnerem propter ipsum
optinendum plenius et diutius *g* quicquid mundus nouit
dulce uel amarum, lene *h* uel asperum. Verum in hiis
rara michi hora et parua mora. Rursum ad certamina,

---

a aerem Xc (*with Vg.*)   *b* contra Xc
c unum Xc   *d* duplicabo Xc
e detestarer QXc   *f* Istud Q
g dulcius Xc   *h* leue Xc

watered my cheeks with my tears. Yet all this, and count-
less other things, I did as one beating the air,[1] until you,
O blessed Samaritan and the protector of Israel who
neither slumbers nor sleeps,[2] laid your hand upon me.
You who watched over me by night, placed your hand
on one left as he thought half dead by the robbers who
had suddenly ambushed and savagely attacked him,[3]
and, lo immediately you removed all these evils.

' Then, perceiving the aridity of my soul, worn out by
the fever of the waves of carnal desires and distracting
thoughts and the fierce temptations ceasing, I marvelled
at what I had been, and what I had now become. Such
struggles against me, nay rather within me, made me
often forget myself, but I remembered you and the land
of Jordan.[4] Wherefore, just as this river derives its name
and origin from two sources, so did I couple the admission
of my sinfulness and your glory. I sang of your mercies,
and confessed my wickedness, feeling that you had
pardoned my iniquity.[5] Dwelling on the little hill of
Hermon, I loathed and detested all the stains of fleshy
lust, humbling myself, and after so fiery an ordeal feeling
myself dust and ashes. Soon, however, you had mercy
on your servant and opened my eyes so that I might
behold the wonders of your law.[6]

' You gave me at times in my weakness and weariness
a foretaste of that hidden manna.[7] That morsel, which
here I was permitted to taste, was so wonderful and so

---

[1] 1 Cor. 9:26
[2] cf. Ps. 120:4 and St Gregory, *Hom. xviii in Evang.* (P.L. 76, 1151), who
applies the name of Samaritan to Christ *quia interpretatur custos* ; cf. also St
Augustine, *Enarratio in Ps.* 30 (P.L. 36, 235)
[3] cf. Luke 10:29 *et seq.*
[4] cf. Ps. 41:7 with the *Glossa Ordinaria in h.l.* and the Gloss of Peter
Lombard (P.L. 191, 419) for what follows.
[5] cf. Ps. 31:5
[6] cf. Ps. 118:18
[7] cf. Apoc. 2:17

rursus ad bella rapiebar. Numquam uero set nec
umquam defuit licet indigno michi piissimi Redemp-
toris miseratio, semper in aure cordis mei uox eius
erudiens et consolans me,*a* semper manus eius mecum
eripiens et coroborans me.'

Et hec quidem ac plurima in hunc modum mente
contrita, non modo pro consolatione nostra set pro
deuotione et humiliatione sua secretius agens de statu
suo, quem in episcopatu deflebat immutatum,*b* de hiis
que in uita priore humanitus uel pertulerat aut diuinitus
perceperat, memorare solebat. Inferebat autem hec in
sui ipsius uehementem sugillationem, quasi Deo pro
beneficiis suis congrue non responderet, aut se post
largiora Domini sui dona, iam in etate robusta, infirmiori-
bus annis uiribus animi imparem exhiberet.

Capitvlvm X

Sententia Pape de prerogatiua ordinis Cartusiensis.
Et de moribus seu uirtutibus monachorum et conuersorum quos ibi Hugo inuenit. Vel quanta inter eos in
rebus ipse spiritualibus auiditate profecerit.

Potitus igitur cupitis tandem amplexibus formose et
luminose Rachel, sedebat nouus heremi accola tamquam
religiosissima Maria, Hugo in cella solitaria.*c*,[1] Sedebat
uero solitarius, qui tamen non erat solus ; set erat cum

a confortans me atque consolans X
b + et c
c solitarius c

unfathomable that to obtain it more fully and for longer I despised all that the world held sweet or bitter, pleasant or harsh. But these times were few and brief. Soon the struggle and conflict were resumed. But, in spite of my unworthiness, the mercy of the most holy Redeemer never failed me, and always I heard his voice in my heart instructing and consoling me, and his hand always held me up and sustained me.'

He often told me when I was alone with him such things and many others about his earlier life, with great contrition and humility, not only for my encouragement, but because he loved to recall what he had then endured and what God had done for him, since he regretted greatly the change caused by his promotion to the episcopate. He bitterly reproached himself for not making a more adequate return to God for his mercies, and for letting his spiritual fervour decline in his later years, after receiving such abundant gifts from the Lord when in his prime.

CHAPTER X

The opinion of the pope on the pre-eminence of the Carthusian order, and the sanctity of the monks and lay brethren whom Hugh found there, and how he advanced exceedingly rapidly in the spiritual life amongst them.

Having attained at last to the desired embraces of the lovely and glowing Rachel, Hugh, the new aspirant to the eremetical life was like the most holy Mary [1] in his

---

[1] The active and contemplative lives were typified by Leah and Rachel (Gen. 29:15 *et seq.*), and by Martha and Mary (Luke 10:38 *et seq.*). cf. St Gregory, *Hom. in Ezechielem*, 2, 2, 8-10 (P.L. 76, 953).

eo Dominus, per quem erat in cunctis prospere [a] agens.[1]
Sedebat multa quidem humilitate pedibus adherens
dulcissimi sui Ihesu, auiditate summa audiens uerbum
eius. Hic illam sibi precipue familiaritatis confidentiam
ad suum conciliauit Ihesum, que illum in tantam
extulerat superbiam ut de cetero in totum uite sue
reliquum omnem mundi gloriam, omne culmen arbi-
traretur ut stercora, omnem superborum et sublimium
huius seculi fastum,[b] uelud in imo positum, ipse in sublimi quodam fixus rerum uertice longe despiceret. Hic
illam sibi uocem assumpserat qua diceret Sapientie :
'Soror mea es,' apud quam 'opes superbe sunt et gloria.'[2]
Quibus participans tamquam frater copiis bone sororis,
positus est a Domino in superbiam seculorum,[3] sicut
inferior huius scripti textus planius [c] edocebit.

Erant quidem [d] ut semper, tunc temporis quam
maxime in congregatione illa iustorum, uiri tam clerici
quam laici mire sanctitatis et grauitatis, ipsisque summis
principibus et ecclesiarum prelatis admodum reuerendi.
Prior domus, proprio uocabulo dictus Basilius,[4] pre
meritorum eminentia et uirtutum prerogatiua non
aliud [e] quam sanctus ab hiis qui eum nouerant communiter uocari consueuerat. Sequebantur eum et
ceteri nec a remotis per culmina religionis consummate,
nec erat facile quis feruentior, quis perfectior inter illos
censeri potuisset dignoscere. In grege laicorum com-
plures [f] eminebant eximiis prediti donis gratiarum.
Plurima de horum uirtutibus que utiliter scriberentur
agnouimus ; uerum quia ad ea que specialius referenda

[a] proprie B
[b] factum B
[c] plenius c ; om X
[d] quidam ut semper sunt Xc
[e] aliter cd
[f] + quidem Xc

cell alone. He was solitary but not alone, for God was with him, who caused all his deeds to be attended by success.[1] He sat meekly embracing the feet of the most sweet Jesus, and hanging on his words, turning to him with a confidence and affection, which raised him to such heights, that for the whole remainder of his life he reckoned the glories and highest honours of the world as dung, and all secular pomp and dignities, however great, as nothing, for being established on so lofty a peak, he despised them from afar off. Here he could apply to himself the words which were addressed to Wisdom: ' Thou art my sister, with whom are riches, honour and glory.' [2] Sharing in these like a brother in the fortune of a bountiful sister, he was, as my narrative will later describe, promoted by God to the honours of this world.[3]

There were always in this holy community, but especially at that particular time, monks and lay brothers of great sanctity and prudence, who were much venerated both by the chief secular princes, and the rulers of the Church. The prior, Basil,[4] was generally called a saint by all who knew him, because of his pre-eminent and exceptional merits and virtues. The others followed him, not afar off, but had attained to such heights of monastic perfection that it was not easy to judge who among them was the most fervent or the most perfect. Amongst the lay brothers also, there were many outstanding personalities, highly endowed with the gifts of the Spirit. Much could profitably be written about their virtues,

---

[1] cf. Gen. 39:2   [2] Prov. 7:4, 8:18

[3] cf. Is. 60:15

[4] Basil of Burgundy, formerly a Benedictine of Cluny, became prior of the Grande Chartreuse in 1151. He made definitive the institution of the General Chapter. Died 1174.

suscepimus, nos insufficientes uidemus, digressionum etiam necessaria diuerticula studiose declinamus.

Tantus ibi [a] in domandis corporibus rigor, tanta in rigore seruabatur discretio, ut medium cum beatis tenendo, nichil infra uires quis aggredi contentus esset, nichil quod uirium metas excederet exercere, etiamsi uellet,[b] sineretur. Feruebat in commune studium inter eos rigide paupertatis, superfluitatis odium, necessariorum parcitas, obliuio temporalium, ambitus eternorum, communis humilitas et cordis contritio, omnibus etiam communis [c] sui ipsius abiectio, prelatio sociorum. Hec enim ut monachis ita et conuersis indifferenti studio inoleuerant. Iam uero inter monachos legendi assiduitas, contemplandi sublimitas, meditandi et orandi defecata suauitas sic palmam tenebant ut uideretur incredibile. Quantum etiam laicis gratia in hiis affluebat, excepto quod per se litteras atramento deformatas legere nesciebant, uix haberetur fides referenti, si publicis niteretur auribus tradere quam acute et ipsi sensum capiebant lectionum, quam ignitas et clericis etiam ignotas, spiritualis inde elicere sciebant intelligentie scintillas, sicut et nobilis ille Girardus, comes olim Niuernensium [d] permagnus,[1] tunc conuersus minimus, ut ipse reputabat, Cartusiensium.

Cum aliquando, eo presente, conferentibus quibusdam magnis uiris de Salomone, utrum constaret quia salutem cum sanctis esset consecutus, cum et ille quid sibi uideretur proferre rogaretur, ' Ita sane,' inquit,[e] 'nemo dubitet de salute eius. Cum enim Dominus Ihesus Christus infernum spoliaturus patrem suum Dauid

---

[a] igitur B
[b] etsi uellet ocv
[c] in commune Xc
[d] Niuernensis c
[e] ita facere infit B ; ita sane infit c

but realizing that what I have specially undertaken to describe is beyond my powers, I must carefully avoid even the smallest and most necessary digressions.

In their treatment of their bodies they tempered too great austerity with prudence, and thus, like the saints, achieved a happy mean. No one was content with mortifications below his capacity, but, even if he wished to he was not permitted to undertake anything beyond the limits of his strength. They were united in their zeal for extreme poverty, their opposition to anything super-fluous, their contentment with the barest necessities, and their indifference to all temporal matters and aspiration after things eternal.

All alike, whether monks or lay brethren, were conspicuous examples of humility and contrition, self-contempt and submission to their fellows. Amongst the choir monks diligence in reading, loftiness in contemplation, and a pure delight in prayer and meditation were so marked as to seem incredible. The lay brethren had received similar graces, except that they were unable to read letters formed by the pen. Indeed, anyone who attempted to tell the world how well they grasped the meaning of what was read to them, and how they were able to draw from it fiery sparks of spiritual intelligence would scarcely be believed.

An example of this is the noble Gerard, formerly the celebrated count of Nevers, then the least, as he supposed, of the Carthusian lay brothers.[1] He was present on one occasion when certain learned men were discussing whether it could be held that Solomon had been saved and was with the saints. On being asked his opinion, he answered, ' Most certainly, no one can have any

---

[1] cf. below, II, p. 56

honorabiliter acciperet secum, non dubium quin et de Salomone fratre suo curam habuerit, qui tanta eius preconia cecinit. Nam et pater utriusque Dauid diceret utique ei : " Domine fili, hunc talem fratrem tuum ne relinquas,[a] set tecum ut decet assumas." ' Nec dicebat iste uir piissimus quia dampnatis in gehenna crederet per sanctorum quorumlibet interuentum absolutionis beneficium prouenire, sicut hereses quedam delirando sompniant ; immo, plenius a sanctis uiris eius questionis solutione instructus, ueracis sententie rationem tali urbanitate, ut erat per omnia illustrissimus, condiendam putauit.

Sic enim utriusque instrumenti [b] hystorias et moralia precepta huius plerosque ordinis conuersos didicisse nouimus, ut uix falleretur qui statuta de more hystoriarum lectiones aut sacros euangeliorum expositores in ecclesia recitabat quin citius hoc illi deprehenderent et subtussiendo [c] idipsum ut audiebant [d] indicarent. Nam et ipsi negotiationem sapientie Dei, ut quidam nundinas seculi, frequentabant pro uiribus [e] et exercebant. De ordine siquidem isto in registro Pape cuius tempore canonizatus est,[f] ita legitur : ' Ordo Cartusiensium in eo alios ordines antecedit quod cupiditati modum imposuit.' [g],[1]

Quid uero hic egisse, quantumue profecisse [h] Hugonem putamus ? Vbi inolitus ei a primeuis, ut ita dicatur,[j] mensibus discendi amor, tum [k] libris, tum magistris, tum ingenio preclarissimo, tum otio quam oportuno tam

---

[a] derelinquas X
[b] + uel testamenti X
[c] subtiliando Xc
[d] audebant B
[e] pro uiribus / om c
[f] approbatus canonizatus est v ; noster Hugo canonizatus est Q
[g] posuit Xcp
[h] profuisse Xc ; + uel profecisse tv
[j] dicam Xc
[k] cum . . . cum . . . cum . . . cum . . . QX

doubts about his salvation. When our Lord Jesus
Christ despoiled Hell, he triumphantly took away with
him his father, David, and must undoubtedly have taken
care of Solomon, his brother, who had so often proclaimed his Advent. Indeed, their father David would
have said to him, "Lord and Son, do not leave this
brother of yours behind, but take him with you, as is
right." ' This holy man did not say this because he
believed that the damned in Hell could receive the
benefit of absolution through the intercession of any
saint, as certain heretics madly dream, but rather,
being well instructed by certain holy men, he put
forward the orthodox view on this problem, seasoned
with the wit for which he was universally famous.

We have heard that most of the lay brethren of
the order knew the historical and moral parts of both
Testaments so well, that, if a slip were made during the
reading of the usual lessons from the Bible and the
gospels, they immediately let the reader know that they
had noticed this by coughing. They showed in acquiring
the wisdom of God, the assiduity and energy commonly
displayed in secular business. It is thus written of the
order in the register of the pope who gave it his approval.
' The Carthusian order excels the others, in that it has
restrained all desire for wealth.' [1]

What shall we say of Hugh's life there and the progress he made? The love of learning which he had
possessed from his earliest years was here given the
books, masters and leisure, which enabled his natural
genius to develop with the rapidity of a forest fire. He
passed whole nights and days in these studies, and the
only cloud on his happiness was that time was too short,

[1] Untraced

ferme *a* et continuo, tantum iuuari et promoueri potuit,
quantum siluis infinitis ignis inexplebilis. In hiis dies
in hiis studiis continuabat et noctes. Nec aliud suis
causabatur profectibus nouercari et gaudiis nisi temporis
breuitatem, cui mirum in modum legenti semper aut
meditanti uel oranti, omnis dierum noctiumque pro-
lixitas minori quam optasset spatio tendebatur.

Capitvlvm XI

Quod senior cui in seruitorem Hugo deputatus fuit,
spiritu prophetico quod episcopus fieret pronuntiauerit.

Itaque Hugo cum Maria uacabat quidem uerbo Dei,
cum qua nichilominus ministerio quod ei competeret
feruenti animo insistebat. Nam sicut Maria nunc capud,
nunc totum corpus, nunc pedes Domini ungere gaudebat,[1]
ita et Hugo modo prioribus, modo coequalibus, modo
etiam inferioribus suis dulcis obsequii gratiam impendere
et quadam deuotionis sue beniuolentia eos gratius
refouere *b* cupiebat. Quod dum circa uniuersos quam
sincere tam et impigre exerceret, iniungitur ei cura et
obsequela senis cuiusdam monachi, magnarum uirtutum
uiri. Hunc iam ualetudinarium et pre etate ac debilitate
suprema cellule sue parietes nusquam excedentem, Hugo
in horis regularibus decantandis uel quibusque *c* necessariis suppeditandis, seruitor deuotus et indefessus tamquam nutrix alumpnum aut mater filium iuuabat et
mulcebat, nec aliter quam ipsi Domino Ihesu Christo *d*
in omnibus ei ministrabat.

a firme X ; tam . . . continuo / *om* B
b + curebat et X
c quibuscumque Q ; quibuslibet X
d + et B

for, although in a most remarkable way, both by day and night he was always occupied in reading, meditation or prayer, he still had less time than he desired for these activities.

Chapter XI

How a senior monk, whom Hugh was ordered to serve, prophesied that he would be a bishop.

Thus Hugh like Mary drank in the word of God and nevertheless at the same time eagerly performed the duties with which he was entrusted. Just as Mary had delighted to anoint now the head, now the whole body, and now the feet of the Lord,[1] so Hugh desired to render voluntary courtesies to his superiors, equals and inferiors, and to show his affection for them by unenforced acts of kindness. Although he served the whole community wholeheartedly and indefatigably, he was enjoined to take charge of and wait on one aged monk, of remarkable holiness, who was already an invalid and unable through his age and infirmities to leave his cell. Hugh chanted the offices with him and supplied his every need, attending to him devotedly and unceasingly just as a nurse cherishes her nurseling, or a mother her son. Indeed, he served him in everything as he would have served the Lord Jesus Christ himself.

---

[1] cf. John 12:3

Contigit aliquando tempus sacrorum ordinum ab episcopo loci celebrandorum instare *a* annis iam aliquantis in tali conuersatione eius peractis. Hoc sciens uir Dei, Hugonis pariter institutor et alumpnus, cepit dicere illi quasi temptans eum : 'Ecce,' ait, 'fili, iam in te est, an uelis, sacerdos fieri. Si adquieueris, ad hunc gradum modo promoueberis.' Ad hec ille, cui iam olim nil dulcius, nil eque dulce erat quam sacris deseruire misteriis,*b* quam diuinis sacramentis saginari ; Ihesumque suum quia sibi dulcissimum ut inferius plenius docebitur, cordis faucibus et corporis in hostia liberius contingere salutari, estuanti ad audita desiderio, mox simpliciter *c* et pure quod optauit aperuit. Ait ergo : 'Quantum in me est, pater, nichil sane magis appeto in uita ista.' Tum uero senex ad eum ; 'O quid dixisti ? O, inquam, quid dixisti ? O quis crederet ausurum te aut dicturum ista ? O miraculum ! O totiens legisti : Ad sacerdotium qui non accedit inuitus, accedit indignus ; et tu modo non inuitus, immo et auidus, ut ipse fateris, accedere non metuis.'

Ad hanc uocem territus et quasi fulmine tactus, tota *d* corporis strage ad pedes obiurgantis prosternitur, flens ubertim et ueniam presumptionis tante gemebundis uocibus petens. Qui ad modicum uelud dissimulans *e* anxiantem, cum ad tantam illius deuotionem et humilitatem totis et ipse uisceribus concuteretur, tandem ita leniter et flebiliter : 'Surge,' inquit, 'surge.' Quo etiam ad iussum eius sedente, hec spiritu prophetico uir Dei *f* locutus est : 'Ne turberis,' inquit, 'non iam fili set domine mi ; ne, inquam, turberis. Scio et uere scio quo

a tempore . . . instante X
b ministeriis p
c suppliciter Xo
d tanta B
e assimulans Xc
f Domini B

It happened after some years, that the season for ordination by the bishop of the diocese approached. The man of God who was Hugh's master and instructor, in order to test him, spoke thus to him, ' Now, my son, you can be priested, if you wish. If you consent, you can now be raised to that rank.' Hugh had already felt for a long time that he desired nothing so much as to celebrate the holy mysteries and be sated with the holy sacrament, for, as I will show more fully later, nothing delighted him so much as to receive his beloved Jesus between his lips and in the depths of his heart in the host that is our salvation. His desire being kindled by what he now heard, he frankly confessed it, saying, ' As far as it concerns me, Father, there is nothing in the world that I desire more.' The old monk answered ' Do you realise what you have said ? Who could have believed that you would have dared to say this ? It is amazing. Have you not read many times : ' He who is not raised to the priesthood against his will, is unworthy to be raised to it.' but you are not only not reluctant, but aspire to it, as you yourself confess, without any sense of unworthiness.'

This reproof made him so ashamed and conscience-stricken that he prostrated himself at his feet, weeping bitterly and, in broken tones, seeking pardon for such great presumption. The other was deeply moved by such humility and devotion, but it was a little time before he reassured him. At length he said gently and sadly ' Rise '. When he had sat down at his command, the man of God spoke thus prophetically ' Do not distress yourself, my son, I should say my lord, for I know, indeed I know, the devotion which prompts your words.

spiritu, quo affectu *a* locutus sis uerba hec. Tibi igitur
dico et uere dico tibi : mox quidem sacerdos, et post, cum
tempus a Deo prescitum *b* aduenerit, etiam episcopus eris.'

CAPITVLVM XII

Quod promotus ad presbyteratus gradum, quantum
creuit ordine, tantum profecit in deuotione ; et de
abstinentie rigore qua ante episcopatum perdomuit
carnem suam.

Promotus itaque, iuxta uerbum uiri Dei, ad gradum
sacerdotii, quantum creuit ordine, tantum in sacra
profecit deuotione. In altaris officio ita quidem uersa-
batur ac si uisibilem manibus contractaret Dominum
Saluatorem. Videbatur astantibus diuina celebranti *c*
opere et ueritate ipsum cum sponsa illud epithalamicum
decantare : ' Dilectus meus michi et ego illi,' [1] tantam ei
dilectus deuotionem interius *d* conferebat, tantam ille
dilecto attentionem exterius impendebat.*e* Itemque *f*
panis et uini uisibilem speciem intuitus, ad inuisibilia
mentis intendens aciem, ' Dilectus meus,' inquit, ' candidus et rubicundus.' [2] Ad duo ista que et quanta cordis
eius uterus conceperit et parturierit, ' Que uox, que poterit
lingua retexere? ' [3]

Interdum etiam crucis lactucam cum agno paschali [4]
expressius, immo impressius gustans et interius dentibus
terens, totis anime sue uocibus clamabat : ' Fasciculus
mirrhe dilectus meus michi, inter ubera mea commorabi-
tur.' [5] Nec enim perfunctoria afficiebatur compunctione
ad horam ac postmodum ad leuia mentem relaxabat,*g*

---

a affatu B   *b* tempus prestitutum a Deo X
c celebrans X   *d* *om* Xc
e ipsi dabat c   *f* Iterumque Xc
g relaxat B

Therefore I tell you, and I speak truly, you will soon be a priest, and later, when the time ordained by God shall come, you will even be a bishop.'

CHAPTER XII

How, being raised to the priesthood, his new rank increased his devotion, and how, before he became a bishop, he kept his body in subjection by extreme abstinence.

He was then promoted to the priesthood as the servant of God had foretold. His devotion increased to correspond with his new rank. At the consecration it was as if he were handling the living body of his Lord and Saviour, and when he celebrated mass it seemed to those present that in deed and in truth he sang like the bride the bridal song ' My beloved is mine and I am his.'[1] His beloved inspired him with so much internal devotion, that his whole being seemed to be concentrated on the beloved. His gaze was fixed on the visible species of bread and wine, but his mind was intent on what they represented. 'My beloved,' he said, 'is white and ruddy.'[2] No words can describe the innermost feelings of his heart.[3]

Partaking of the bitter herbs of the Cross and the Paschal Lamb,[4] he tasted them inwardly and not merely physically, his whole soul proclaiming, ' A bundle of myrrh is my well-beloved unto me, he shall dwell between my breasts.' [5] Nor was he moved merely

---

[1] Cant. 2:16   [2] Cant. 5:10
[3] Hymn *Sanctorum meritis*, ascribed to Rabanus Maurus, sung at Vespers on Martyrs' feasts
[4] cf. Exod. 12:8-9   [5] Cant. 1:12

set animum in uigore districtionis *a* continens, illud
prophetisse et peccatricis egregie sibi uendicabat, 'Vultus
eius non sunt amplius in diuersa mutati.'[1]

Domabat corporis menbra uigiliis, ieiuniis, flagellis,
et iuxta morem ordinis usu cilicii et potu aque cum
arido pane. Nichil omittebat de austeritate ulla *b* quam
communis regula uel maiorum admittebant exempla.[2]
Peculiaria etiam complura supererogare non desistens,
genua flectebat crebrius, corpus totum sternebat in
terram ; iacensque pronus cum Moyse et Aaron, cum
Iosue et Daniele diuinam exorabat clementiam quatinus
a populo suo furorem suum auerteret et propitiationem
acceleret.[3] In omni Quadragesime septimana ferias
tres in aque *c* et solius panis edulio, nullo penitus con-
dimento adhibito,*d* nisi forte salis adderetur prelibatio,
transigere consueuit. In ultima uero ebdomada sabbati
adiciebatur obseruantia in simili dieta.[4] Numquam
infirmitas aut debilitas seu casus alius ante sumptum
episcopatum, alio cibo uel potu istud quadriduum eum
compulit aliquatenus releuare.

Abstinentie uero huic ascribebant medici in etate
progressiori stomachi illius nimiam infrigidationem,
unde plures interdum perferebat dolores et iuges pene
molestias. Hanc quoque designabant causam qua
uirtus in eo appetitiua, uirtute digestiua potentior,
corpulentiorem *e* eum iam quinquagenarium faciebat
quam fuerat pridem adholescens. Sic ergo non modo
sobrie, iuste et pie, immo parce, benigne et deuote Deo,
proximo et sibi uiuendo, ad summum sacerdotii gradum
dignissime subeundum diuinitus meruit preparari.

---

a discretionis Xc   *b* *om* X
c B *omits* in ; aqua X   *d* *om* B
e corpulentioremque erat X   [1] 1 Kings 1:18
[2] *Rule of St Benedict*, c. vii, 8th degree of humility

for a short time, afterwards turning his attention to trifles, but his mind remained concentrated on God. It could in fact be said of him as of the celebrated prophetess and sinner, ' His countenance never altered.' [1]

He kept his body in subjection by watching, fasting and the discipline, and, as was the custom of his order, wore the hair shirt and lived sometimes on water and dry bread. He omitted no austerity which the rule, or the example of his superiors suggested,[2] adding to these very many other individual practices, such as frequent genuflections and prostrations. When lying on the ground he would, like Moses and Aaron, Joshua and Daniel, beseech the divine mercy to turn away its wrath from the people and speedily be merciful to them.[3] Throughout Lent for three days in the week, he partook only of bread and water with no flavouring, except possibly salt, and in the last week observed the same rule on the Saturday.[4] Before he became a bishop, neither sickness nor physical weakness, nor any other happening would make him alter his diet on these four days.

The doctors ascribed the numbness of his digestive organs, which caused him so much pain and discomfort in his later years, to this abstinence. They attributed the fact that at fifty he was fatter than he had been in his youth to his requiring more food than he could digest. Living thus, not merely temperately, righteously and piously, but serving God with great devotion, and showing kindness to his neighbour and harshness only to himself, he was prepared by divine grace for the highest grade of the priesthood. He did not ascend the ladder

---

[3] cf. Exodus 32:11 ; Daniel 9:16

[4] This fast on bread and water for three days a week during Lent was originally ordered for three days a week throughout the year. cf. *Consuetudines Guigonis*, c. xxxiii (P.L. 153, 705-6)

Scalam nempe uirtutum haut segniter diatim con-
scendens, cuiuslibet dignitatis apicem sanctitatis *a* culmine precellebat.

CAPITVLVM XIII

Quod beato Petro Taretasiensi *b* archiepiscopo
familiare obsequium Hugo impenderit ; et de quibusdam aliis que utrumque, archiepiscopum uidelicet et
predictum eius ministrum contingunt.*c*

Per idem tempus uir sanctissimus Taretasiensis
archipresul Petrus, Cisterciensis monachus,[1] Cartusiam
sepius adire solebat, ibique in cella solitaria *d* infra
sanctorum illorum habitacula uelud intra mellita quedam aluearia, pluribus per interualla mensibus ut apes
prudentissima commanebat.   Aut certe ut columba
mitissima et mansueta,*e* in archa quadam *f* tutissime
quietis, ibi cum Noe respirabat, fugiens seculi tumultum
quasi impetum aquarum inundantium, uniuersam fere
terrarum faciem misere obruentium.   Hiis *g* uero sacris
meditationibus et spiritualibus sanctorum uacans collationibus, alterum cum Paulo se paradisum credebat
inuenisse unde persepe ad tertium rapiebatur celum
sublimis theorie.[2]

Huius itidem Hugo mancipatur obsequio, seruitio
delegatur.   Quis enim *h* dignius tanti uiri interesset
archanis ?   Quis menbra sanctissima purius contrectaret,
foueret dulcius, sollicitius obseruaret ?   Quis denique
illo deuotius seruiret tanto presuli ?   Quis sciret, quis

----

a + iam Xc   *b* Cartusiensi B
c contigerunt X   *d* solitarius c
e mansuetissima Xc   *f* quidem X
g Hic Xc   *h* + Hugone Xc

of perfection slowly day by day, but soon attaining to the highest degree of sanctity, was worthy of any office, however pre-eminent.

CHAPTER XIII

How Hugh became the attendant of Blessed Peter, archbishop of Tarentaise, and of certain things which befell the archbishop and his servant.

During this period Peter, the most venerable Archbishop of Tarentaise, a Cistercian,[1] used often to come to Chartreuse, and, there alone in a cell among those of that holy community, dwelt for several months like an industrious bee making honey in his hive. He might also be compared to the mild and gentle dove living in security and tranquillity with Noah in the ark, and fleeing from the tumult of the world as from the onrush of the waters of the flood sent to overwhelm almost the whole face of the earth. Passing his time in meditation and in converse on spiritual matters with these holy men, he believed that like Paul he had found himself in Paradise, and was often on the wings of contemplation borne up to the third heaven.[2]

The duty of waiting upon him was allotted to Hugh. Who was more fitted to be the companion of such a

---

[1] Peter, a monk of Cîteaux under St Stephen Harding, was appointed bishop of Tarentaise in 1142, where he showed himself a zealous reformer and a staunch defender of the Church's rights against Barbarossa. Famous for his miracles and love of the poor, he was described by Walter Map (see below II, 131) as ' a man of joyous nature, modest and humble ; he seemed a model of virtue.' He died in 1175 and was canonised in 1191.
[2] For this paragraph cf. Gen. 8:8-12 ; 2 Cor. 12:2-4

posset tam facetum, tam acceptum exhibere famulatum
sancto Dei ? Si lectio recitari, si quelibet sententia in
tanto librorum pelago inquiri petebatur et inueniri, quis
utrumque competentius set celerius, set libentius adim-
pleret ? Ad manum ei omnis que posceretur Scriptura
fuit.ᵃ Si de Veteris, si de Noui Instrumenti ᵇ paginis
sermo erat, si gesta sanctorum, si tractatus doctorum
inquisitionem mouebant, Hugonis sollertiam nichil
latebat. Cumque sanctus ille loqueretur, hic auditor
erat mansuetus et docilis ; cum loqui iuberet,ᶜ pro-
nuntiator acutus, et mirum in modum eloquio efficax
et suauis. Si illum senem, si hunc iuuenem pariter
uideres, iterum Petrum et Iohannem sibi redditos et
coniunctos estimares. Et ille quidem etate et nomine
Petrus erat, hic Iohannes gratia et obsequela. Obse-
quebatur in cunctis namque gratiose que sancti poterant
aut reuerentie congrua aut animo grata esse. Abluebat
frequenter pedes eius et osculabatur osculo cordis sui,
quia oris osculo non sinebatur. Diluente autem illo,
ut referre solitus erat, plantas illius et tibias, aiebat ei
sanctus : ' Fili, etiam superiora lauari indigent ; laua
secure et bene.' Asserebat enim hoc genus fomenti
infirmiori corpusculo suo plurimum conferre.

Extat usque in presens sub decliui montis latere quo
itur a monachorum mansionibus ad fratrum diuersoria,
sedes quedam pro sancti pontificis illius pausatione, illic ᵈ
frequentius in eundo et redeundo usque ad sudorem
fatigati, parata. Neque enim ibidem equitare, quia uel
priori loci hoc minime licebat, archiepiscopo aliquatenus
libebat.ᵉ Est autem sedes huiusmodi. Stant ᶠ cominus
due proceritatis immense abietes, locum sessionis humane

ᵃ erat X
ᶜ iuberetur Xp
ᵉ licebat X

ᵇ + uel Testamenti X
ᵈ ac sic Xc
ᶠ ita ut Xc

man? Who would handle his venerable limbs with such modesty, or serve him with such gentleness and care? Who else possessed the knowledge and ability to wait on the holy man with such readiness and intelligence? If he wished to be read to, or wanted to have some particular passage found for him in so vast a collection of books, who could do it as competently, rapidly and willingly? Whatever volume he wanted was produced. If they were discussing either the Old or the New Testament, or examining the lives of the saints, or the works of the fathers, nothing escaped Hugh's investigations. When the holy man spoke he could not have had a more willing or attentive listener, if he asked him to talk, what he said was intelligent, well-phrased, and very much to the point. To see the old man and the young one together you would imagine that Peter and John had once more returned and been re-united. The former was Peter in age and not only in name, the latter John in grace and attentiveness. He did everything he could to show his veneration for the holy man and to give him pleasure. He frequently washed his feet, and, as he was not permitted to kiss them with his lips, he kissed them in spirit. He told us how when he bathed his feet and legs, the saintly man used to say ' My son, I need to be washed further up, don't be afraid to wash me thoroughly ', for he declared that this warm fomentation was very beneficial to his fragile frame.

There still exists on the side of the mountain, on the way from the cells of the monks to the lodgings of the lay brothers, a seat made as a resting place for the holy bishop, who became tired and sweaty through often passing up and down. The archbishop would seldom ride when there because the prior was forbidden to do so. The seat was of this type. There were two large firs

capacem medio inter se spatio prebentes. Hiis pertrans-
uersum incisis modice insertus est uectis taxeus quadrus
nec multum grossus. Hoc erat totum cathedre huius
pontificalis opus.

In hac sedentem uidimus aliquotiens iam episcopum
Hugonem, de suo quondam archiepiscopo, iam regnante
in celo, hec et alia nobis gratissime referentem, et
sudorem sancte sue faciei extergentem ; nec enim parum
laborabat et ipse in ascensu uie illius. In throno excelso
isto etiam nobis qui ab eo hec audiebamus *a* sedere
iocundum fuit, mirantibus lignum aridum crescentibus
arboribus ita insolubiliter compaginatum ut obduci pene
uideretur cicatricis utrimque incisio. Quidam et hoc
miraculi loco ducebant quod *b* abietibus per quaterdenos*c*
uel eo amplius annos in aera crescendo in tantum eleuatis,
sedile trabis inserte *d* in sublime nullatenus euectum, ita
solo esset contiguum ut etiam hominis sessioni exigui
cerneretur accomodum. Quod ita recens apparebat ac
si succum natiuum necdum exuisset.

De archiepiscopo etiam hoc *e* memorabat quia post
stratus sui ingressum, ut fatigata diurno labore quiete
nocturna menbra releuaret, dum hunc Hugo in lecto
componeret et uestibus operiret, cotidie hanc eum orationem proferre audiebat : 'Presta quesumus, Domine,
ut de perceptis muneribus gratias exhibentes, beneficia
potiora sumamus.'[1] Cotidie uero et benedictione com-
petenti *f* ministrum suum Hugonem muniebat et auctor-
itate pontificali a peccatis omnibus absoluebat et monitis
spiritualibus instruebat. Nichil denique utilium sub-
trahebat, set omne consilium Dei quod sciret esse profuturum ei et pluribus per eum illi sollicite manifestabat.

---

a audiuimus X   *b* pro Xc
c quater ternos X ; quaternos c   *d* quatinus sedile trabis insertum X
e om B   *f* potenti Bp ; benedictionem petentem X

growing side by side with a space between them. Horizontal cuts were made in these into which a squared pole of yew wood of no great thickness was inserted. This was the only seat provided for the bishop.

We sometimes saw Hugh sitting on that seat, telling us affectionately this and certain other anecdotes about his former archbishop, now reigning in Heaven, and wiping the perspiration from his venerable countenance, for the ascent was no small labour to him. It was a pleasure also to us, who heard these stories from him, to sit on that lofty throne. It amazed us that as the trees grew the timber plank became so firmly fixed that the mark left by the incision could scarcely be detected. It also seemed wonderful that, although the trees had been growing vigorously upwards for fourteen years or more, the seat was never any higher, but remained near enough the ground for a small man to sit on it in comfort. It always seemed as fresh as if its original sap had not yet dried.

He related also this about the archbishop. When he had gone to bed and was resting his tired limbs after the labours of the day during the quiet of the night, and Hugh himself was settling him in bed, and covering him with the bed clothes, he heard him utter this prayer daily ' Grant we beseech thee, O Lord, that giving thanks for the gifts that we have received, we may obtain greater benefits.' [1] Every day he gave his blessing to his servant Hugh, and by his episcopal authority absolved him from all his sins, instructing him also in spiritual matters. He withheld nothing profitable from him, but was careful to make known to him all the counsels of God which he deemed would be useful to him, and through him to very many others.

[1] Postcommunion for feasts of bishops

Capitvlvm XIV

Quam industrie familiam gubernauerit, uel quam sollicite predicationis studio insudauerit. Quamque in diuinis siue in rebus temporalibus, omnibus in commune a se consilium petentibus, iam procurator constitutus domus Cartusiensis, consultor extiterit efficax et deuotus.

Post hec cum iam Hugo in quietis sue nidulo per bina circiter lustra moratus, et mundo plene mortuus plumis undique et pennis fultus solidissimis ad uolatum esset aptissimus, procurationem totius domus ei inquantum licuit renitenti prior suus delegauit. Huiusmodi uero columba hec pulcherrima satis exhorrebat uolatum. Horrebat corporaliter circumuolare officinas materiales et diuersoria corporalia, qui spiritualiter uolare didicerat ad domus *a* Patris qui in celis est multas mansiones, et Domini uirtutum spiritualia *b* cogitatione et auiditate perambulare tabernacula. Volatus quippe iste fuit ad requiem, ille ad fatigationem. Ad hunc dabantur ei penne ut diceret cum psalmista 'uolabo et requiescam', ad illum sumebat pennas *c* diluculo et habitabat in extremis maris,[1] que iccirco *d* maris sibi extrema erant quia tenebris *e* curarum et sollicitudinum amaritudinibus respersa erant,*f* extra negotiationum tamen secularium mare erant.

Viderat autem prior illius ut erat prudentia sicut et beniuolentia unice preditus, uiderat, inquam, illum uas

---

a domum Xc
b spirituali . . . perambulare eterna tabernacula Xc
c pennas suas diluculo Xc, ut habitaret X
d cuius itinera X ; cuius iterum maris sibi proxima extrema erant c
e in tenebris X
f respersus erat, extra negotiorum c

CHAPTER XIV

How when he was made Procurator of Chartreuse, he provided assiduously for the community, and was an earnest and indefatigable preacher, and how his counsel was sought by everyone and what wise and admirable counsel he gave both in spiritual and in temporal matters.

After this, when Hugh had been in his quiet nest for nearly ten years, dead to the world, and his wings and feathers were ready for flight, obedience compelled him, much against his own inclination, to accept the office of procurator of the community committed to him by the prior. Flight of this type, this lovely dove abhorred. He shrank from flying in person round the various departments and the huts, for he had learned to fly in spirit to the house of his heavenly father in which there are many mansions, and to roam in thought and desire round the heavenly tabernacles of the lord of hosts. That flight indeed was repose, the other wearisome. For the first he was given wings that he might say with the Psalmist, ' I will fly away and be at rest ', for the second he ' took the wings of the morning and dwelt in the uttermost parts of the sea '.[1] These matters were truly to him the uttermost parts of the sea, since their obscurity caused him bitter anxiety and disquiet, though only on the outer edge of the sea of secular business.

His prior had noted his exceptional sagacity and kindliness and had seen that he was a chosen vessel,

---

[1] cf. Ps. 54:7, 138:9, and Gloss of Peter Lombard *in h.l.*, according to whom the psalmist, borne on the wings of charity, dwells with God alone at the ends of the earth and not in the sea of cares where he would sink.

effectum in honorem, utilem in omnibus et ad omne opus bonum sufficientem.[1] Sciebat enim eum, seruiendo fidelissime Ihesu Christo, affatim didicisse bonis quibusque preesse operibus. Reputabat igitur incongruum aliis eum de cetero manere infructuosum, qui sicut oliua speciosa et uberrima fructificauerat sibi in domo Dei.[2] Nouerat illum et igne caritatis splendescere et pinguescere oleo pietatis. Nec censebat oportunum ut lucerna lucens et ardens, sub modio diutius latens, sibi tantum luceret, que lucem omnibus qui in domo erant[3] sufficiens erat ministrare. Exponitur itaque in publicum, et ponitur super candelabrum, quatinus ad lucem eius non modo ad horam, immo ad eternitatem gaudeant uniuersi.

Regebat ergo industrie commissam sibi familiam, fratres sollicite instruebat, et iuxta illud de sancto Honorato Arelatense dictum quod frequenter in ore habebat multumque laudabat: 'Torpentes semper excutiens a desidia,[a] feruentes spiritu cogebat ad requiem.'[4] Exhibebat priori suo se[b] alterum Ioseph qui optime nouerat[c] esse Dominum cum eo. Vnde, creditis sibi omnibus, nichil ipse nouerat nisi panem tantum quo uescebatur. Ipse uero fidelis in omnibus tamquam Dauid, egrediens et ingrediens ad imperium eius, in cunctis se prudenter habebat. Erat reuera Dominus manifeste cum eo et omnia opera eius dirigebat.[5] Vnde ad ingressum illius benedixit Dominus domui sue ualde, exuberare eam faciens[d] in omnibus bonis.

Erat quoque in sermone prudens et efficax, in consilio acutus et circumspectus. Qui ad illum accedebat, cellam

---

[a] ad desideria X
[b] om B
[c] sciebat Xc
[d] exuberare omnia faciens Xc

profitable in everything and sufficient for every good work.[1] He knew that he, as a most faithful servant of Jesus Christ, had learnt to excel in all good works, and therefore judged that it would be wronging others to allow one to continue to remain unfruitful, who had grown up in the house of God as a beautiful and most flourishing olive tree.[2] Since he knew that he was aflame with the fire of charity and full of the oil of holiness, he did not consider that it was right that a burning and shining light should be hidden any longer under a candlestick, and illuminate only himself, when he was capable of giving light to all who were in the house.[3] He was therefore brought out and placed on a candlestick, so that all might rejoice in his light, not only at that time but for ever.

He faithfully ruled the community committed to his charge and was most conscientious in instructing the lay brothers, living up to that description of St Honoratus of Arles which he often used to quote with marked approval, ' He made the lazy shake off their sluggishness, and compelled those who were fervent in spirit to rest.' [4] He behaved to his prior like another Joseph and he, having fully realized that the Lord was with him, entrusted everything to him, and dissociated himself entirely from all administrative work. Like David Hugh acted prudently and loyally in everything, going out and returning as he commanded him. God was obviously with him and directed all his activities,[5] and when he took charge blessed the monastery exceedingly, causing it to have all good things in abundance.

His words were discreet and sensible, and his advice

---

[1] cf. 2 Tim. 2:21 [2] cf. Ps. 51:10 [3] cf. Matt. 5:15
[4] St Hilary, *Vita S. Honorati*, c. iv (P.L. 50, 1259)
[5] cf. Gen. 39:3, 6, 23

se uinariam putabat introisse aut certe promptuarium
eructans ex hoc in illud.[1] Si enim de temporalibus alicui
consuleret, siue ab aliquo consuleretur, mox consilium
pro negotio instanti referebat oportunum consulens eum,
uel ab eo consilium accipiens ; set confestim consilio
salutari, de caducis ad mansura consulentem et con-
sultum transferebat.

Irrideant, si uidebitur,[a] talia prosequentem aut
nimium litterati aut parum creduli. Illi sillabas captent
et cauillent, isti sententiis derogent et discredant. Ego,
ut uerum fatear, litteratis satisfacere [b] nescio, incredulis
non sufficio. Hiis autem quibus sola per seipsam ueritas,
etiam nullo fucata ambitu uerborum placet, id quod
uerum noui celandum non duxi, set fiducialiter imperanti
cedendo caritati ut facultas tulit exposui. Sillabas
calumpniantibus utpote doctis indoctus cedo, dis-
cutientibus sententie ueritatem ad defensionis mee
patrocinium omnes qui Hugonem nouerunt interpello.
Quis ab Hugone consilio etiam in temporalibus destitutus,
non consilium retulit necessitatibus suis profuturum,
sapientibus quoque huius seculi admirandum ? Quem
uero in temporalibus erudiuit [c] quem mox ad perpetua
non incendit ?

Loquebatur in capitulo monachorum uerbum Dei,
et spiritualibus spiritualia comparans, quasi musto
quodam pretiosis [d] rerum spiritualibus pigmentis condito
iocundissime debriabat, uino licet meracissimo Scriptu-
rarum iugiter potatos. Loquebatur in auditorio fratribus

---

[a] Arrideant si uideatur X ; Arridebunt si uiderint c
[b] sufficere B
[c] non erudiuit X
[d] pretioso Xc

shrewd and wise. Whoever approached him thought he had entered a rich wine-cellar or a garner full to overflowing with good things.[1] If he gave counsel to anyone, or anyone consulted him concerning temporal matters, he received excellent advice on the subject at issue, and then immediately he and his adviser turned their attention from transitory things to eternal ones.

Let the scholars and the sceptics mock, if they wish at the narrator. Let the former take exception to and criticise the style, and the latter question and cast doubts upon the truth of what I relate. I admit that I cannot hope to please scholars, or convince the incredulous. I write for those who prefer the simple truth without any ambiguity or circumlocutions. I have not concealed the truth as I knew it, but have faithfully set it down to the best of my ability, at the request of those to whom I gave way out of affection. I accept all criticisms of my style, but against those who impugn my truthfulness I defend myself by appealing to those who knew Hugh. Would anyone, now deprived of Hugh's counsel even in temporal matters, not confess how much more valuable it was when in desperate straits than that of men with experience of the world, and was there any who consulted him about secular business whom he did not quickly inspire with a love of spiritual things ?

He preached the word of God to the monks in chapter and, by the subtlety of his exposition, he made his hearers who had already imbibed the ancient wine of the scriptures, drunk with a heady new wine, laced with the precious spices of allegorical interpolations. Speaking to the lay brethren, in accordance with the apostle's counsel, he gave great draughts of milk to those as yet

[1] cf. Ps. 143:13

et lactentibus lac apostolicum affluenter immulgebat.[1]
Secularibus qui forte aduenissent loquebatur et docebat [a]
diuites non sperare in incerto diuitiarum.   Pauperes
recreabat, ut licebat pro rigore ordinis, diurnis [b] etiam
subsidiis.   De hoc uero iocundum aliquid uolente
Domino referemus et utile, cum illa scribemus que apud
Cartusiam ipsum iam episcopum uidimus egisse.[2]   Istos
uero, cum rebus nequiuit, consolabatur sermonibus,
illud adimplens uiri sapientis: 'Ecce,' inquit, 'uerbum
bonum super datum optimum.'[3]

Omnes interea Hugonem loquebatur ; siue prior
siue monachus siue conuersus gratiam attollebat collatam
Hugoni.   Diues Hugonem laudibus efferebat, egenus
Domino precibus Hugonem commendabat, coegenus [c]
commendandum supplicabat.   Istud uero ille uotiuum
ducebat, illud tamquam friuolum contempnebat.   Nec
tamen [d] nullus ex hoc fructus procedebat, quod tamen
melius alterius libelli textus exponet.   Nam et lectori
parcendum et prospiciendum labori et intentioni :   et
iam recessurum a Burgundia nouis Anglia dicendi
principiis competentius suscipiet, quem ad innouationis
sue gratiam felici suscepit auspicio, rectorum maxime
suorum iamdiu uitiis misere inueterata.

[a] dicebat X
[b] diuinis cd
[c] coegenis B ; et coegenis c ; *om* X
[d] Cum X

unweaned.[1] If laymen happened to arrive, he exhorted the rich not to trust in the transitoriness of riches and assisted the poor as far as the meagre resources of the order permitted with daily alms. If God wills it, we will later on give a description of what we ourselves saw him do at Chartreuse when he was already a bishop,[2] as this should prove interesting and profitable. When material help was not available, he comforted them with words, in accordance with the maxim of the sage, ' Lo, good words are the best of gifts.' [3]

All spoke well of Hugh: the prior, the monks and the lay brethren extolled the grace vouchsafed to him, the rich were loud in his praise, the needy commended him to the Lord in their prayers and begged their fellow sufferers to pray for him. For the prayers he was grateful but treated the praises with contempt, but these, as is better explained in another book, were not completely fruitless. I must, however, spare my readers, and proceed with my narrative, since Hugh is about to leave Burgundy, and his arrival in England is a good beginning for a new book. That miserable and sinful land, which had endured for so long the vices of its rulers, received in him a happy augury of better fortune.

---

[1] cf. 1 Cor. 3:2
[2] see below II, pp. 162-7.
[3] Ecclus. 18:17 (also cited in *Rule of St Benedict*, c. xxxi)

LIBER SECVNDVS

Proemivm [a]

Cum Lincolniensis ecclesie presulatum annis iam Hugo bissenis, diebus quinquaginta tribus, gloriosissime administrasset,[1] placuit sanctitati sue paruitatem meam de uite claustralis dulcedine in sollicitudinum suarum qualecumque solatium assumere, suoque inseparabiliter lateri sociare. A quo tempore per annos tres et dies quinque, quamdiu scilicet in corpore postea uixit, ab eius numquam nisi [b] per unam solam noctem abfui comitatu, die semper et nocte adherens ipsi et ministrans ei. Huius igitur spatio temporis omnia fere que de eo libellus presens continebit aut propriis uidi oculis aut a sanctis ipsius labiis audiui. Causam qua in nostrum uenit orbem tum et ab eo tum et ab illis [c] qui huius aduentus sui procuratores extiterunt [d] accepi ; similiter et modum quo a dilecta sua Cartusia decessit,[e] quo domum Withamensem a fundamentis construendam disposuit, instituit et uiris optimis adimpleuit, ac post hec ad episcopatum accessit.

De hiis que in episcopatu gessit antequam ei adherere cepissem, de industria pretereo innumera certissime comperta, notitia cunctorum dignissima. Quia enim plurima ex hiis quosdam me longe doctiores litteris mandasse accepi, superfluum immo et presumptuosum esse iudicaui ab hiis [f] congruentius exposita insipidiore

[a] prologus Qc
[c] aliis o
[e] discessit Xco

[b] *om* B
[d] + audiui et X
[f] aliis QXc

45

BOOK TWO

PROLOGUE

WHEN the venerable Hugh had ruled with great distinction over the church of Lincoln for twelve years and
fifty-three days,[1] it pleased him to remove me, an obscure
monk, from the peace of the cloister and make me his
constant companion and some small consolation to him
in his onerous office. Thenceforth until his death, which
took place three years and five days later, I never left him
except for one night, but was always with him, ministering to him night and day. The things I have here set
down are what I saw with my own eyes during this time,
or what I heard from his own venerable lips. It was
from him and those who had brought it to pass, that I
learned the cause of his coming to our land. These also
told me how he had left his beloved Chartreuse, and had
ruled over and directed the building operations at
Witham almost from its beginnings, and how he had
made it a model community, and finally how he was
raised to the episcopate.

I have purposely omitted much valuable material
concerning his episcopate, belonging to the period before
I became his companion, although it would be of great
interest to everyone, because I have learnt that more
competent scholars than myself have already set it down
in writing. It would therefore be waste of time and
presumptuous for me with my lack of literary skill to
repeat what others have already much more adequately

---

[1] Here and elsewhere Adam assumes that St Hugh's episcopate lasted
for 15, not 14 years. In reality Adam joined St Hugh's household in the
11th, not the 12th year of his episcopate. See Introduction, p. xvii.

eloquio replicare. Ad ea uero seriatim referenda,
quorum istos notitiam minus ad liquidum credimus
assecutos, calamum pariter intendentes et animum, tale,
inuocato Spiritus Sancti adiutorio, sumamus exordium.

Capitvlvm I

Quod rex Anglorum domum ordinis Cartusiensis in
Bathoniensi *a*,1 territorio nomine Witham fundauerit, et
Bathoniensem episcopum Cartusiam direxerit ut Hugo-
nem ad illius regimen mitti optineret.

Ea igitur tempestate qua bono Christi odore inter
ceteros domus Cartusiensis spirituales uiros Hugonis
nomen celebre, multorum circumquaque corda mul-
cendo, etiam ora repleuerat, contigit ad regis Anglorum *b*
Henrici secundi notitiam uirtutum illius famam tali
occasione peruenisse. Quadam die rege in transmarinis agente, uenit ad eum uir quidam nobilis de
Morienne partibus.*c* Rex uero de ordine Cartusiensium,
inter alia mutue sermocinationis uerba, pleraque ab
eodem inquirere cepit. Nam dudum sancte illius conuersationis fama preuentus, asciuerat de domo prefata
quosdam fratres, quibus et locum quem ipsi elegerant
in Anglia contulerat, uillam scilicet Witham appellatam
in Bathoniensi territorio sitam, cum terris et siluis, cum
pascuis et uiuariis necnon et aliis fundande illius ordinis

a Lincolniensi c
b Anglie X (*and in title*)
c + (*blank space*) nomine B

described. I have thus decided to confine myself to dealing in order with matters about which they have not, as I think, given sufficient information, and having invoked the aid of the Holy Spirit, I shall now begin.

Chapter I

How the king of the English founded a Carthusian monastery at Witham in the diocese of Bath,[1] and sent the bishop of Bath to Chartreuse to secure Hugh as its prior.

At that time, Hugh having won the hearts of many persons in the vicinity, his fame like the fragrance of Christ was spread abroad with that of the other holy men of the Carthusian order, and it chanced that a report of his holiness reached Henry II, king of the English. The cause was this. Once when the king was across the sea, a nobleman from Maurienne came to him, and in the course of their conversation the king questioned him about the Carthusian order. Having heard of its holy life some time before, he had received certain brothers from that monastery, and had given them a site selected by themselves, a vill named Witham in the diocese of Bath, with the lands and woods, pasture and fishponds and other appurtenances necessary for the foundation

---

[1] The foundation of Witham was begun in 1178; the first founders included Prior Narbert, Albert of Portes, Br. Gerard and Br. Aymard. cf. below pp. 64-8, II, 62-9 and Introduction, pp. xxiv-vii

domui necessariis. Qui uero predictis fratribus prior
fuerat designatus, ad breue uix tempus in Anglia degere
adquieuit. Vacationi namque et quieti solitudinis *a*
assuefactus, negotium sollicitudinis tante constructioni
debitum mente delicata non ferebat. Tedebat eum,
immo et socios eius pene cunctos, ritus gentis alienigene,
diete insolite, et ceterorum que moribus aduenarum *b*
et uotis in solo peregrino de facili pariunt offensionem.
Nam et prouincialium nonnullis formidolosus uidebatur
eorum esse in suos fines accessus, frustra scilicet istis
metuentibus sibi ne illi, propriis minus contenti limitibus,
eorum iugeribus occupandis inhiarent. Quem indi-
genarum aduersum se uiri innocentes motum pullulare
sentientes et in futurum precauere quieti sue satagentes,
priorem suum ad domum suam redire permiserunt,
quatinus, communicato cum uiris sanctis consilio, uel
animequior ipse rediret siue alium loco suo ad hec magis
sufficientem destinari optineret. Rediit ergo, et loco
eius alius mittitur, qui tedio simili affectus, morte beata
finem laborum et uite initium citius accepit. Reliqui
inter ista fratres uariis perturbationum procellis immani-
ter fluctuabant. Rex ipse angebatur medullitus ad hec.
Cepit namque ymaginari iam et pertimere futuri notam
ruboris, qua inurendum *c* se nouerat apud magnates
multarum in circuitu nationum, si cepta adeo salubria,
adeo cunctis exteris gentibus fauorabiliora *d* nequiuisset
consummare.

A uiro igitur memorato super hiis tale recepit *e* consilium. 'Ab hiis,' inquit, 'domine mi rex, fluctibus, unico
uos et efficacissimo liberare potestis consilio. Est in domo
Cartusie quidam monachus, natalibus quidem clarus set
morum strenuitate longe preclarior, nomine Hugo de

---

a quiete solitudini Xc   *b* om B   *c* mirandum Xc
d honorabilia Xc   *e* accepit X

of a house of their order. The first prior remained only for a very short time in England, for being accustomed to a life of peace and retirement he was too sensitive to bear the responsibility which the business of the new foundation demanded. He and almost all his companions were dismayed by the unfamiliar food and habits of a foreign people and all the other things contrary to their own customs which vex and annoy strangers in a foreign land. Their arrival in the district alarmed some of the natives, who feared quite needlessly that, being dissatisfied with the extent of their own territories, they would do their best to gain possession of their lands also. These guileless men, becoming aware of the growing ill-will of the inhabitants and being anxious to secure a peaceful future, allowed their prior to return home, so that after taking counsel with holy men, he might either come back in a more tranquil frame of mind, or be replaced by someone more capable of dealing with the situation. He therefore departed, but his successor was equally discouraged, and soon ended his trials by a holy death and entry into life eternal. The rest of the brethren however had to endure many difficulties and afflictions. The king also was seriously disquieted, since he foresaw and dreaded that he would become the laughing stock of neighbouring rulers, if a project so well begun and which had won general approval from all foreign nations should end in failure.

The man I have already mentioned gave him this advice. ' My lord king,' he said, ' there is only one means of freeing yourself effectively from these difficulties. At Chartreuse, there is a monk of noble birth but far nobler character, named Hugh of Avalon. He has been endowed with every virtue, and all who know him are so much attracted by him that they love him at first

Aualun. Hic omni uirtutum gratia decoratus, ita est
omnibus qui eum nouerunt acceptus et gratiosus ut solo
aspectu omnium in se rapiat affectus. Qui uero [a]
uerbum ab ore eius audire merentur, tamquam [b]
diuinum se uel angelicum gaudent oraculum percepisse.
Hunc si nouella in partibus adhuc uestris sanctissimi
ordinis huius plantatio cultorem habere meruerit atque
rectorem, uidebitis eam letissime ad omnem subito
gratiam fructificando proficere. Tota insuper ecclesia,
ut certus sum, Anglicana illius purissime religionis et
religiosissime puritatis nitore uenustius decorabitur.
Ceterum quia hunc sui non de facili emittent de domo
sua, ipse quoque non nisi coactus et inuitus alterius
habitationis adibit sedem, fauorabili et strenua opus est
legatione, operosa etiam precum ambitione nitendum
quatinus, hoc solo quamtocius impetrato, et uester de
cetero animus a sollicitudinis huius molestiis releuetur,
et hec sublimis religio ad gloriam excellentie uestre
insignius propagetur. Inuenietis in uno homine isto cum
ceterarum uniuersitate uirtutum quicquid longanimitatis
et dulcedinis, quicquid magnanimitatis et [c] mansue-
tudinis, in aliquo mortalium poterit reperiri.[d] Nulli
huius ingrata esse uicinitas aut cohabitatio ualet, nullus
hunc uitabit ut alienigenam, nullus non ut ciuem,[e] ut
domesticum, ut fratrem aut amicum intimum illum
respiciet. Nam et ipse omne humanum genus non aliter
quam propria attendit uiscera, uniuersos homines
amplectitur et fouet ulnis et gremio [f] unice caritatis.'
Hec et in hunc modum plurima ille dixerat. Dicenti
quoque rex multum applaudens et gratias agens, dirigit
quam celerrime cum litteris regiis ad domum sanctam
legatos uenerabiles, dominum uidelicet Reginaldum [1]

---

[a] etiam X ; uero etiam Qc   [b] om B   [c] dulcedinis . . . et / om B
[d] inueniri Xc   [e] + nullus Q   [f] et gremio / om X ; unice / om c

sight. Anyone who has the honour of hearing him speak, perceives to his great delight that his words are like those of an angel or even of God himself. If you were able to secure him to take charge of and rule the new foundation of his holy order in your land, you would rejoice to see how soon it would flourish in every way. I can assure you that the fame of his piety and integrity would bring lustre to the English church. Since, however, his superiors would be reluctant to send him away, and he himself would be unwilling, except under compulsion, to go to another foundation, you will need the services of persuasive and determined ambassadors making energetic representations. Having, however, obtained your petition your mind will be relieved of these troubles and anxieties and this illustrious order will flourish to the increased glory of your highness. You will find united in this one individual all the patience, courtesy, courage, gentleness and other virtues possible in any mortal man. His presence will annoy nobody, he will not be shunned as a foreigner, rather everyone will treat him as a neighbour, an old and intimate friend, or even as a brother. The whole human race is as dear to him as himself and his superabundant charity embraces and cherishes all men.' He said very much more to the same effect. The king heard him gratefully and with warm approval. He immediately sent a distinguished embassy consisting of Reginald,[1] bishop of Bath surnamed the Lombard, and

---

[1] Reginald of Bath, the son of Jocelin, later bishop of Salisbury, was born c. 1140. Called ' the Lombard ' from his Italian education, he became archdeacon of Salisbury, and was first a friend, then an enemy of Thomas Becket. He was Henry II's ambassador to the Pope and was consecrated bishop of Bath at S. Jean de Maurienne in 1174 by Richard of Canterbury and St Peter of Tarentaise. He attended the 3rd Lateran Council in 1179 and probably made this visit to the Grande Chartreuse on his way back. In 1191 he was elected archbishop of Canterbury, but he died very soon after.

Bathoniensem episcopum cognomento Lumbarh et
cum eo uiros quosdam strenuos et industrios.

Capitvlvm II

De temptatione carnis, qua uehementius, imminente
iam uocatione sua ad prelationis gradum, uexatus est ;
et de uisione qua *a* per sanctum Basilium uisitari meruit et
curari.

Mirabilis Deus uero in sanctis suis,[1] futurorum
prescius, quin potius auctor et conscius iam preuenerat
sanctum suum dispensatione *b* mirabili. Visitaturus
namque eum diluculo, subito probauit illum ;[2] in
probatione subita infirmitatem eius ostendens illi, in
uisitatione diluculi suam conferens salutem ei. Vt enim
apostolorum principem Dominus sub passionis articulo
negare se permissum prius ostendit sibi, in breui postmodum loco sui aliis preficiendum, ita egit erga fidelem
et peruigilem suum seruum super familiam suam mox
constituendum. Ostendit namque illum sibi ipsi,
' multiplicans uulnera eius,' ut ait sanctus Iob, ' etiam
sine causa ;'[3] et sic eum prefecit aliis, sanans prius supra
humane modum infirmitatis contritionem eius speciali
gratia. Quid enim potuit esse cause in homine iam
circiter quadragenario, iam corpus portanti contritione
multiplici perualide edomitum,*c* iam cor habenti medita-
tione defecata, necnon et oratione quam continua tam et
pura mundissimum ; quid, inquam, habuit,*d* aut in hoc
quid potuit esse cause ut repente traderetur angelo

a quam B
b + sua Xc
c castigatum Xc
d huic B

other active and energetic men with letters to that fervent monastery.

CHAPTER II

How on the eve of his promotion to the rank of prior, he was severely assailed by carnal lusts, and how in a vision he was visited and cured by St Basil.

God who is glorified in his saints,[1] and who knows, nay rather directs, what is to come, had guided his beloved by his marvellous providence. He suddenly tempted him in order to send him consolation at dawn,[2] so that through unlooked for temptation he might show him his weakness, and through his consolation at dawn give him confidence in his mercy.

Just as at the time of his passion the Lord showed the chief of the apostles, whom he was shortly to set over the others in his place, that he would be permitted to deny him, so now he acted in a similar way towards his loyal and devoted servant, whom he was soon to place over his household. He revealed him to himself, by multiplying his wounds, as St Job says, without cause,[3] and then set him over others, after he had healed him of his exceptional infirmity by a special manifestation of his grace. What cause could there be that a man already about forty, with a body well tamed by his many austerities and a heart purified by assiduous meditation and continuous contemplative prayer, what cause could there be, I repeat, that such a man should suddenly be handed over to an

---

[1] cf. Ps. 67:36
[2] cf. Job 7:18
[3] Job 9:17

Sathane, stimulis carnis sue colaphizandus¹ usque ad desperationem pene uite sue? Stimulis *a* quidem carnis paulo minus *b* usque ad mortem accessit carnis; uite namque anime etsi timere potuit, set desperare nullatenus ualuit; que iam in tuto fuit, colligata nimirum 'quasi in fasciculo uiuentium apud Dominum.'² Vt autem quid athlete fortissimo contigerit, quomodo *c* impugnatus fortiter fortius repugnando uicerit et *d* uincendo triumph-auerit succincte referamus et plane.

Tanta ei carnis temptatio subito exorta est, tam continue tamque importune in eum debachata est, ut mallet gehennalibus interim *e* tradi penis quam tantis urgeri *f* flammis. Tam ingens pugna, tam forte certamen fuit, ut solius diuine non dubitetur uirtutis fuisse quod humanitus non cessit, set uiriliter resistendo triumphum reportauit. Quia uero ad plenum huius modum congressus nemo referre posset quibus lacrimis, quantis gemitibus, quam crebra confessione, quam aspera flagellatione uel diuinum expetierit adiutorium uel cor contriuerit uel corpus cruciauerit proprium, euentum huius belli breuiter absoluamus.

Diei cuiusdam diluculo uisitauit eum hoc ordine oriens ex alto sol iustitie, mittens angelum suum et eripiens eum de potestate tenebrarum harum.³ Egerat noctem illam sicut in tenebris, sic ipse insompnis *g* pene totam; luctabatur namque angelus ille tenebrarum aduersus eum, ut eum traderet in teterrimam uesperam consensionis *h* inique. Ille uero non solum reluctabatur ei, immo et cum alio luctabatur angelo usque ad mane⁴ triumphalis palme, illud apostolicum expetens et expectans in se impleri: 'Nox precessit, dies autem

a Stimulus Xc   *b* + ei X
c quonam modo Xc   *d* om Bc
e om B   *f* urgeret X
g in sompnis ot   *h* contentionis Xc

angel of Satan to be chastised by the thorns of the flesh [1]
until he almost despaired of his life ? The thorns of the
flesh almost caused his physical death, but although he
feared for the salvation of his soul, yet could he not
despair, for it was already safe, and had been gathered up
in the harvest of those predestined to live with God.[2] I
will describe clearly and briefly what befell this valiant
warrior, how, being fiercely attacked, he defended himself
even more stoutly and conquered, winning a magnificent
victory.

A great temptation of the flesh suddenly assailed him,
and attacked him so violently and frequently, that at the
time he would have preferred to endure the torments of
Hell, rather than the violence of his own desires. The
conflict was so terrible that undoubtedly it was through
divine power alone that his human nature was not
defeated ; but by resisting manfully he emerged
victorious. As the struggle itself and the tears and
groans expressive of a tormented heart, and the frequent
confessions with which he implored God's help and the
hard scourging with which he tortured his body all
defy description we shall proceed to the end of the fight.

One day at dawn the Sun of justice and Day-spring
from on high visited him in this manner, and sending his
angel snatched him from the power of darkness.[3] He
had passed the whole night in gloom, and almost without
sleep, for the angel of darkness fought with him to deliver
him into the dark night of evil consent. Not content with
resisting this one, he also strove with another angel [4]
till dawn, when he triumphed, remembering and await-
ing the fulfilment of the words of the apostle ' The night

---

[1] cf. 2 Cor. 12:7   [2] cf. 1 Kings 25:29
[3] cf. Luke 1:78 ; Acts 12:11 ; Col. 1:13   [4] cf. Gen. 32:24

appropinquauit.'[1] Sic cum duobus congreditur unus,
hunc inuitans, illum deuitans, repellens illum, attrahens
istum. Nimirum ab isto extorquere nititur benedictionem
qua consequeretur de illo ereptionem. Palestra adeo
uirilis pugne area fuit celle sue, in qua demum athlete
fortissimo, prostrato quidem non [a] superato, non uicto
set fatigato, tenuis obrepsit sopor. Erant quippe oculi
eius pre uigiliarum prolixitate grauati, cui dicere
competebat Domino : 'Preuenerunt oculi mei ad te
diluculo, ne preuaricarer eloquia tua,' iam uero
'dormitauit anima mea pre tedio.'[2] Nec uero huiusmodi
telis leniter [b] uulnerabat eos cum quibus congrediebatur,
unum ut compateretur et auxiliaretur, alium ut con-
funderetur et fugaretur. Summis tandem uiribus iaculum
hoc tergeminum emittens, uno impetu uicit utrumque
colluctuantium, sic exclamans : 'Per passionem, crucem
et mortem tuam uiuificam libera me [c] Domine.'[3] Hoc
dicto, solo prosternitur, 'Adhesit,' inquiens, 'pauimento
anima mea, uiuifica me secundum uerbum tuum[4]
Domine, qui mortuus es pro me.'

Continuo uelud in excessu positus, uidit uirum Dei
qui eum susceperat ad ordinem illum, sanctum quondam
priorem Cartusie Basilium[5] uultu et amictu angelico
radiantem astitisse sibi, seque sic uoce blanda compel-
lantem : [d] 'Quid tibi,' inquit, 'est, fili karissime? Cur
ita iaces pronus in terra? Surge et uelle tuum fiducialiter
enarra.' Ille uero ad eum : [e] 'O,' ait, 'pater bone et
nutritor [f] meus piissime, affligit me usque ad mortem lex
peccati et mortis que est in menbris meis[6] ; et nisi more
solito auxilieris michi,[g] en morietur puer tuus.' Vix
dictum compleuerat, et sanctus sic paucis : 'Bene,'

---

[a] nec Q
[b] leuiter Xc
[c] nos Xc
[d] appellantem X
[e] Ille . . . eum / om X
[f] enutritor Xc
[g] + subito X

is far spent, the day is at hand.'[1] One man struggled against the two, pleading with the latter and repulsing the former, resisting the first and imploring aid from the second, endeavouring with all his might to win the blessing which would free him from the attacks of the other. The lists for the combat in which he fought so manfully was his cell, where finally the stout-hearted champion, prostrate but unconquered, worn out but undefeated, snatched a short sleep. His eyes were heavy with long watching and he could truthfully say to the Lord, ' Mine eyes prevent the night watches, lest I should forget thy word, my soul melteth through heaviness.' [2] Nor did he lightly wound with these darts those whom he fought, the one that he might have compassion on him and assist him and the other that he might be confounded and put to flight. At last hurling three javelins with all his force, he conquered by one thrust both his assailants, crying aloud ' Deliver me, O Lord, by thy passion, cross and life-giving death.' [3] When he had spoken thus, he prostrated himself on the ground, exclaiming, ' My soul hath cleaved to the ground, quicken me, O Lord, who died for me, according to thy word.' [4]

Almost immediately afterwards, being as it were in an ecstasy, he saw the man of God who had received him into the order, Basil [5] the late holy prior of Chartreuse standing at his side in shining robes and with the countenance of an angel, who greeted him kindly, and said, ' What ails you, my dear son, that you lie prostrate on the earth? Rise and tell me frankly what you desire.' He answered, ' My loving father and venerable master, the law of sin and death which is in my members [6]

---

[1] Rom. 13:12   [2] Ps. 118:148, 28
[3] cf. Litany of the Saints   [4] Ps. 118:25
[5] Prior Basil died in 1174 (*La Grande Chartreuse par un Chartreux,* 1952)
[6] cf. Rom. 7:23

inquit, 'auxiliabor tibi.' Moxque patefactis nouacula,
quam manu tenere uidebatur, uisceribus eius quasi
strumam igneam inde uisus est exsecuisse et longius
extra cellam proiecisse ; dataque benedictione, medicus
discessit. Eger sanatus et sibi redditus, sompno fugiente
resedit, letatusque *a* supra modum de ostensa sibi
claritate nutritii sui qui ante *b* aliquot annos *c* migrauerat
ad Dominum, omnimodis et in corde et in carne se
repperit immutatum.

Horum summam cum ab ipsius ore Hugonis,
secretius mecum loquentis, pluries acceperim, in extrema demum egritudine sua planius et diligentius totius
euentus ordinem, sicut eum modo digessi, michi
enarrauit. Querenti uero utrum aliquem postea huiusmodi senserit in carne sua motum, 'Reuera,' inquit, 'quod
aliquem senserim non nego, set simplicissimum et quem
non minus contempnere quam comprimere esset facilli-
mum.' Hec iccirco dixerim quia aliter de hiis alium
quemdam scripsisse accepi, asserentem uidelicet quod
per beatam Virginem dominam nostram Dei genitricem,
sibi apparentem uisitatus, eunuchizatus et curatus ita
fuerit quod nullam deinceps carnis titillationem *d* omnino
expertus sit. Verum que ab ore illius de curatione et
curatore eius audiui, uerissime expressi.[1]

---

a letusque Qc
b + per B
c dies d *and le Couteulx, wrongly*
d temptationem X

torments me to the death, and unless you assist me as you were wont to do, your disciple will assuredly die.' He had scarcely uttered these words when the holy man said briefly ' It is well, I will aid you.' He immediately cut open his bowels with a knife which he seemed to be holding in his hand, and extracting something resembling red hot cinders, he flung it out of the cell a long distance away. The doctor then withdrew after giving him his blessing. Sleep having left him, the sick man sat down, healed and restored to himself. He rejoiced exceedingly at the vision of the glory of his master, who had departed to God a few years before, and realized that he had been completely cured both in spirit and body.

Hugh briefly narrated this to me many times in private conversations. The full and detailed account which I have now given I heard from his own lips in his last illness. When I asked him if he had afterwards felt any stirrings of the flesh, he answered ' I will not deny that I have felt some, but these were so insignificant that I did not have to fight against them but could simply ignore them.' I have written thus about this, because I have heard that someone else gave another version in which our Lady, the blessed virgin mother of God, appeared to him and made him a eunuch, so that he was completely cured and did not thereafter experience the slightest carnal inclination. I have therefore set down truthfully what I heard from his mouth about the circumstances of the healing and who healed him.[1]

[1] Accounts of somewhat similar occurrences are to be found in Cassian, *Collatio* 7, c. 2 (P.L. 49, 669-70), St Gregory, *Dialogorum liber I*, I, c. 4 (P.L. 77, 165), and in the *Gemma Ecclesiastica* (P.L. 74, 293-4). These accounts had been read by St Hugh and doubtless conditioned his vision or dream. The other author referred to by Adam is probably Giraldus, II, 247 and VII, 76.

Capitvlvm III

De aduentu nuntiorum regis [a] Cartusiam cum
uenerabili episcopo Gratianopolitano, et super illorum
postulatione prioris fratrumque diuersa sententia, et
Hugonis allegatio dissuasoria.

Ita leuites Domini, quem ab utero matris sibi
assumpserat electio Dei Patris, iam feriata a preliis, iam
celebrante iubileum optate quietis terra corporis sui,
post diutinam et deuotam ministrationem tabernaculi
custodiendis preparabatur uasis sanctuarii. Misticum
enim legis quinquagenarium [1] ante moribus optinuit quam
annis, prius attigit et impleuit sanctitate quam etate.
' Consummatus siquidem in breui impleuit [b] tempora
multa ; placita enim erat Deo anima illius. Propterea
et properauit illum educere de medio iniquitatum,'[2]
libidinis uidelicet et elationis. Miscuit ei celestis medicus
arte mirabili confectam potionem, ueneno et balsamo
temperatam. Venenum quippe temptantis [c] libidinis
uenenum extinxit in eius mente elationis ; at uero bal-
samum superni medicaminis uenenum deuicit in carne
eius totius libidinis. Illo fundatus est in humilitate, isto
in incorruptione [d] solidatus. Sic, sic duobus illis famosis
et principalibus antiqui serpentis capitibus in eo con-
tritis,[3] a reliquis eius menbris, id est a uitiis secundariis,
facile imposterum triumphauit. Ita uero optabilius a
figurali, quam olim Petrus a materiali eductus Herodis
carcere nesciebat quia uere ista fiebant per angelum,[4]
estimans se tantum uisum uidisse, non etiam uisus ef-

---

[a] + Anglie X   [b] compleuit Xc
[c] temptationis X   [d] corruptione B

Chapter III

Concerning the arrival of the king's envoys and the venerable bishop of Grenoble at Chartreuse and the different opinions of the prior and brethren about their request and Hugh's dissuasory speech.

Thus the Levite of the Lord, chosen and set apart by God the Father from his mother's womb, enjoyed for a short time after the conflict the repose and peace which he had so long desired and after his long and devoted ministry in the tabernacle was ready to take charge of the vessels in the sanctuary. In holiness and virtue although not in years he had already attained to the symbolic fifty of the Mosaic law,[1] and 'being made perfect in a short time, had fulfilled a long time ; for his soul pleased the Lord.' Therefore, ' hastened he to take him away from the midst of wickedness,' [2] I mean lust and pride. The divine physician had mixed for him a subtly compounded draught of poison and balsam. The poison of carnal temptation extinguished spiritual pride, but the balsam in the celestial medicine destroyed the poison of fleshly lust. By the one he was grounded in humility and by the other his purity was made invulnerable. Thus, the two principal and most deadly heads of the ancient serpent were crushed in him,[3] and he easily extracted himself from the lesser evils, that is from the more venial sins. Indeed, Peter's release from Herod's prison was less happy than his from that prison of the spirit : like Peter, he knew not that it was real and the work of an angel, supposing that he had merely seen a vision [4] without realizing its effects. He knew

---

[1] cf. Num. 8:25   [2] Wis. 4:13-14   [3] Gen. 3:15   [4] Acts 12:9

fectum percepisse. Sciebat se ad presens alleuiatum, nesciebat imposterum ab hac febre *a* esse sanatum. Dominus uero, qui procurabat iam in remotis mundi partibus promotionem eius, sic eo nesciente operabatur salutem in intimis sensibus eius.*b*

Venientes autem regis legati Cartusiam, assumpto secum uenerabili Gratianopolitano episcopo [1] ipsius loci diocesano, litteras domini sui priori et fratribus presentatas, persuasoriis *c* uerbis suppliciter et strenue prosecuntur. Omnibus uero ad primum contristatis auditum, prior [2] quam maxime conturbatur ; procrastinatur eorum responsio ; conscientie et uota super negotio discutiuntur interim singulorum. Prior prius *d* petitioni penitus contradicit ; fratrum in diuersa uariatur sententia. Hii talem uirum et uniuersitati ordinis adeo profuturum in tam remota dirigi nullatenus oportere dicebant ; alii, quorum unus dominus *e* Bouo fuit, quem postea priorem Withamie [3] hec sepius referentem audiuimus, a Deo exisse uerbum regis asserebant, nec tutum esse contradicere plurimis rationibus edocebant. 'Vos,' inquit Bouo, 'nescitis quicquam,[4] nec cogitatis quia superna dispositio facit hec omnia, ut ordinis huius sanctitas per uirum sanctum usque in supremos *f* mundi limites splendidius elucescat. Set neque putetis illum diu sub modio latebrarum uestrarum *g* posse cohiberi. Credite mee paruitati, inter precipua ecclesie sancte luminaria ipsum in breui audietis super candelabrum ecclesiastici regiminis sublimari. Dudum michi uir-

---

a + se c
b c *ends ch. II here*
c persuasoribus B
d primus QXc
e *om* Xc
f extremos Xc
g nostrarum X

that he had been freed for the present, but did not know that his fever had been permanently cured. In this way the Lord who was procuring his promotion in far distant regions, had without his knowledge purged him from the defects of his animal nature.

The royal envoys came to Chartreuse, bringing with them the diocesan, the venerable bishop of Grenoble,[1] and having presented their lord's letters to the prior and brethren, supported these by their own earnest persuasions and prayers. They were all at first dismayed at what they heard, and especially the prior.[2] No immediate answer was given ; and in the meantime they discussed the matter to ascertain what each of them felt and thought about it. The prior's first reaction was to refuse, whereas the brethren were divided. Some said that in no circumstances should a man so useful to the whole order be sent to so distant a land ; others, amongst whom was Dom Bovo, whom afterwards as prior of Witham [3] we often heard describing what had taken place, declared that the king's request was inspired by God. These gave many reasons why it would be unwise to refuse it. Bovo spoke as follows, ' You do not know[4] what is in store, nor do you consider that divine providence has brought this to pass in order that the fame and glory of our order may by means of this holy man be spread to the uttermost parts of the world. You cannot expect that he can long be concealed under a bushel in your wilderness. Believe me, you will soon hear

---

[1] John of Sassenage, bishop of Grenoble 1156-1219. Like other bishops of Grenoble at this period he was a Carthusian, which, together with the friendly relations existing between the Grande Chartreuse and the bishops of Grenoble since the days of St Bruno and St Hugh of Grenoble, explains the prominent part taken by him on this occasion.

[2] Guigo II, prior 1174-1180 and author of the *Scala Claustralium* (P.L. 184, 457-84) and other spiritual writings. He died in 1188 with a reputation for holiness.   [3] *c.* 1192-1201   [4] John 11:49

tutibus Hugo episcopus potius uisus est quam monachus extitisse.'

Postulatus demum Hugo super hoc suam proferre sententiam, suam aperire uoluntatem, ita citius ait : ' Voluntati mee super statu meo nichil penitus reseruare iampridem edoctus fui.[a] Quid autem de hiis uere sentiam libere exponam. In medio uestre sanctitatis tamdiu conuersatus, monitis et exemplis uestris in tantum adiutus, numquam uel per unum diem animam meam custodire sciui. Vnde miror quomodo in sapientis alicuius animum ascenderit quod ad aliorum regendas animas per memetipsum [b] mitti longius debuissem. Qualiter uero instituere nouam domum sufficerem, qui antiquorum instituta seruare nequiui ? Puerilia sunt ista que audio et nec deliberationis tante spatio, saluo reuerentie uestre beneplacito, aliquatenus digna. Omissis de cetero igitur talibus, cum et negotium arduum sit nec patiens dilationis, uestraque intersit solerter prouidere, ne regis illius cepta ad periculum animarum et ordinis sancti dedecus protelentur diutius imperfecta, e uobis aut ex ceteris domibus uestris [c] uirum quempiam ad hoc opus ydoneum eligite et cum istis mittite. Viris autem istis tamquam sapientibus et uos sapienter respondete, uelle eorum melius quam ipsi postulent [d] adimplete, assignantes eis non quem utpote decepti, set qualem ut religiosi et discreti querunt. Non expedit deceptos in persona postulati inconsultius exaudiri, qui [e] decipi in qualitate persone nec ipsi uolunt. Sic denique in sua petitione exaudiantur, ut gaudeant se utilius quam petierint [f] exauditos.'

---

[a] sum Xcm
[c] nostris X
[e] quia Q
[b] meipsum QXc
[d] postulant X
[f] petierunt Qv ; petierant c

that he has been set upon the candlestick of the ecclesiastical hierarchy, among the highest luminaries of holy Church. For a long time I have considered that Hugh's qualities are more those of a bishop than of a monk.'

Hugh was finally asked to express his own feelings about the matter. He replied at once ' I have long been taught to have no personal preferences concerning myself. I will, however, say frankly what I feel about this. I have lived a long time in your holy company, and have been assisted by your advice and example, and never even for one day have I been responsible for my own soul. Wherefore, it surprises me greatly that it would occur to any reasonable person that I ought to be sent far away and be entrusted with the souls of others. I cannot even observe the customs of our founders, so how can I have the ability to make a new foundation ? What I hear is arrant nonsense, and, with all due respect to you, not worth further discussion. As this business is important and must be dealt with immediately let us pass on to it. It is your duty to make careful provision to prevent the king's project remaining any longer uncompleted, to the detriment of souls and the disgrace of our holy order. Therefore, choose from amongst yourselves, or from another of our houses, someone with the gifts for this task and send him with these men. They are reasonable people and you should treat them as such. Give them a better answer than the one asked for, by providing them, not with the man they have sought for owing to a misconception, but one whom, being pious and sensible men, they really require. As they were not wilfully deceived about the character of the person they petitioned for, you ought not to grant a request made on misleading information. Let their prayer be so answered that they are luckier than if it had been granted.'

CAPITVLVM IV

Quod Hugo, instar sancti omniumque *a* iustorum spiritu pleni Benedicti, carnis euicta impugnatione in seipso, regendis aliis prefici dignus fuit. Et quod tandem cum regiis nuntiis *b* compulsus Withamiam uenit, et a fratribus ibidem consistentibus cum inestimabili gaudio susceptus est.

Reuera enim temptationis, ex parte et perhennius quam intelligeret *c* deuicte, metu nimium adhuc trepidabat, quam itineris huius occasione aliquatenus *d* excitari aut reaccendi summo studio precauebat. Nesciebat tale quid secum in presenti, quale dudum cum omnium spiritu iustorum pleno gestum legerat Benedicto, diuinitus fuisse actitatum. Nam et iste modo sicut quondam Benedictus, carnis temptatione uehementissime impugnatus est, set cum Benedicto et Hugo repugnauit, cum Benedicto uicit, cum Benedicto triumphauit, cum Benedicto quoque, hoste superato, aliorum dux Christi militum effici, et institutor sacre conuersationis, cum Benedicto sanctissimo et ipse in omni sanctitate probatissimus meruit inueniri.¹ De quo, sicut inferius planius dicetur, quidam uersificator egregius uerissime et breuissime, multa illius *e* bona paucis complexus, ita ait :

Pontificum baculus, monachorum norma, scholarum
     Consultor, regum malleus, Hugo fuit.²

Qui licet hec que premissa sunt seu et alia pro sui excusatione instantius prosequeretur, interna tamen

---

         a sancti / *om* B ; que / B¹, *crossed out by corrector*
         b + ire X   *c* intellexit X
         d aliqualiter X   *e* unius B ; *om* c

CHAPTER IV

How Hugh, like St Benedict who was filled with the spirit of all the just, having overcome in himself the assaults of the flesh, was worthy to rule over others. How at length under compulsion he came to Witham with the royal envoys, and was welcomed by the brethren there with indescribable joy.

He still dreaded exceedingly the recurrence of his former temptation, not realizing how completely it had been overcome, and feared greatly that it would return if he went away.

He did not know that God was dealing with him now as he had read that he had formerly dealt with St Benedict who was filled with the spirit of all the just. Hugh, like Benedict, had been fiercely assailed by carnal temptation, like Benedict he had defended himself, and like him had conquered and overcome.   Like him also, once the enemy had been defeated, he was to be the leader of other soldiers of Christ, a pillar of monastic life and a conspicuous example of sanctity.[1]   As I shall show more fully below, his many virtues were exactly and succinctly summarized by a celebrated poet :

> The bishop's prop and stay, the model monk,
> Patron of scholars, hammer he of kings :
> E'en such was Hugh.[2]

Although he put forward very strongly many other arguments as well as the ones already given, God's wise

---

[1] cf. St Gregory, *Dialogorum liber II* (P.L. 66, 125-204), whence is drawn the phrase *omnium iustorum spiritu plenus*
[2] cf. below, II, p. 231–2, where these lines are attributed to John of Leicester.

dispositio cuncta suauiter moderantis sapientie Dei [1] nullatenus potuit nutus sui [a] effectu priuari. Set nec prioris quidem patrocinium, Hugonem retinere cupientis, ei contra dispositarum a Deo rerum ordinem poterat suffragari. Vtriusque uero contradictio, et prioris uidelicet et Hugonis, dum nescienter nititur refragari, compellitur necessario famulari operanti inuisibiliter maiestati. Nam quo pertinacius prior resistebat, quo instantius Hugo se ad hec insufficientem asserebat, eo uehementius episcopi presentes cum suis consiliatoribus, iunctis tandem sibi quibusdam fratrum de conuentu natu maioribus, ut fieret quod rex tantus petierat perurgebant. Quid plura ? Fratrum tandem uniuersitas, tum precibus tum et rationibus eorum [b] qui aduenerant uicta, petentibus cedit.

Hugo, assentire flagitatus a cunctis, in priorem cum aliud [c] non posset, transfundit [d] sententiam. Sciebat id sibi ab illo, qui eum ut animam suam diligeret et a se nullatenus elongari optaret, uix aut numquam iniungi posse. Quem monitis sui episcopi, cunctorum etiam gemebundis precibus qui aderant interpellatum, sic dicunt qui intererant respondisse. ' Viuit Dominus, numquam sermo iste egredietur ex [e] ore meo que iubeam Hugonem meam senectutem deserere, suaque dulcissima et pernecessaria presentia Cartusiam uiduare.' Qui nimia importunitate uniuersorum tandem obrutus et quid faceret potius non inueniens, conuersus ad dominum Gratianopolitanum, ait : ' Iam quidem ratum est quod de me dixi : Hugonem a me uox mea aut mens mea numquam remouebit. Tu iam uideris, tu episcopus noster es, tu et pater et frater noster. Si hoc ei iniungas,

[a] uirtute sui X ; sue uirtutis cv
[b] om B ; orationibus eorum X
[c] in alium Xc
[d] transfudit Xc   [e] de Xc

providence which governs all things[1] could not be diverted from its purpose. Even the support of the prior who was anxious to retain him was of no avail against what God had decreed for him. Their resistance was forced of necessity to give way to the invisible workings of the Almighty, which in their ignorance they strove to oppose. For the prior's categorical refusal, and Hugh's earnest protests in regard to his insufficiency merely made the bishops and their counsellors and at last the senior monks, whom they had won over, insist the more energetically that the request of so powerful a ruler should be obeyed. There is little more to say. The whole community was finally convinced by the prayers and arguments of the envoys and granted what they asked.

They all begged Hugh to consent, and he, since he could not do otherwise, left the decision to his prior. He knew that since he loved him as his soul, and in no circumstances wished him to be far away, he would be unlikely to command this. The eye-witnesses describe how he, when urged by the exhortations of the bishop and the prayers and tears of the whole company present, replied : ' By the living God, I cannot utter the command which would cause Hugh to leave me in my old age, and deprive Chartreuse of his much loved and most necessary presence.' At last, shaken by the earnest pleading of all those present, and being at a loss as to what he ought to do, he turned to the lord bishop of Grenoble and said, ' What I have said about myself still holds. No decision or word of mine shall remove Hugh from me. Do what seems best to you, since you are our bishop, our father and our brother. If you order and enjoin it, I will neither gainsay you nor resist.' He said no more, but

[1] Wis. 8:1

si precipias, ego non contradico, non resisto.' Nec plura
locutus, iam uocem fletu interrumpente, lacrimis indulgebat quibus mentis anxie leniret dolorem.

Videres [a] iam per ora cunctorum riuos fluere [b]
lacrimarum. Episcopus et ipse, ut erat piissimus et
monachus ualde honestus et mansuetus, compellentibus
omnibus ut permissa sibi a priore in Hugonem uteretur
potestate, ita primum uniuersos alloquitur : ' Quia
uobis, fratres karissimi, quos non minus conuersatione
quam professione Christiane perfectionis apicem con-
scendisse manifestum est, nos desides et a culmine uestre
sanctitatis longe inferiores, non necesse est ostendere quid
in hiis [c] que Dei sunt agere debeatis, aut etiam uos
monere quatinus uobis melius cognita strenue compleatis,
qui in omni uita uestra non que uestra sunt, set que
Ihesu Christi [1] uos querere comprobatis ; hoc unum ad
memoriam uobis, domine prior, set et uestre, fratres,
uniuersitati reuocandum putaui, quo uobis ante oculos
ponatur qualiter in casu simillimo se habuerint pre-
decessores uestri.[d] Cum enim ad instantiam sancti
Cenomanensis tunc episcopi Berticramni in occiduas
Galliarum partes sanctissimus Benedictus dilectum et
sanctum discipulum suum Maurum, fundande gratia
religionis monastice destinaret, similem ibi luctum ex [e]
luctus causa non dissimili legitis [f] exortum.[2] Quem
suum pariter et fratrum dolorem ea sanctus Dei ratione
compescuit, ut ostenderet non oportere seruos Dei [g]
ullatenus contristari super hiis que uelle nouerint [h]
Dominum suum. Vbi et uerbum intulit memoria
dignissimum : ' Ne forte ' ait, ' hac ipsa nostra tristitia
Deo, quod absit, inueniamur contraire.' [j]

[a] Videns Bo   [b] effluere Xc
[c] quid . . . hiis / *om* B   [d] habuerunt . . . nostri X
[e] et Q   [f] legistis Xc   [g] *om* B   [h] nouerunt Xc
[j] . . . nostra iustitia, quod absit, inueniemur contraire X

broke off weeping, and by giving way to tears relieved the anguish of his mind.

Everyone was now weeping copiously, and begged the bishop to make full use of the power given him by the prior over Hugh. He was a very holy man and an excellent and compassionate monk, and now addressed the whole gathering : ' My dear brethren, whose lives and profession have clearly attained the height of Christian perfection, we who are so inferior and so far below your standard of sanctity cannot presume to show you what you should do in the things of God, or even to advise you to carry out wholeheartedly what you understand better than we do ourselves, since your lives are a proof that you seek not your own advantage but Christ's.[1] I think it advisable, however, to recall to your memory, lord prior and brethren, how your predecessors acted in a very similar case. When at the request of St Berticram then bishop of Le Mans, the most holy Benedict sent his beloved and saintly disciple Maurus into Western Gaul to establish the monastic life there, you must have read that there was similar grief there for a not dissimilar cause.[2] Which sorrow on the part of himself and his monks the saint of God justly rebuked and showed that it was not right for the servants of God ever to sorrow over what they knew to be his will. On this occasion he spoke words well worth remembering ' Lest perchance by our sadness, we are resisting God, which Heaven forbid.'

[1] cf. Phil. 2:21
[2] *Acta S. Mauri*, c. III. cf. *Acta Sanctorum*, II, 324

'Set et te, Hugo frater karissime, in hoc quoque
imitari conuenit quem sequi *a* semper dulce habuisti,
unigenitum Filium summi Patris, qui de altissimo
secreto sue Deitatis pro multorum salute ad publicum
dignatus est exire humane conuersationis. Et tu igitur
peregrinari ad modicum a tuis karissimis, postposito
interne *b* quietis adeo dilecte silentio, pro eo ne cuncteris
in presentis uite exilio, ut ei perhenniter postmodum
socieris in beatitudinis sue regno. Hoc ego licet
indignus uice ipsius, in remissionem peccatorum tuorum
ob compensationem etiam *c* eternorum premiorum, tibi
iniungo et in ui obedientie firmiter precipio. Perge
itaque sospes et felix cum uenerabilibus uiris istis qui te
uocare uenerunt, curamque suscipe domus Withamie
in Anglia, fauente Domino construende. Presis quoque
constanter et prosis instanter loco et fratribus ibi con-
gregatis in nomine Domini et congregandis.'

Hanc Hugo diffinitionem aliquamdiu pedibus se
pontificis deuoluendo *d* irritare nitens nec quicquam
proficiens, cessit postremo ; seseque orationibus omnium
presentium commendans, fratribus in osculo pacis
ualefaciens, cum legatis illis profectus est, ad regem
uenit, tandemque cum fauore maximo ab ipso dimissus
et ad Witham cum honore deductus, tamquam angelus
Domini a paucis fratribus qui tunc ibi erant in priorem
suscipitur cum gaudio ineffabili. Hec nos aliquantulum
diffuse prout gesta sunt retulisse, nulli sit onerosum,
quibus et Hugonis modestia et humilitas, quibus et
fratrum suorum in eum *e* beneuolentia et caritas euidentius commendatur. Habent preterea in hiis unde sibi

---

a om B
b interim QXc
c om B
d aduoluendo QXc
e eorum B

'You also, my dear brother Hugh, must imitate in this him whom you have always desired to follow, the only-begotten Son of God the Father Almighty, who for the salvation of many deigned to come from the lofty mystery of his Godhead to live on earth as a man. During the exile of this present life you must be ready for his sake to abandon those dearest to you and the silence and peace you love so much for a little while, that afterwards you may live with him eternally in the bliss of his kingdom. I, as his unworthy representative, charge and command you under obedience to do this for the remission of your sins, and in the hope of an eternal recompense. Go then confidently and willingly with these venerable men who have come to summon you. Take charge of the house of Witham which will, God permitting, be founded in England, and rule it and the brethren already there and those who shall join them, faithfully and diligently, and may it prosper under your rule.'

Hugh cast himself at the feet of the bishop and tried for a short time in vain to make him alter his decision. Finally he gave it up and, commending himself to the prayers of the whole company, he exchanged the kiss of peace with the brethren and bade them farewell. He accompanied the envoys to the king who received him with marked kindness and taking leave of him, had him honourably conducted to Witham. The few brethren there greeted him as if he were an angel of God and were exceedingly glad to have him for their prior. No one ought to blame me for describing these events somewhat fully, exactly as they happened, since they are clear evidence of Hugh's humility and self-effacement, and of the great affection felt for him by his brethren. These events should be a lesson for those to take to heart, who,

metuant, qui nulla *a* regulari disciplina probati ipsi regulariter uicturos quibus presint coaceruant ; habent simul et prelati qui talibus auctoritatem talia presumendi administrant. Qui si forte et nobis qui hoc *b* scribimus ceperint indignari, nouerint profecto et uere nouerint se ab Hugonis ingenio *c* alienos. De quo sane manifeste constat quia in religione perfecta et perfectissima ab infantia perfectissime conuersatus,*d* promotionem suam in huiusmodi procurantes exhorruit, impedire conantes artius dilexit.

CAPITVLVM V

De solerti prouisione Hugonis super uniuersis que utilitas flagitabat ecclesie Withamensis. Et quam fauorabilem se beneficumque prestiterit pristinis illius loci indigenis in transmigratione ipsorum.

Inuenit autem fratres uelud alter Ioseph in Dothaim[1] quod interpretatur defectus. Consistebant equidem in silua, haut procul a regia tunc uilla uocabulo Witham, que futurorum quodam presagio tale nomen creditur sortita. Dicitur namque Latine mansio siue habitatio sensus ; quod excellenter per aduentum ueri huius Christi philosophi *e* locus ipse effici meruit in re, attractis undique ad odorem notitie sue uiris sensatis, in omni uerbo et in omni sensu prestantissimis. Qui manentes ibidem et habitantes corpore, ad illam eternam patriam, cuius perfectis iam sensibus gaudia pregustant,*f* cogitatione et auiditate inhiare non cessant.[2] Quos autem

---

a in illa B   *b* illi quibus hec X ; nobis quibus hec c
c + esse c   *d* + est, quod X
e uiri huius Christi (*om* philosophi) X   *f* pregustabant Xc

without a long training in the religious life, collect a band of would-be monks in order to rule over them, and also one for bishops who enable such persons to behave so presumptuously. If, perchance, the writer arouses their indignation, it is because they cannot but realize the vast difference between Hugh's attitude and theirs. In his case it was abundantly clear that his prejudice against those who caused his advancement and affection for those who tried to hinder it was due to his membership from infancy of two religious orders, one strict and the other much more so, and to his perfect observance of the rules of both.

CHAPTER V

Concerning Hugh's careful provision for all the needs of the Church of Witham, and his consideration and generosity towards its former inhabitants on their departure from it.

Like another Joseph, he found his brethren in Dothan,[1] which is a synonym for penury. They were living in a wood near the royal vill of Witham, a prophetic name. It means in Latin, house or home of the mind, which is exactly what the place became by the coming of Christ's true philosopher, for its fame in this respect brought learned men there from all sides, who were conspicuously eloquent and intelligent. They stayed on and lived there, with their hearts concentrated on the eternal home for which they so eagerly longed and whose joys they already sensibly tasted.[2]   But Hugh

[1] cf. Gen. 37:17 and *Glossa Ordinaria in h.l.*: 'Dothain interpretatur defectio.'
[2] cf. Responsory *Iste Sanctus* (Common of Bishops)

inuenit fratres habebant cellulas ex asseribus contextas,
uallo perexiguo et palis circumseptas. In hiis utcumque
usque ad tempus correctionis sese recipientes, omnibus,
ut breuiter dicatur, aut pene omnibus necessariis ac [a]
debitis ordini suo adminiculis, erant carentes. Neque
enim diffinitum erat usque adhuc ubi maior, ubi minor
ecclesia, illa monachorum cum [b] cellis et claustris, hec
cum fratrum domunculis et hospitum [c] diuersoriis
aptius construi debuisset. Villam supradictam, eorum
iam ditioni cessuram,[d] habitatores pristini incolebant ;
necdum prouisum eis fuerat ut sedes auitas sine murmure,
sine sui lesione, nouis uellent aut possent successoribus
cedere. Hiis et aliis de situ, de qualitate loci, necnon
et de ceteris que necessitas ordinis flagitabat loco
conuenire uel utilitati ibidem conuersantium inseruire,
diligenti solertia perspectis et singillatim pernotatis,
Hugo, nam et inter eos ita condictum fuerat, ad regem
citius repedauit. Cumque de singulis quod sibi uideretur[e]
exposuisset, rex in omnibus prudentiam illius et modestiam admiratus, quecumque ille disposuit et ipse appro-
bauit, que postulauit libenter [f] indulsit.

Ac primo quidem uniuersos conuocari fecit prediorum
uel rerum quarumlibet possessores quos loco cedere
oportebat, ne quolibet strepitu aut frequentie cuiuscumque accessu solitudinis sue alta silentia interrumpi
aut saltem interpellari [g] uel modice potuissent. Quibus
ex parte regis optio in commune data est ut e duobus
quod maluisset [h] unusquisque eligeret ; agros scilicet et
habitandi loca, conditione pari ut apud Witham fuerant
sortiti, in regiis ubi elegissent maneriis reciperent, aut

---

[a] aut B   [b] illa . . . hec / *om* c ; cum / *om* Bc
[c] hospitium B   [d] ditioni collatam per censuram X
[e] que sibi uiderentur Xc   [f] clementer X
[g] interpolari Xc ; interpellari uel interpolari Q
[h] maluissent X ; mallent cv

found the brethren living there in cells made of stakes surrounded by a narrow ditch and a stockade. At the time of his arrival and until he could reform it, to put it briefly, they lacked everything or almost everything essential even for the modest requirements of their order. It was not yet decided where the greater church, with the cells and cloister for the monks, or the smaller one, with the quarters and houses for guests and lay brethren, could best be erected. The former inhabitants were still living on the site which was to be handed over to the monks, nor had provision been made to enable them to give up their ancestral homes to their successors without indignation and serious loss to themselves. After Hugh had made a thorough and detailed examination of these problems and of others connected with the site and its character, and had ascertained what was needed to make it conform to the regulations of the order, and conduce to the welfare of the community there, he returned by arrangement to the king, and gave him his views on all these matters. The latter was greatly impressed by his sense and moderation and fully approved of all his suggestions, promising him everything he had asked for.

First of all Hugh held a meeting of those who had holdings or other possessions and would have to give them up because the noise and the frequent visitors would destroy or at least disturb the monks' privacy and perpetual silence. On the king's behalf he offered them the choice of two alternatives : either to be given fields and dwelling-sites of the same type as at Witham on any royal manor they chose, or to be freed from villeinage and go and live wherever they wished. When some had chosen lands and others freedom, Hugh, who was determined to temper justice with generosity, said to

pristine seruitutis iugo absoluti, quas uellent regiones
libere incolandas adirent. Tunc aliis terras, aliis
petentibus libertatem, Hugo iuris benigni emulator
tenacissimus regi ait : ' Iam, domine, hoc etiam prouideri
necesse est, ut pro domibus uel pro quibusque *a* in
culturas et uarias structuras sumptibus aut sudoribus
istorum compensatio pecuniaria tribuatur, quatinus in
nullo detrimentum sustinentibus per nos, letis leti *b* et
beniuolis succedamus grati.' Ad hec in primis cum
uelud difficilem se exhiberet rex, ille in bonitate precipuus, in interuentu strenuus, adiecit dicens : ' Reuera,'
inquit, ' domine mi, nisi usque ad obolum nouissimum
super omnibus hiis satisfactum fuerit *c* prius hominibus
istis, locus idem non poterit conferri nobis.' Ita uero
mercem sibi, ut putabat, in nullo profuturam rex emere
compulsus, tuguria scilicet *d* uetustissima, tigna cariosa
et parietina semiruta, multum effudit aes pro breui
commodo. Venditores autem, accepto pretio, nouo
negotionis genere exhilarati quia ditati, nouum bene-
dicebant institorem, qui de longe portauerat panem
suum ; [1] panem utique confortantem, primo utique cor
proprium, ne regi quod esset audire dignum reticeret, et
ut quod esset congruum mediocribus exhiberet. Deinde
etiam ipse rex et illi mediocres eodem pane roborati et
confortati sunt, utique ad edificationem anime, set illi
qui egebant etiam ad solatium huius uite.

Verum negotiator iste bonus, tantillo non contentus
lucro ubi iustitiam *e* seruasse potius quam fecisse
misericordiam sibi uideretur, ita regi ore faceto rursus
infit : ' Eya, domine mi rex, ecce in terra tua propria
diuitem te domibus numerosis aduena ipse et egenus feci.'

---

a quibuscumque QXc   *b* om Xc
c fuit B   *d* uidelicet Qc
e instantiam X

the king, ' Now, my lord, you must also see that they are given monetary compensation for their homes, and for whatever expense or labour they have bestowed on their holdings and buildings of every kind. If they sustain no loss through us we shall gladly and joyously take over from contented people who wish us well.' The king at first made difficulties, but Hugh's great kindheartedness made him persist and he continued : ' Sire, unless these men are first paid for everything down to the last halfpenny, I cannot accept this place.' Thus, the king was compelled to buy goods which he thought completely worthless, old hovels, decayed beams and half-destroyed walls, laying out a considerable sum of money to little advantage. The sellers when they were paid were absolutely delighted at this new type of sale which enriched them considerably. They blessed the new prior who had brought his bread from afar ; [1] the bread which strengthened everyone, and which had given him the courage to tell the king what he ought to know, and what was the right thing for him to do for these poor people. Finally, both the king and these humble folk were both sustained and nourished by the same bread, to the edification of their souls. The latter however, also received material consolation in their poverty.

This good business-man was not, however, content with a deal which seemed to him to be just but not generous, and therefore once more spoke to the king with a smile. ' See, my lord king, how I, a poor stranger, have enriched you in your own land with many houses.' He laughed at this and replied ' I had no wish to receive this sort of riches, which have made me almost

---

[1] cf. Prov. 31:14. Documentary evidence of the transfer of the former inhabitants of Witham to Knapp, in North Curry, about 30 miles away, can be found in Thurston, Appendix A and references.

Ad hec subridens ille, ' Sic,' inquit, ' ditescere non ego cupiebam. Diuitie iste iam pene egenum me fecerunt. Set nec scio cui sunt *a* usui opes iste.' Tum Hugo, hoc modo elicita per eius responsum occasione *b* quod intendebat proferendi, ' Bene,' inquit, ' bene ; en, ut uideo, paruipenditis commercium istud. Fiat igitur quod uestrum decet *c* magnitudinem ; michi non habenti ubi capud reclinem [1] dentur edes iste.' Stupens ad hanc postulationem rex et postulantem cum admiratione intuitus, ' O te,' inquit, ' dominum mirabilem ! Non putas quod nouas uobis domus nequeamus extruere?*d* Dicito tamen quid tu inde faceres.' Et ille, ' Non decet,' inquit, ' regalem amplitudinem de quibusque minimis interrogare. Hec prima est petitio mea ad te ; et cum sit modica, cur moram patior in exaudiendo ? ' Tum rex alludens, libenter enim ingenium uiri, ut erat prudentissimus, longa concertatione uerborum explorabat, ' O,' inquit, ' hominem in solo peregrino pene iam uiolentum ! Iste, si uiribus niteretur, quid ageret qui uerbis ita extorquet ? Ne uero duriora nobis inferantur ab eo, fiat quod exigit.' Tunc ille concessas sibi edes omnium pristinis dedit possessoribus, quarum illi iam pretium possidentes, iterato ipsas aut pretio distrahunt aut transferunt *e* alias iterum inhabitandas. Sic ille, non iam in sanguinibus edificaturus Iherusalem,[2] Neemie solertia preditus et deuotione, fauore Salomonis, sollicitudine Dauid, locum ut modo cernitur exstruere festinabat.

---

a sint QXc
b eliciens . . . occasionem Xc
c deceat QXc
d Num . . . nequeamus Q ; non . . . ualeamus Xc
e distrahant aut transferant X

destitute. I don't even know anyone to whom they could be of any use.' His answer gave Hugh the opportunity he had sought for. ' Very good,' he said, ' I see you don't think much of your bargain. It would be an action in keeping with your munificence to give these buildings to me who have not where to lay my head.' [1] The king was dumbfounded at the request and stared in amazement at the petitioner. ' You are,' he replied, ' an extraordinary prior. Do you really believe that I cannot erect new buildings for you ? At least tell me what you are going to do with these.' He answered ' It is unworthy of your royal generosity to ask about such trifles. This is my first request to you, and, as it is so trivial, why shouldn't it be granted at once ? ' The king, who had a sense of humour, thoroughly enjoyed his ready wit, and intentionally prolonged the verbal duel. ' Can a man on foreign soil be so bold ? What would happen if he were to use his fists, when his tongue is so violent ! Lest worse should befall us, let him have what he asks.' Hugh then gave back the buildings he had received to their former owners, although they had already been paid for them. These either sold them once more, or took them away to live in them elsewhere. Thus he, being endowed with the foresight and devotion of Nehemiah, the favour of Solomon and the zeal of David, was enabled to build Jerusalem without blood,[2] and immediately set about the erection of the edifice which we now see.

[1] Luke 9:58
[2] cf. Mich. 3:10

Capitvlvm VI

Quomodo rex, modestiam expertus et longanimitatem uiri Dei, iurauerit illum, se uiuente, de regno ipsius nullatenus discessurum, seque consilia salutis sue illi communicaturum asseruerit.

Accidit interea, maiori[a] constructionis iam parte conuenienter explicita, regem, uariis regni curis detentum, minus intendere quibusdam fabricis perficiendis quarum usus pernecessarius uideretur. Inde sumptibus in stipendia deficientibus, artifices queruli priorem et fratres importunis crebro uerbis lacessebant. Hinc quosdam e fratribus ad curiam prior destinauit qui regi super huiusmodi defectu oportune suggererent, huncque suppleri optinerent. Ille prouisurum se negotio et necessaria citius pollicetur esse missurum. Redeunt qui missi fuerant, nichil preter uerba reportantes. Dissimulante interim principe quod promiserat adimplere, cessatum est funditus ab opere. Prior sub silentio sustinendum credidit, ut rex motu proprio quod expedire nouerat exequi studuisset. Verum ipso diutius negligente, iterata legatione interpellatur, iterumque sicut prius uerbum, non datum, reportatur. Inter hec, multa dilatione protracta, tedium subrepsit fratribus. Quidam ex hiis etiam, bile commoti, uerbis in priorem asperioribus inuehuntur. Desidie eum simul et negligentie incusant, qui per seipsum regem, licet in remotis agentem, pro tanto negotio iam olim non adisset.

---

[a] maioris X

Chapter VI

How the king, having experienced the patience and understanding of the man of God, swore that as long as he lived he should never leave his kingdom, and declared that he would take counsel with him for the welfare of his soul.

When the more important buildings had been erected, the king, being absorbed in political matters, took very little interest in the completion of the other essential ones. There being no money to pay them, the masons became indignant and frequently made insulting and wounding remarks to the prior and brethren. The prior sent some of the monks to the king to tell him about the arrears and obtain what was needed. He promised that he would soon arrange matters and send the necessary supplies. Thus, the envoys returned merely with empty promises, and as the king did not fulfil his undertakings, the building operations stopped altogether. The prior believed that no protest should be made, and that the king should be given the chance, on his own initiative, to interest himself in the completion of what he knew was needed. As he failed to do so, after a considerable time he was approached by other envoys, who as before received empty promises, but no gifts. Meanwhile, the protracted delay proved wearisome to the brethren, and some of them waxed indignant and bitterly reproached the prior, taxing him with laziness and indifference, because since the business was important he had not already himself gone to the king, even though the latter was far away.

Fratrum autem quidam Girardus[1] nomine, uir austeri quidem ingenii set bene religiosus et sermone inter magnates et principes efficacissimus, talibus priorem affatur : ' Quousque, domine prior,' inquit, 'palpandum iudicatis hominem durissimum, nec potius ei palam denuntiatis ut consummet citius edificia, quibus carere non debet forma ordinis nostri ; aut, si ulterius differre maluerit, ualefacientes ei, ad patriam et domum propriam redire una cum nobis omnibus maturius festinetis ? An minus animaduertitis *a* quia in ordinis nostri redundat iniuriam tanta circa nos illius incuria et nos ipsi pateamus cunctorum in circuitu derisioni, qui tot iam temporibus hic commanentes, exiguis nequeamus mansiunculis istis culmen imponere ? Quod si uerecundia uos innata cohibet, ne homini huic que decet *b* proferatis, adeamus ipsum pariter et que ei *c* dicturus sum ego ipse audietis.' Conuocatis autem cunctis *d* fratribus et negotio in commune prolato, placuit omnibus Girardum cum priore proficisci ad regem. Et prior ' Consilium,' inquit, ' uestrum et ego gratanter accepto. Verumptamen uobis, frater Girarde, prouidendum erit ut quemadmodum libere, ita et modeste uos habeatis in uestro sermone. Cum enim sit, ut uere comperi,*e* princeps iste sagacis admodum ingenii et inscrutabilis fere animi, forsan ut temptet nos dissimulat exaudire nos. Scit procul dubio perfectionis quam professi sumus quam maxime interesse illud dominicum implere documentum quo dicitur nobis : ' In patientia uestra possidebitis animas uestras,'[2] necnon et illud beatissimi Pauli: ' In omnibus exhibeamus nos sicut Dei ministros, in multa patientia.'[3] Multa uero patientia in eo comprobatur,

---

a aduertitis X   *b* dedecet o ; decent Xc
c *om* B   *d* *om* B
e Cum sicut uere comperi X

One of the brothers named Gerard,[1] a man of rather harsh temperament but nevertheless a good monk, whose words had considerable force with kings and magnates, spoke thus to the prior, ' How long, lord prior, do you intend to go on humouring this hard man, instead of bluntly telling him that he must either quickly finish the buildings which are essential in our way of life—or else, if he goes on procrastinating, you will take your leave of him, and return home with us as soon as possible. Can't you see that his obvious neglect of us is bringing discredit on our order, and that our being here for such a long time without being able to put roofs on our poor huts is making us the laughing-stock of the whole neighbourhood ? If your natural shyness prevents you giving this man a piece of your mind, let us go to him together, and you shall hear what I have to say to him.' The brethren all met to discuss the matter, and it was unanimously decided that Gerard should go with the prior to the king. The prior said ' I willingly accept your advice, but take care, brother Gerard, to be courteous as well as frank. I have discovered that the king is crafty and his mind is almost unfathomable. It is possible that by postponing his assistance, he is testing us. He must know that the perfection to which we are pledged consists especially in fulfilling our Lord's instructions ' In patience possess your souls ',[2] and those of Paul ' Show yourselves in all things the ministers of God, in much patience.' [3] It is a sign of

---

[1] This brother Gerard was known to Peter of Blois, archdeacon of Bath, who described his knowledge of the faith, his compunction and his austerities ; cf. *Compendium in Job*, c. ii (P.L. 207, 815-6).

[2] Luke 21:19

[3] 2 Cor. 6:4

si multa contraria siue aduersa in multa lenitate
supportet longanimitas multa. Patientia enim sine
longanimitate non multa set curta erit ; absque lenitate
uero, prorsus nulla erit.'

Assumptis itaque prior secum predicto *a* Girardo et
alio fratre nomine Einardo, uiro grandeuo et proba-
tissime in sancta religione uirtutis, ad regem profectus
est. Quos ille omnes ac si celestes angelos uenerabiliter
excipiens, ad insinuationem instantis negotii blanda
locutus, bona pollicitus, dilationes excusans,*b* celerius
omnia perficienda promittens, sumptus tamen inpre-
sentiarum non contulit, nec quando esset collaturus
certius intimauit. Tum uero infrendens frater Girardus,
sue *c* potius deliberationis pristine quam admonitionis
sibi facte memor, regem aggreditur durius arguere.
' Demum quicquid,' ait, ' de cetero uisum uobis fuerit,
domine rex, de faciendo uel omittendo opere inchoato,
mea ulterius non intererit presentia.*d* Totum uobis
regnum uestrum quietum cedo ; ad nostram potius
Cartusiensem heremum,*e* uobis ualefaciens, mox redibo.
Putatis uos nobis gratiam exhibere si uestro nos uel pane
sustentetis, cum eo penitus non egemus. Verum satius
nobis est ad saxa nostrarum confugere Alpium quam ad
talem hominem habere conflictum, qui totum quod pro
salute sua geritur tamquam perditum arbitratur. Habeat
sibi, citius amissurus et cui nescit ingrato relicturus, opes
quas tantum amat, nec Christus hiis dignatur nec quisquam bonus Christianus participari.' Hec ita, immo et
hiis satis duriora, Girardi blandimenta ad tantum
dominatorem fuisse referuntur. Quid uero pio inter
ista et modesto priori suo animi fuit ? Referebat sepius
iam episcopus talia eum et tanta prosecutum, ut horum

----

a predictis o   *b* + metas X ; causam v   *c* sueque QXc
d *om* QXc   *e* *om* B

patience to bear trials and adversities with gentleness and forbearance. Patience without forbearance is of little account, and without gentleness it is worthless.'

Taking with him therefore, as we have said, Gerard and another brother named Einard, a very old but exemplary monk, the prior went to the king, who received them as reverently as if they had been angels from Heaven. He was very gracious when they explained their business, and made lavish promises, apologising for the delay and undertaking that everything should soon be completed. He did not, however, supply the money, or give them any guarantee when it would be forthcoming. Then the fiery brother Gerard, remembering his first intention and not the warning he had received, turned furiously upon the king. ' Whatever you may finally decide, lord king, about completing or not completing this work you have begun, is no concern of mine. I shall not trouble you further, but bid you farewell, as I shall shortly return to my hermitage at Chartreuse. You think you are being generous, if you provide us with bread, for that at least we have. I prefer to return to my barren Alpine crags, rather than to struggle with a man, who regards anything spent on his salvation as mere waste. Keep the treasure you love so much, and which you will soon have to lose and leave to some unknown and ungrateful person : neither Christ nor any good Christian will deign to share it.' Such blandishments as these, and even more biting ones, Gerard is said to have used to this most powerful monarch. What was passing through the mind of the holy and courteous prior during his outburst ? The bishop often declared that he had said such terrible things that even after all this time he still shuddered when he recalled them. Indeed the words

post tantum temporis ipse reminiscens totus inhorresceret.
Tunc uero, cum ista proferebat heros ille, cui ex Spiritu
Dei tanta libertas fuit, hic tanto uice regis suffundebatur
rubore, ut uix confusionem cordis sui ipse toleraret.
Monebat *a* fratrem modestius effari, talibus parcere
aut penitus silere. Verum is, ut erat conscientie purioris
et reuerende canitiei, sanguinis etiam generosi, nichili
ducebat quecumque dixisset, si iam dictis *b* alia atque
alia quibus principem corrigeret aut erudiret, nec adhuc
dicenda subnecteret. Putares eum cum Eliu, amico beati
Iob, musto zeli debriatum loqui : 'En uenter meus
quasi mustum absque spiraculo quod lagunculas nouas
dirumpit,' itemque 'Conceptum sermonem quis poterit
cohibere ? ' *c*,1

Verum interea regem uideres philosophantem. Non
uultus *d* immutauit, non uerbum edidit ; immo tacitus
et tranquillus dicentem sustinuit quousque uniuersa que
mente concepisset ore parturiret. Tandem ille satiatus
precordialique parturitione exoneratus, finem fecit
obiurgationibus, et silentio labia flagellantia concedens,
spiritum continuit, uocem repressit.*e* Habito post hec
ab uniuersis aliquamdiu alto silentio, priore uultum pre
confusione deprimente, rege autem subaspiciente, estus-
que mentis illius ex gestibus ipsius perpendente, sic
tandem ipse rex orsus est loqui. 'Quidnam tu,' inquit,
'meditabundus deliberas tecum, uir bone ? Num etiam
tu abire disponis et cedere nobis regnum nostrum ? ' Ad
quem ille submisse et leniter : 'Non adeo de uobis,'
inquit, 'domine, despero. Potius compatior impedi-
mentis uestris et occupationibus quibus prepediuntur *f*
salutaria studia anime uestre. Occupati enim estis ; et

---

a + autem prior X
b si iam dominus o ; set cum iam dictis X ; qui iam dictis c
c prohibere X   *d* Nec uultum . . . nec o
e pressit X   *f* per que prepediuntur o ; quibus impediuntur Xc

of this valiant man to whom the spirit of God had given such amazing boldness, made him blush on the king's behalf, and feel overcome with shame. He cautioned the monk to speak less bluntly, and either to moderate his language or be silent altogether. He, however, with all the assurance of a good conscience, old age and noble birth, took no notice of what was said to him as long as he could find any other words with which to rebuke the king and tell him what he thought of him. Like Elihu the friend of blessed Job he seemed drunk with the wine of his own eloquence. ' From my stomach without a pause gushed out wine which broke the new wine-skins,' or again ' Who could prevent the utterance of my thoughts.' [1]

In the meantime the king seemed lost in thought. His face did not change and he said nothing, but listened silently and calmly until the speaker had poured out everything he had in his mind. At last even Gerard, having unburdened himself completely, was satisfied and ended his reproofs, and allowing his biting tongue to be silent, refrained from further words. For some time there was deep silence. The prior lowered his head in confusion and the king looked covertly at him, guessing his discomfort from his behaviour. At last he began to speak. ' You are lost in thought, reverend father. What are you deciding ? Do you also intend to go away, and leave me to possess my kingdom in peace ? ' He replied gently in a low voice : ' I have not lost confidence in you, lord king. Rather I pity the distractions and occupations which prevent you from occupying yourself with the salvation of your soul. You are busy, but with God's assistance you will yet complete the good work

---

[1] Job 32:19 and 4:2

cum Dominus adiuuerit, bene prosequemini cepta
salutaria.' Tunc rex complexus eum,[a] cum iuramento
ait : ' Per salutem anime mee, dum uitales spirabo
auras, tu a meo regno non discedes. Tecum enim partiar
consilia salutaria, tecum et studia anime mee necessaria.'
Misit extemplo et sumptus, opusque summa cum instantia
iussit compleri.[1]

CAPITVLVM VII

De singulari erga priorem Withamie regis fauore,
propter quem illum genuisse carnaliter ipse rex estima-
batur a multis.   Et de monitis ipsius circa salutem
uariamque utilitatem, tam ipsius regis quam et quorumlibet aliorum.

Post hec princeps ille magnus uiri Dei crebrius
fruebatur colloquio, consilio amplius delectabatur. Nec
erant multi set nec, ut a multis credebatur, uel unus sub
omni eius erat potestate in quo magis requiesceret
spiritus eius quam in priore Withamie.

Erat autem potestas eius multa : cui tota, cum parte
maxima Hybernie, seruiebat Anglia, cui Neustria cum
Andegauia, Aquitania quoque uel Gasconia, necnon
et finitimarum regionum tractus multi et magni subiace-
bant.   In omnibus uero terris hiis nulla inueniebatur
persona cuiuscumque gradus aut ordinis cui libentius
auscultaret, cui promptius [b] obtemperaret quam homini
huic, in omnibus que ratio salutis anime sue ab eo inquiri
uel exaudiri exigebat.   Tanta denique familiaritate illi
seipsum committebat, tam singulari [c] amoris priuilegio

      [a] + ita Qc
      [b] pronius Xc
      [c] singularis Xc

you have begun.' The king then embraced him, and
said with an oath, ' By the salvation of my soul, as long
as I am alive, you shall not leave my kingdom. I will
take counsel with you on what concerns the salvation
of my soul.' He immediately sent the money and
ordered that the buildings should be finished as speedily
as possible.[1]

Chapter VII

Concerning the king's marked affection for the prior
of Witham, which led many people to believe that he was
his son, and concerning the counsels which he gave to
the king and certain other persons, which were profitable
for their salvation and in other ways.

After this the powerful monarch had frequent inter-
course with the man of God, and found his counsels
acceptable. There were few persons in his dominions,
indeed many would say none, with whom his soul
found as much peace as it did with the prior of Witham.

His territories were vast. The greater part of Ireland,
as well as England, Normandy and Anjou, Aquitaine
and Gascony, and great tracts of many of the neighbouring regions were under his sway. In all these territories
there was nobody, whatever his rank or profession, to
whom he listened more readily, or obeyed more
promptly than this man, in all matters connected with
the welfare of his soul, about which he either sought his
advice or granted his requests. He admitted him to such
intimacy, and showed him an affection so much in

---

[1] For Pipe Roll entries relevant to this statement see Introduction p. xxv

cunctis fere hominibus illum preferebat, ut crederent et assererent pertinaciter nonnulli hunc illius filium naturalem, huius illum genitorem fuisse carnalem.

Vidimus post mortem regis Ricardi, huius de quo loquimur regis filii et successoris, cum esset Hugo in finibus Aquitanie,[a] innumeras undique diuerse conditionis et dignitatis turmas ad ipsum concurrere, nec aliter quam a regis defuncti germano super statu suo ipsum consulere. Contendebant nobiscum plures, illum fratrem regis nuncupantes ; nec cedebant [b] nobis de illius cognatione aut progenie quod uerum noueramus asserentibus. ' Nos,' inquiunt, ' quid uerum habeatur [c] de hiis melius scimus, agnouimus euidentius. Dominus noster [d] quondam rex Henricus numquam externum hominem ut istum amabat, ut istum honorabat, de nullo ut de isto confidebat, nemini ut isti seipsum credebat. Nisi esset iste filius eius, quod etiam corporis forma consimilis fateri probatur, numquam se et sua tam specialiter illi exponeret, nec in tantum honoris culmen hominem alienigenam tanta cum instantia promoueret.'

Et hec quidem illi. Verum nos quod uerissime scimus firmissime asserimus, quia non istam ei penes regem gratiam conciliauerat caro et sanguis set reuelatio et inspiratio Patris qui est in celis.[1] Ita tamen in hac quoque parte gratie complebat in famulo suo Dominus quod suis promiserat in euangelio discipulis, omnia propter ipsum relinquentibus : ' Accipietis [e] in hoc seculo centies tantum, et in futuro uitam eternam.'[2] Nam conscius ipsius qui in excelsis erat manifeste nouerat quam sincero quamque perfecto affectu cordis ipsum, relictis omnibus, ille sequeretur qui nisi propter ipsum nichil preter ipsum amare sciebat.

---

[a] *lege* Andegauie (=Anjou)   [b] credebant Qcv   [c] asseratur Xc
[d] *om* B   [e] + inquit c

excess of that which he displayed to almost everyone else that some people believed, and even asserted with conviction, that Hugh was his natural son, and that Henry was in fact his father.

I saw how when Hugh was in Aquitaine after the death of King Richard, the son and successor of the king I have mentioned, large numbers of people of various ranks and conditions hastened to consult him about their position, under the impression that he was the brother of the deceased king. Many of them argued with me, insisting that he was the king's brother, and would not give way when I told them what I knew to be true about his birth and descent. ' We,' they said, ' are much better informed as to the truth, and can see it clearly for ourselves. Our late king Henry never loved or honoured a stranger as he did this man, nor was there anyone else to whom he gave so much of his confidence or trusted to the same degree. If he had not been his son, and their physical resemblance proves it, he would never have done so much for him, nor would he have worked so hard to raise a foreigner to so lofty a position.'

So much for them. I, who know the truth, can say with conviction that it was not any physical tie which won him the king's favour, but the spirit and grace of our heavenly Father.[1] This particular favour towards his servant was a fulfilment of our Lord's promise to his disciples in the gospel : ' You shall receive in this world a hundred fold and in the world to come eternal life.' [2] God who is in heaven knew well with what sincere and perfect affection he had left all things to follow him, loving nothing apart from God except for God's sake.

[1] cf. Matt. 16:17   [2] Mark 10:30

Rex quoque id ipsum acute peruidens et perpendens, sicut hanc a Deo gratiam noscitur percepisse, ut
uiros bone conuersationis testimonio probatos artius
diligeret, tanto eum pre ceteris coluit eminentius quanto
senserat illum diuini amoris facibus flagrare excellentius.
Nec enim in sermone assentationis, nedum adulationis
aliquando fuit apud eum ; enimuero qualem nouerat
expedire, sibi primo, deinde suis, postremo uniuersis
illum cupiens exhiberi, instabat oportune, importune [a]
pro causa et negotio, pro tempore et loco, arguens,
obsecrans et increpans eum in omni patientia et suaui
doctrina ; [1] ' miscens,' iuxta Sancti Benedicti egregiam
sententiam, ' temporibus tempora, terroribus blandimenta.' [2] Tam uero solerter et circumspecte, adeo ef-
ficaciter et modeste, nunc subtilius quarumdam rerum
argumentis, nunc splendidis uirorum illustrium exemplis,
regis animos alliciebat, et quo uellet sepius ducebat,
ut uideretur, iuxta illud dominicum ad beatum Iob,
rinoceros uoluntarie seruire sibi ; uideretur et ipse rino-
cerontem alligare loro suo. Nec erit absurdum si etiam
dicatur quia et [b] glebas uallium post eum rinoceros iste
confregerit,[3] qui duritiam hominum terrena sapientium
adeo emolliuerit ut post eum in odore unguentorum ipsius
currere [4] et eum sibi in ducem et preceptorem eligere
dulce tandem habuerint.

Verum de hiis subsequens sermo planius que fuerint
dicenda, prout Dominus dedit,[c] explicabit. Nunc seriem
cepte narrationis prosequamur. De illis itaque rebus
duntaxat seu negotiis consiliabatur iste cum illo, que
Christum, que ecclesiam, que regni tranquillitatem, que
populi pacem, que denique suam ipsius [d] contingebant
salutem. Curas terrenorum tam in nullo cum illo
tractabat quam sola ipse celestia curabat, solus quibus-

The king also observed this and it weighed much with him. His love of men with a reputation for holiness, a grace he had received from God, is well known. He therefore honoured him more than others because he realized that the flame of divine love burnt more brightly in him. Hugh was not complaisant, and never flattered, rather he desired to point out to him what was right, firstly for himself, then for his companions, and lastly for everyone. This he preached in season and out of season, in every case and business, at all times and in all places, reproving, exhorting and rebuking him with all long-suffering and pleasant doctrine,[1] and, acting on the excellent advice of St Benedict, he alternated according to the times between sternness and persuasion.[2] By a combination of earnestness and prudence, and of firmness and courtesy, now by a witty exposition of certain matters, now by inspiring stories of illustrious men, he so won the king's heart, that he could generally make him do whatever he wished. Indeed, to use God's words to blessed Job, it would seem that the rhinoceros obeyed him willingly and that he had bound the rhinoceros with his thong.[3] It is not far-fetched to say that this wild ox broke the clods of the valleys in his wake, since he so softened the hardness of worldly-wise men that they ran after him, attracted by the odour of sanctity,[4] and were delighted to choose him as their guide and teacher.

What follows, if God so wills, will make this clearer, but now I will resume the thread of my narrative. The king consulted him on all matters relating to Christ and the Church, and to the general peace and tranquillity of the realm and his subjects, as well as on his own

[1] cf. 2 Tim. 4:2   [2] *Rule of St Benedict*, c. ii
[3] Job 39:9-10   [4] Cant. 1:3

cumque posset amanda, querenda et optinenda inculcabat. Quam multis tamen bona quoque terrena
Hugonis hortatu ille contulerit, quotiens iras in clementiam per Hugonem mutauerit, et hiis et *a* a quibus
offensus esset ueniam concesserit, quot ecclesias et loca
religiosa Hugonis optentu prouexerit rebusque necessariis
ampliauerit, perlongum esset singillatim recensere.
Monebat hunc assidue, non in uana uentoque *b* fugatiore
mundi prosperitate atque potentia confidere, non in
incerto diuitiarum sperare, set in Deo uiuo qui uera est
fortitudo, qui certa et eterna est beatitudo sperantibus et
confidentibus in se. Suadebat ei facile tribuere, perituris
permansura comparare, indigentibus communicare bona
momentanea cum *c* quibus sortiretur eterna.[1]

Super uariis excessibus sepius arguebat eum,*d* ad
correctionem sedulo inuitabat. Corripiebat eum
uehementissime pro ecclesiis cathedralibus et cenobiis
uacantibus, que in manu sua illicite sepius ac diu
detinebat, que per manus suorum pessime tractabat.
In proficiendis tandem episcopis et abbatibus abuti eum
usurpata a predecessoribus suis potestate conuincebat.
Insinuabat omnium pene *e* malorum causas et materiam
in *f* populo Dei per indignos pullulare prelatos, per
eosdem foueri, per ipsos augeri, per eos et uigere. Pro
hiis uero omnibus, in illos precipue penas diuino
asserebat iudicio retorquendas, qui talibus in eorum
promotione auctores se aut fautores non timuissent
exhibere. ' Et quid necesse est,' aiebat, ' o princeps
sapientissime, ut pro uano cuiuscumque fauore persone

---

a *om* QXc   *b* uentosaque X
c pro Xc   *d* + et X
e *om* B   *f* *om* B

spiritual welfare. Hugh discussed temporal business with him as little as possible, since he was only interested in spiritual things, and, by whatever means he could, impressed on the king that these only should be loved, sought after and obtained. It would take too long to mention individually how many people he gave alms to, or how often his wrath was turned to clemency and how many were pardoned by him at Hugh's intercession, and also how many churches and religious houses he provided for and assisted with the goods they needed. Hugh urged him earnestly not to put his trust in the hollowness of wordly pomp and power, which are as transitory as the wind, nor to set his hopes on the uncertainty of riches, but in the living and omnipotent God, the certain and eternal happiness of all who hope and trust in him. It was not difficult to persuade him to be generous, and to purchase lasting security with perishable goods, and by sharing his temporal wealth with the poor, to purchase with it an eternal recompense.[1]

Hugh frequently reproved him for his various sins, and constantly urged him to make amends. His most vigorous rebukes were in connection with the vacant cathedrals and monasteries, which he often retained for a long time illegally, and which his officials plundered remorselessly. He also accused him of abusing the powers which his predecessors had usurped in connection with the appointments of bishops and abbots, and pointed out that almost all the shortcomings and misfortunes of the people of God were due to bad prelates, and that these were fostered by them and so increased and flourished. Because of these things he declared that divine

---

[1] Henry's will, made in 1182, included large bequests to various religious Orders of monks and nuns and the provision of dowries for poor girls, and may perhaps be attributed to St Hugh's influence. cf. Rymer, *Foedera*, I, 47

tot animabus mortem perniciosam inferas, tot de
perditione multorum Christi morte redemptorum dispendia Deo irroges, tibique perinde tot suppliciorum
cumulos in futurum reponas ?   Quanto satius liberas
quibusque electiones iuxta canonum scita relinqueres et
teipsum tot malorum laberintho explicares, tuas ad hoc
tantum partes imponeres,[a] ut Deo acceptum et in hiis
que Dei sunt populo tibi subdito profuturum, ut qui
eligerent preualerent, in contrarium nitentes in suis
molitionibus elisi deficerent.   Hac enim ratione prouida
sanctorum patrum dispensatio in preficiendis ecclesiarum
rectoribus, Christianissimis olim principibus locum
noscitur accomodasse non extremum ;   quo per eorum
sincerissimam diligentiam, ambitiosorum si qua emersisset
temeritas facilius premeretur, religiosorum [b] unanimitas
in studiis suis robur, in uotis [c] effectum expeditius consequeretur.'   Talibus Hugo insistebat eloquiis, huiuscemodi erga principem uacabat monitis quotiens occasione
quacumque [d] eius utebatur familiari accessu, quotiens
secretiore illius potiebatur affatu.   Et quidem ratione
ipsum multiplici adibat frequentius, nunc accersitus
ab ipso, nunc pro uariis domus quam fundabat et regebat
necessitatibus ultro ad eum pergens.   Emergebant uero
creberrime tunc temporis regi hinc inde aduersa
perplurima [e] que iugiter uiri spiritualis uaria consolatione
ferebat leuius, nonnumquam uero superabat fretus
orationibus eius facilius, plerumque autem eius instructus
consiliis circumspectius uel [f] prudentius declinabat.

---

[a] interponeres Xc ; imponeres . . . subdito / *om* B
[b] + uero Qc
[c] + et B²t
[d] qualicumque QXc
[e] plurima Qc
[f] uel / *om* BX ; prudentius / facilius X

vengeance would fall heavily upon those who had
shamelessly caused or furthered their promotion.
' Why,' he said, ' must you, a ruler of such renown for
your wisdom, promote the advancement of such unworthy persons, bring the risk of eternal damnation upon
so many of the souls whom Christ redeemed by his death,
and heap up for yourself for this cause so many torments
in the life to come ? Would it not be much better to
permit freedom of election in accordance with the rules
of canon law, and free yourself from such a labyrinth of
evils, by making it a rule in your domains to do only in
the things which belong to God what is acceptable to
him and profitable to the people under your sway ? This
would mean that the will of the electors would prevail
and the efforts of their opponents be defeated. For this
reason the holy fathers in their wisdom formerly con-
ceded to Christian rulers no small part in ecclesiastical
appointments, so that by their disinterested care any
unscrupulous endeavours of ambitious men might be
easily countered, and through their authority unanimity
amongst the monks in making an election might be
achieved more readily.' Hugh made use of such arguments, and took full advantage of any private interview
or conversation to drive his point home. This was why
he frequently went to him, sometimes at Henry's special
request, and sometimes of his own accord on the business
of his monastery. At this time the king had often to face
many misfortunes of every kind, which he bore with
more resignation owing to the consolations of this holy
man. Some of these he surmounted thanks to his
prayers, and many others, by taking his advice, he was
able to avoid by using prudence and discretion.

Capitvlvm VIII

Qualiter in mari Brittanico regia classis pene nau-
fragata optatum litus sedata tempestate subiuit, rege
inuocante per merita prioris Withamie Deum, et
uouente quod eum promoueri satageret in episcopum.

Contigit uice quadam regem cum classe non modica
medium *ᵃ* pelagus quod inter Neustriam Brittaniamque
limitatur sulcantem, nimia repente suborta tempestate,
pene naufragari. A prima denique uigilia noctis mare
intumescens furentibus uentis,*ᵇ* nimiis motibus aut
obsistere aut alludere *ᶜ* uisum, naues medias *ᵈ* nunc
astris inserere, nunc immergere abysso laborabat. Hoc
elementorum ludo nescio an aliquid in hoc mundo
humana pertulerit conditio luctuosius. Sub hac morte
ipsa amariore, mortis ymagine, non modicum temporis
expensum docebat singulos nauigantium, omne uite
mortalis spatium uix exiguum reputari posse momentum,
si sagax inspector rerum illius contempletur occasum.
Nil rex, nil consul, nil potens, nil fortis aut diues, nil
quilibet senior aut iuuenis totum illud causabatur quod
eatenus uixisset, quod serenum aliquando uidisset et
tranquillum. Iam *ᵉ* sub oculis presens mortis ymago
cogebat nonnullos habere in uotis, ipsius pridem aculeum
pertulisse. Quibus mens sanior erat confessioni peccatorum insistebant, ex desperatione uite presentis sollicitu-
dinem *ᶠ* future capientes. Precibus plerique gemebundis
uotisque ad Deum,*ᵍ* ad sanctos ac sanctas succlamitant.*ʰ*
Rex tandem et ipse in hec uerba prorupit : ' O,'

ᵃ om B
ᶜ allidere X
ᵉ + enim Xc
ᵍ + et Xc

ᵇ uentorum Xc
ᵈ mediis Xc
ᶠ sollicitudines X
ʰ succlamabant Xc

CHAPTER VIII

How when the royal fleet was nearly wrecked in the English Channel, the tempest ceased and it reached the haven it desired, since the king invoked God, through the merits of the prior of Witham, and swore to do his utmost to make him a bishop.

On one occasion, a large fleet with the king on board was ploughing its way across the sea which divides Britain from Normandy, and a sudden violent storm arose so that it was nearly wrecked. From the first watch of the night, the swelling seas seemed now to resist, and now to mock at the immense fury of the driving winds, and now to raise the ships to the stars, and now to plunge them into the depths. I do not know if men on this earth can endure any worse disaster than to be the sport of the elements. Any considerable period spent under the threat of death, more terrible than death itself, should teach any voyager, if one with a taste for philosophising on human affairs should be involved in such a disaster, to regard the whole span of this earthly life as one brief moment. All of them, whether king or count, or however noble, courageous and wealthy they were, felt that by comparison their whole lives up till then had been tranquil and serene. The obvious proximity of death now made some of them wish that they had already endured its sting. The more sensible among them hastened to confess their sins, since their despair of saving their lives caused them to prepare themselves with care for the future life. Most of them called upon God and the saints, with prayers, lamentations and vows.

The king at length burst into speech. ' If only my

inquit, 'si uigilaret nunc Cartusiensis Hugo meus, si
secretis intenderet modo precibus, si uel sollempnibus
cum suis fratribus interesset modo diuinorum officiorum
excubiis, non ita in longum mei obliuisceretur Deus.'
Tunc altius ingemiscens, 'Deus,' inquit, 'cui seruit in
ueritate prior Withamie, illius interuentu ac meritis,
nobis in tanta pro peccatis nostris angustia iuste
deprehensis, clementer miserere.' Ferunt quidam etiam
uouisse eum quod ad pontificalem niteretur gradum
quamtocius illum promouere, si meruisset incolumis ad
portum peruenire. Nec mora ; pelagi fragor, uentorum
turbo subsedit et euanuit ; cadunt fluctus, redit aura
lenior, fretum funditus complanatur *a* ; naues uniuerse
optato potiuntur littore ; referuntur ab uniuersis gratiarum actiones diuine clementie.*b* Rex de cetero
uenerationi uiri Dei se totum deuouit.

Capitvlvm IX

Quod expleta constructione habitationis monachorum et conuersorum, Hugo sacris uite contemplatiue
otiis feruenti deuotione animum impenderit.*c* Et quod
per soporem, spiritu uigilante et orante etiam uocaliter,
Amen repetere sepius consueuerit. Et quod semper totus
et integer inueniebatur in eo ad quod eum intendere
cuiusque temporis ratio prescribebat.

Ipse, completa iam edificatione utriusque mansionis,
fratrum scilicet et monachorum, solitis sancte conuersationis exercitiis quo liberius eo et impensius uacabat.
Tempus omne quod sompnii sola necessitas sibi minime

---

^a + equor X
^b Xc *end chapter here.* V *adds :* uotaque seruati referunt in littore naute
^c intenderet X

Carthusian Hugh were now watching, and praying alone in his cell, or along with his brethren he were celebrating the divine offices with due solemnity, God would not forget me for so long.' Then he groaned aloud, ' God,' he said, ' whom the prior of Witham serves so devoutly, through his intercession and merits have mercy on us, who are justly for our sins brought to such straits.' It is even alleged that he vowed that he would try to make him a bishop as soon as he could if he were permitted to come safely to port. Immediately, the roaring of the sea, and the force of the winds subsided and ceased, the waves sank, a gentler breeze blew, and the whole sea became calm. All the ships reached the shore they desired, and everyone gave thanks to the divine mercy. From henceforth the king's reverence for the man of God was complete.

CHAPTER IX

How, once the buildings for the monks and lay brethren had been finished, Hugh with great devotion, gave himself entirely up to contemplation. How, even when he slept, his spirit was awake, and he prayed aloud, often saying Amen repeatedly. How he always concentrated on the duties which fell to him at a particular time.

Once the buildings for both monks and lay brethren had been erected, Hugh resumed his usual holy manner of life more fully and intently than ever. He scarcely slept at all, but spent his time in prayer or reading, in meditation or spiritual instruction. Although his body rested, if you had been with him you would have

uindicasset, orationi aut lectioni, meditationi uel spirituali
indulgebat collationi siue exhortationi ; quamquam et
dormienti corpore mentis numquam dormitionem sur-
ripere *a* credidisses, si familiarius ei adhereres, si dor-
mientem sollicitius obseruares, si referentem que cordi
uigili inter soporis nexus spiritu *b* liber percepisset studiosius attendisses.   Audires hunc centies cum uehementi
spiritus impulsione, cum forti labiorum impressione,
siue interdiu siue noctu *c* quiescentem, misticum illud
ore totiens Dominico iteratum Amen quasi in con-
clusionem premisse orationis proferre.   Nichil uero aliud
ab ore dormientis, sicut plerisque moris est aut uoces
aut uerba sompniando emittere aliquando procedebat,
set leniter, silenter et quietissime pausando,*d* nunc per
interualla rarius, nunc uero frequentius, protracta
aliquantulum prima sillaba et ultima in acutum ueluti
iaculando emissa, Amen innumeris uicibus repetebat.

Quotiens hoc a dormiente prolatum audiuimus,
totiens illud sponse de Canticis illi congruere sentiebamus,
ut loqueretur celesti sponso anima ipsius, dicens :
'Ego dormio, set *e* cor meum uigilat,'[1] immo etiam
orat.   Quotiens uero ea nobis que per soporem sensisset
aut uidisset *f* referebat, ymnicum illud ei competere
perpendebamus quod ille uigilando etiam attentius
sepe canebat :

> Exuta sensu lubrico,
> Te cordis alta sompnient.[2]

Nec uero mirum si dormienti non deerant interna
serenitas,*g* intima claritas, mera suauitas, quem uigilantem externa uanitas, ceca curiositas, impura uoluptas,
suis irretire illecebris nullatenus preualebant.

---

a subrepere Xc
c in die siue in nocte X
e et Xc (*and Vg.*)
g sinceritas B ; seueritas c

b spiritum X ; spiritus c
d + et Xc
f audisset c ; percepisset aut audisset X

believed that his soul was always awake, and if you had been on close enough terms to watch over him whilst he slept, you would have noticed how he repeated what his spirit which remained free from the bonds of sleep dictated to the alert heart. You would have heard him, whether he was resting by day or by night repeat a hundred times with immense fervour and with an obvious movement of his lips that mystic Amen so often uttered by our Lord, as if he were ending the prayers we have already mentioned. Although many people are accustomed sometimes to make sounds or talk in their sleep, no other word ever was uttered by him when asleep except this, said slowly, almost inaudibly, and very quietly after a pause. Sometimes it was said very occasionally with long intervals between each, and at other times frequently, and over and over again, the first syllable being somewhat slow, and the last as rapid as an arrow.

Whenever I heard this word uttered by the sleeper I thought that the words of the bride in the Canticles where the soul addressing her heavenly bridegroom says ' I sleep, but my heart waketh ',[1] or better, prayeth, were applicable to him. Whenever he related to me what he had heard or seen when sleeping, I considered how apt in his case was the hymn which he so often sang with great fervour when he was keeping vigil : ' When the deceptions of the senses have been put off, the depths of the heart dream of thee.' [2] No wonder he enjoyed internal peace, spiritual enlightenment, and immense consolations when asleep, for when he was awake earthly vanities, purblind curiosity and impure desires never ensnared him.

[1] Cant. 5:2
[2] Hymn of St Ambrose, *Deus creator omnium*, from the Carthusian breviary

Cum uero corporalia sumebat alimenta, cum faucibus tereret cibi nutrimenta terreni, tunc potissimum aures eius esuriebant et hauriebant uerbum Dei. Si cum fratribus pro more, iuxta consuetudinem diei festi, refectorium ingressus una cum illis pranderet, prout ipse ceteros et monebat et docebat, oculos in mensa, manus in scutella, aures ad librum, cor ad Deum [a] habebat. Si solus edebat in cellula, partiebantur sibi liber et mensula oculorum officia ; tunc enim lumina eius sibi detrahebant uicissim, hinc liber apertus, hinc panis appositus, nam pulmenta rarius adiciebantur. Aqua sola sepius poculum simul et iuscellum fuit. Condimentum hiis epulis pretiosissimum numquam defuit sermo Dei. Codicem uero celeri perstringens obtuitu,[b] uelud raptim animo potius transmisit quod ruminaret quam desiderio quod illud satiaret aut studio quod illi satisfaceret.

In omni namque tempore et in omni loco, quod loci quod temporis flagitaret ratio, hoc et ipse faciebat, hoc et aliis agendum monebat. Quam adeo uelud in habitum sibi uerterat ordinatissimam et saluberrimam institutionem, ut cum semper totus et integer esse uideretur in eo ad quod eum intendere prescribebat loci presentis aut hore dispositio, hoc etiam ipsum tempore quiescendi obseruaret in lectulo. Numquam eum lectulus, dummodo esset incolumis, uel [c] ad momentum tenuit uigilantem. Mox ut eius menbra stratum excepisset, et ipsa sopor pariter excipiebat, set [d] quando intempestiue quolibet casu excitaretur a sompno, confestim uel ad orationem surgebat uel sub momento soluebatur rursus in soporem.

---

[a] + semper Xc
[b] obtutu X
[c] uelud B
[d] si QXc

When he took bodily nourishment, his teeth chewed material food, but his ears were thirstily drinking in the word of God. If he entered the refectory to eat with the brethren as was customary on feast days, in accordance with his own instructions to his companions his eyes were on the table, his hand was beside his plate, his ears were engrossed in the book, and his heart fixed on God. When he was eating alone in his cell, his eyes were on his book and on his food, and turned alternately to each of them, now to the open book and now to the bread set before him, for he rarely added relish of any kind. Water alone generally sufficed him both for drink and for broth. The word of God never failed to be the most precious condiment to his meal. Reading with great rapidity and complete absorption, his object was to give his mind food for meditation rather than personal enjoyment or satisfaction of his desire for information.

At all times and in all places he did what was required of him on that occasion and at that moment, and advised others to do the same. This wise and excellent rule had become so much a matter of habit with him that he seemed totally absorbed in what the circumstances of time and place dictated must be done. This applied even when he was in bed, for unless he were ill he never remained there awake even for a moment. As soon as he lay down, he fell asleep, but if he were unexpectedly awakened too early, he either immediately rose to pray, or almost instantaneously fell asleep again.

Capitvlvm X

De eo quod sublimes in eruditione uiri, tam de clericorum quam et de monachorum ordine, agnita perfectione Withamensium, abdicata mundi huius sapientia, Christiane inter eos philosophie mancipari festinauerint.

Hiis et huiusmodi spiritualis discipline studiis, florente apud Witham Hugone et cum suis condiscipulis[a] salubriter philosophante, confluebant ad eum plurimi diuerse conditionis seu professionis uiri religiosi aspectu illius et affatu edificari,[b] instrui et munere optate consolationis refoueri, certius presumentes. Nec uero sua quempiam spes fallebat ; nullus hac in parte pio fraudabatur cordis desiderio. Cunctis apud Witham exempla dabantur perfecte religionis ; omnes inde reportabant documenta sane instructionis ; quique ibidem affatu replebantur [c] pie deuotionis. Hinc subito per omnes Brittanie [d] fines sancte huius opinionis fragrantia suauiter diffusa, multorum precordia tante dulcedinis afficiebat gratia, ut uiri literatissimi uariisque redditibus ditati, relictis huius mundi [e] pompis, sancte et sincere illius conuersationis humilitatem tota deuotione expeterent, totaque alacritate subirent. Gaudebant illustrissimi disciplinarum secularium magistri sub tanti magisterio doctoris illud implere apostolicum : ' Si quis uidetur inter uos sapiens esse, stultus efficiatur ut sit sapiens.' [1] Abdicata itaque uana mundi sapientia, sub disciplina preceptoris adeo [f] docti, efficiuntur et ipsi

[a] discipulis cm ; fratribus et condiscipulis X
[b] + et X
[c] quisque ibidem affectu replebatur QXc
[d] + uel Anglie X
[e] seculi Xc
[f] a Deo X

Chapter X

How distinguished scholars, both seculars and regulars, realizing the perfection of Witham, hastened to devote themselves to the true Christian philosophy, renouncing the wisdom of this world.

Such were the spiritual ideals and learning which flourished exceedingly at Witham under Hugh and his fellow disciples. A great multitude of holy men of different rank and order flocked to him, counting upon receiving the edification, instruction and consolations which they desired by meeting and speaking with him. Nor were they deceived, for none of them was disappointed in his expectations. To all of them Witham was a perfect example of monastic life, and they all brought back wise and sound religious teaching, and each of them spoke warmly of the piety and devotion they had witnessed. Very soon, a rumour of the fragrance of its holy reputation gently spread throughout all Britain, and the hearts of many people were so touched with affection for such delights that men of great learning and considerable wealth abandoned the ambitions of the world, and sought with utter simplicity and fervour this life of humility and holiness, embracing it with the greatest eagerness. These renowned representatives of secular learning under the guidance of a master of such experience gladly carried out the maxim of the apostle, ' If any man among you seemeth to be wise, let him become a fool that he may be wise.' [1] Having renounced the empty wisdom of this world, under the training of so learned an instructor they themselves

---

[1] 1 Cor. 3:18

docibiles Dei,[1] tramitem Christiane philosophie in-
declinabili uite carpentes rectitudine. Nonnulli quoque
ex monachorum necnon et clericorum ordinibus regularium, sub uirgam *a* solertis se transferre cupiebant
pastoris, sagaci nimirum animo perpendentes, corporee
quidem pascue ariditatem, que penes eum reperiebatur,
pinguedine spiritualis alimonie uberius compensari.

Experientia docente, sentiebant manifeste longius a
pastore isto illam relegari maledictionem qua multatur
in libro beati Iob, qui ' pauit sterilem *b* et uidue non
benefecit.'[2] Huius quippe sub dispensatione pastoris, hec
uice uersa sterilis, de qua et per seipsam Veritas dicit :
' Caro non prodest quidquam,'[3] macerabatur abs-
tinentia, squalebat cilicio, uigiliis pro deliciis in *c* frigore
et inedia exercebatur ; uidua uero, cuius uir abierat uia
longissima nec ante plenilunium *d* reuersurus,[4] set tunc
ab integro meritorum fulgore ad celestis eam thalami
delicias introducturus, hec, inquam, uidua apud fidelem
hunc amicum sponsi epulabatur cotidie splendide,
calceabatur iacintho, induebatur purpura et bisso.[5]
Nichil tamen huic cum illo diuite erat commune qui
post huius nominis cultum et epulum sepelitur in
infernum. *e* Huius namque bissus uidue, secundum
Apocalypsim, iustificationes fuerunt carnis et spiritus ; [6]
purpura, crucis Dominice stigmata ; iacinthus uero
celestia desideria, quibus internorum affectuum munie-

---

a uirga Xc
b que non parit X
c om Xc
d plenissimum B
e sepultus est in inferno Xc (*and Vg.*)
[1] John 6:45
[2] Job   24:21. The soul, according to the *Glossa Ordinaria in h.l.*, is
the widow : Christ is the husband who has gone away.

became capable of learning from God [1] and pursued the path of Christian perfection undeviatingly throughout their lives. Some of them had been monks or canons regular, who wished to transfer themselves to the rule of so skilled a pastor, prudently deciding that the monotony of the material food which they would find with him would be amply compensated for by the sumptuousness of the spiritual fare.

Experience taught them how little this pastor deserved the curse threatened in the book of blessed Job ' against the man who fed the barren, and did no good to the widow '.[2] Under the rule of this pastor the words about the barren could be interpreted by what the Truth himself said, ' The flesh profiteth nothing ' ; [3] for he became emaciated with fasting, was lacerated by his hair shirt, and disciplined himself by watchings, cold and hunger instead of easy living resembling a widow whose husband had gone on a long journey,[4] nor would he return before the full moon, but then would bring her by reason of the absolute brilliance of his merits to the delights of the heavenly bridal couch. This widow, indeed, feasted daily splendidly with this friend of her spouse, shod with jacinth and robed in silk and scarlet. There was no resemblance, however, between him and the rich man who after his renown, luxury and feasting was buried in hell.[5] The fine linen of this widow was, according to the Apocalypse, the redemption of flesh and spirit,[6] her scarlet the marks of the cross of Christ, the

---

[3] John 6:64
[4] cf. Prov. 7:19-20
[5] cf. Luke 16:19 *et seq.*
[6] cf. Apoc. 19:8

bantur uestigia.[1]   Talibus siquidem insignibus ador-
nata, nutriebatur in croceis,[2] et iuxta sententiam uiri
sapientis, 'Epule eius diligenter fiebant.'[3]   Hiis ipsa
cotidie saginanda epulabatur splendide, splendoribus
repleta celestis theorie.

Hec uidentes et cognoscentes plurimi, nitebantur in
sancta suscipi harum triclinia feminarum.   Earum
uero prepositus, ut erat prudens per omnia et circumspectus, nec cito nec facile aperiebat pulsantibus.
Probabat namque spiritus, ut monet apostolus, si ex Deo
essent,[a,4] et quidem non sine cauta dulcedine et leui [b]
quadam asperitate.   Aperuit autem quibusdam post
largiora [c] probamenta perseuerantibus in pulsando,
uerum, ut ex fine patuit, non in omnibus illis bene-
placitum fuit Domino.[5]   Abierunt quippe retrorsum,
etsi forte non omnimodis post Sathanam, ex illis quidam [d] ; declinabant uero cum Loth montem [e] con-
templationis ardue, saluandi forsitan in Segor actionis
pie,[6] non ualentes cum Moyse ad caliginem accedere in
qua erat Deus,[7] set redeuntes in tabernacula sua in
quibus habitauerant prius.

---

[a] sunt Xc
[b] leni QXc
[c] longiora Xc
[d] om B
[e] in montem c ; a monte X

jacinth, celestial desires which directed the deepest affections of her heart.[1]   Made conspicuous by such ornaments, she was brought up in scarlet,[2] and to quote the words of the sage, ' Her feasts were carefully prepared '.[3]   On these fresh meats Hugh banqueted sumptuously daily, being filled with the radiance of heavenly contemplation.

Very many persons seeing and knowing these things, attempted to become guests at the supper of these holy women.   Their prior being prudent and discreet in all things did not readily open to those who knocked. As the apostle counselled he tested the spirits whether they were of God,[4] for his gentleness was not without certain reserve, or even a touch of asperity.   Some he admitted because in spite of a long delay they persisted in knocking, but as the end showed, in all of them the Lord was not well pleased.[5]   Certain of them, indeed, turned back, although perhaps not entirely to their damnation, nevertheless like Lot they departed from the steep mountain of contemplation, to be saved maybe in the Segor of good works.[6]   Unlike Moses they were unable to enter the cloud in which God was,[7] but returned to their tents where they had formerly dwelt.

---

[1] cf. *Glossa Ordinaria* on Exod. 25:4, 26:4, 27:16
[2] cf. Lam. 4:5
[3] Ecclus. 30:27
[4] 1 John 4:1 cited in *Rule of St Benedict*, c. lviii
[5] 1 Cor. 10:5
[6] cf. Gen. 19:17-23 and *Glossa Ordinaria in h.l.*
[7] cf. Exod. 20:21

CAPITVLVM XI

De turbulenta inquietudine Andree et Alexandri, qui
ordinem deseruerunt Cartusiensem. Et quod Alexander,
postea facti penitens, redeundi aditum non inuenit.

Concussa sunt interea materne pietatis in Hugone
uiscera. Collidebantur inter se duo, quos nitebatur
parturire Deo, rei quidem ueritate paruuli, set sua, immo
et publica estimatione magni. Andreas unus, alter
Alexander uocabatur. Posterior secularis, ut uulgus
loquitur, extiterat canonicus, cognomen habens de
Lewes, prenominatus magister, maior habitus in quad-
riuio set minor repertus in euangelio. Prior ille qui et
Andreas, monachus habebatur et sacrista monasterii quod
Muchelia nuncupatur.[1] De horum utroque illud
Rebecce matris [a] que eos parturiebat licuit proferre :
' Si sic michi futurum erat, quid necesse fuit concipere ? '[2]
Vterque istorum sibilo instigatus serpentis antiqui,
sepius in Hugonem, semper uero in sanctum quem
indignus subierat [b] ordinem, dente uipereo seuiebat.
Corde siquidem reuersi in Egiptum, manna celicum
nauseantes,[c] pepones et allia suspirabant.[3] Nec in
longum fraudati sunt miserabili desiderio suo,[4] set
usque ad nauseam ingurgitati, sero intellexerunt quid
distet inter siliquas regionis longinque et panes domus
paterne.[5] Nec uero in sugillationem sacri ordinis, ad
quem alter eorum rediit, alter uero accessit, hec dicimus ;

---

[a] mater B ; matri c
[b] indigni subierant X
[c] + ad X
[1] Muchelney, founded c. 970, was a small and unimportant Benedictine
monastery partly controlled by Glastonbury.
[2] Gen. 25:22, a source also for the second sentence in this chapter
[3] cf. Num. 11:5

Chapter XI

Concerning the disturbance caused by the insubordination of Andrew and Alexander, who left the
Carthusian order. How Alexander later, having repented, was refused re-admission.

Meanwhile, Hugh's almost motherly affection received a shock. He came into conflict with two men
whom he had endeavoured to train for God, but who
were really still spiritually children, although highly
regarded both by the world and themselves. Their
names were Andrew and Alexander. The latter, to use
the colloquial term, had been a secular canon. His
surname was ' de Lewes ' and he was a distinguished
teacher, with a great knowledge of the Quadrivium, but
little of the gospel. The former, Andrew, had been a
monk and sacrist at the monastery of Muchelney.[1] The
words of Rebecca when she was bearing her sons can
most appropriately be applied to them, ' If it was to be
thus for me in the future, why did I conceive ? '[2] At the
instigation of the ancient serpent they both hissed with
viperish spite frequently against Hugh and all the time
against the holy order, which they were unworthy to
join. Their hearts had returned to Egypt and the
heavenly manna nauseated them, for they sighed after
the melons and the garlic.[3] They were not long deprived
of their shameful desires,[4] but after glutting themselves
upon them till they were sick, they understood too late
the difference between the husks of the distant land and
the bread of their father's house.[5] We have nothing to
say against the holy orders to which one of them returned

---

[4] cf. Ps. 77:30   [5] cf. Luke 15:16-17

set quid eis acciderit, qui bonum non bene deseruerunt set nec bene ad bonum accesserunt, ueraciter intimamus.

Versi namque in seditionem ut illi quondam famosi murmuratores Moysem, ita Hugonem isti durus exacerbabant, irritantes eum[a] in uanitatibus suis.[1] Andreas utcumque modestius furebat, Alexander uero[b] sine moderaminis respectu multa suo Paulo mala ostendebat.[2] 'Seduxisti nos,' inquit, 'pessime, et induxisti nos in locum horroris et uaste solitudinis,[3] priuatos et exutos habitationibus amenis rebusque opimis, et quasi non essent religiose quietis habitacula in seculo, ita hic inter feras et frutices nobis ferino more delitescendum prescribis. Habundat omnis terra religiosorum cetibus uirorum, ubi et cohabitantium multitudo ad solatium et perfectio satis superque nobis sufficeret ad exemplum, et ecce soli sine solatio, pre accidia languidi et torpentes, neminem totis diebus uidemus quem imitemur, parietes solos quibus includimur intuemur. Set nec sedent[c] nobis nimium licet argute rationes tue ; manifestis enim et rectissimis sententiis nostris semper aduersatur sermo tuus. Ita uero rarissime adhuc in terris iugum nouelle huius legis portandum ingeritur nobis, ac si perierit ubique preterquam apud Cartusienses Christianitas tota et uix paucissimis homunculis uia sit comperta salutis. Verum quos potiora non latent, hec inutilia et uana diutius tenere nec debent nec ualent. Hiis ergo[d] salubriora quesituri, ulterius recusamus addici.'[4]

Talibus sacrum ordinem illum agebat blasphemiis, talibus uirum Dei afficiebat conuiciis hominis peruicacia

---

[a] exarcebant in eum B, *omitting* irritantes
[b] *om* B
[c] cedent QX
[d] + longe Xc

and which the other entered, but merely relate what happened to them, when they had basely forsaken the perfect way for one good in itself, but embarked upon from unworthy motives.

They were a source of disorder like those well-known conspirators against Moses, reproaching Hugh bitterly and angering him by their futile complaints.[1] Andrew did show some restraint but Alexander gave full vent to his indignation against his Paul.[2] ' Wretch, you have deluded us,' he said, ' and have brought us to this wild and lonely place,[3] taking us away from our pleasant dwellings and a civilized way of life. You have forced us to lurk amongst beasts and thorns, as if there were not places of monastic retirement in the world. The whole land is full of communities of monks, and the mutual support provided by the communal life provides us with a sufficiently good example of religious perfection. Here alone and without companionship, we become torpid and dull through boredom, seeing no one for days at a time whose example can inspire us, and having only the walls which shut us in to look at. Your apparently un-answerable arguments shall not convince us, since what you have to say is always in opposition to our sound and excellent judgment. The yoke of this new law which you tell us must be borne, as if all Christians everywhere would be damned except the Carthusians and the way of salvation were open to very few, is almost unendurable in this world. Since we know better, we must not and cannot endure this unprofitable and narrow way of life any longer. We are going to seek something saner, and absolutely refuse to stay for a further period.'[4]

These perverse and insane men uttered such blas-

---

[1] cf. Deut. 32:21 [2] cf. 2 Tim. 4:15 [3] cf. Deut. 32:10
[4] Peter of Blois, a former fellow-student of Alexander, refuted these complaints in *Epistola LXXVI* (P.L. 207, 262). St Hugh's authentic teaching on the ordinary Christian life is to be found *infra*, II, pp. 45-8.

uesani. Dolebat interea Hugo periculis eorum qui iam firmauerant sibi sermonem nequam apostasie. Timebat quoque scandalis *ᵃ* infirmorum ac recenter conuersorum quos, preter ineuitabiles undecumque prodeuntes temptationum estus, huiusmodi uehementius exagitabant *ᵇ* tempestuose procelle. Erat enim spiritus eorum, male scilicet robustorum, uelud 'turbo impellens parietem' ¹ sancte illius societatis discindensque pro uiribus compagem. Quantum denique mestitudinis, quantumque tedii sacrum istud pectus, in fraterna compassione et uera pietate tenerrimum, occupauerit, pro illorum amara obstinatione, nec ipse qui hoc pertulit ullis potuit, ut sepius fatebatur, uerbis declarare.

Vidimus autem postea hunc ipsum Alexandrum, iam Cluniacensem monachum, rebus aliquantulum sibi cedentibus contra uotum, permutationis sue penitudine ductum, Hugonis tunc episcopi ambitiosius gratiam implorare, nobis etiam preces ingeminare multiplices, quo interuentu nostro reditum mereretur ad ueri, ut asserebat, paradisi incaute perditam mansionem. Verum, sicut per Apostolum dictum est de Esau: 'Non inuenit penitentie locum, quamquam cum lacrimis inquisierit eam.' ² Obstitit enim non solum memorate improbitatis sue in posterum quoque suscepta transgressio, uerum etiam presentis inquietudinis sue notabilis *ᶜ* occasio. Translato enim ad regimen Cluniacensis monasterii Hugone Radingense abbate,³ qui eum ob litterarum prerogatiuam et magni nominis umbram in commensalem sibi et familiarem asciuerat, hic iam uelud inglorium se

---

ᵃ scandalum Qt
ᵇ exagitabat formido X ; exagitabat tempestuosa procella c
ᶜ uariabilis Xc
¹ Is. 25:4
² Heb. 12:17

phemies against this holy order, and reviled the man of God. Hugh was greatly grieved at their peril, for their wicked words showed their determination to desert. He feared also the danger to the weaker brethren and the newly converted, who, in addition to the inevitable temptations of all kinds which novices have to undergo, would be badly disturbed by this continuous wrangling. Their evil influence was like a strong whirlwind raging against the wall of that holy house,[1] and by its fury tearing its joints asunder. When he talked about it, he could not, as he himself confessed, put into words the heaviness and dejection of his heart, which was filled with brotherly compassion, and the most tender pity for their bitter obduracy.

I myself afterwards met Alexander, then a Cluniac monk, who when things turned out somewhat contrary to his expectations, regretted his desertion, and earnestly begged Hugh who was now a bishop to pardon him. He also implored me with many tears, that I would use my influence to gain permission for him to return to what he called the true Paradise which he had rashly forsaken. But, as the apostle said of Esau, ' He found no place for repentance though he sought it with tears '.[2] The obstacle was not only that his former sin and wickedness was still remembered, for the cause of his present discontent was well-known. Hugh, abbot of Reading,[3] who because of his scholarship and un-deserved reputation had made him his constant companion and attendant, had become abbot of Cluny, and he, feeling himself slighted and abandoned, began to

---

[3] The Cluniac Abbey of Reading was founded by Henry I in 1121. Hugh II, abbot from 1186-1199, became abbot of Cluny in the latter year. cf. R. Graham, *English Ecclesiastical Studies*, ' The Relation of Cluny to other movements of Monastic Reform,' especially p. 23 and B. R. Kemp, *Reading Abbey* (1968).

reputans et destitutum, deteriora sentire ceperat de claustrali amplitudine et sodali *a* multitudine quam senserat pridem de angustia celle et solitariorum raritate.

Capitvlvm XII

De eo quod difficillimus semper inueniebatur Hugo ad recipiendos semel egressos de ordine illo, cum assignatione cause *b* huius difficultatis.

Semper quidem Hugo difficilius inueniebatur ad recipiendos semel egressos ab ordine, seu monachos seu conuersos, asserens huic quam maxime religioni cauendam sedulo instabilium leuitatem palearum.[1] Hoc siquidem nomine illos exprimebat, qui ad facilem motus temptationis separantur a collegio bonorum, excussi ab area inite professionis. Huiusmodi homines in aliis commodius habitare posse locis religiosis dicebat, in quibus uite actiue disciplina etiam istos quandoque promouet ad salutem. Eo autem ipso quod talium experta et probata societas repudiatur ab ordine Cartusiensi, tam illis consuli aiebat, qui ne ingrediantur repelluntur, quam et illis qui intro admissi quieti interius morantur ; cum et istis id ad quod minus ydonei sunt non confertur, aliis uero eorum accessu impedimentum non irrogatur. Nullius uero, quamlibet dilecti, quamlibet preminentis uiri, ullatenus *c* admittebat in hoc casu preces, omnibus in commune aditum claudens redeundi qui sponte deseruissent, in quibus se prius intractabiles exhibuissent, septa ouilis sui. Zelabat per

a sodalium cv
b *om* B
c nullatenus QX

find a magnificent cloister, and membership of a large community even more distasteful than a small cell and the comparative loneliness of an eremitical life.

Chapter XII

Hugh's extreme reluctance to re-admit those who had once left the order, and its cause.

Hugh was always found to be very reluctant to re-admit monks or lay brethren who had once left the order.[1] He declared that the levity and instability of such chaff must be most carefully guarded against in his order. Such was his term for those who when faced with the slightest temptation deserted the society of the good, and were winnowed from the threshing-floor of monastic life. He said that men of this type could live more successfully in other religious orders, in which the discipline of an active life could sometimes bring about the salvation even of such persons. He said it was as the result of experience that they were rejected by the Carthusian order ; they were refused re-admission both for their own sakes and so that those who had been admitted might remain there without having their peace of mind disturbed. Thus, they were not given something for which they were completely unfitted, and their re-admission did not act as a hindrance to others. In these cases the prayers even of his greatest friends, or of the most important people were useless, and without exception the door was firmly closed against all who had left his sheepfold of their own accord, having first shown their

---

[1] St Hugh's attitude was that of Guigo's *Consuetudines* (P.L. 153, 749-750)

omnia suorum quietem tamquam suam *a* ipsius salutem ;
unamquamque commissarum sibi animarum non aliter
attendebat, non aliter omni studio spiritualis pulchri-
tudinis excolebat quam sponsam amantissimam Domini
sui. De qualibet ipsarum, omnibus quidem set specialius
sibi uel cuilibet illius ordinis rectori, uoce celestis sponsi
illud de canticis estimabat proferri : ' Adiuro uos per
capreas ceruosque camporum ne suscitetis neque eui-
gilare faciatis dilectam quousque ipsa uelit.'[1] Videbatur
ei non solum ipsos hanc adiurationem spernere,*b* qui
aliqua improbitate sabbatum illorum sanctum et delicatum presumerent infestare,[2] immo et illos qui infestos
dissimularent uel inclusos reprimere, uel infestaturos et
exclusos ne ingrederentur negligerent arcere. Rediit
autem, ut prelibauimus, et memoratus Andreas, nominis
sui honore mutilatus, ad nota infantie sue cunabula.[3]

CAPITVLVM XIII

Quod sacris codicibus sollicite adquirendis plurimam
impendit operam ; et de bibliotheca Wintoniensium
monachorum, quam regi datam et Withamensibus
collatam, Hugo pristinis restituit possessoribus ; et de
prerogatiua dilectionis inter utrumque collegium.

Libet succincte quiddam ex gestis uiri spiritu pleni
gemine dilectionis, Dei uidelicet ac proximi, referre, quod
eiusdem que in illo uehementer enituit, sincerissime
caritatis insigne documentum fuit. Igitur pene iam pro

---

a sui Xcp
b quietem hanc perturbare Q

perverseness. The peace of his flock was in every way as important to him as his own salvation. He considered each soul committed to his care as the beloved bride of the Lord, and to be trained as such in the pursuit of heavenly beauty. He believed that to each of these but especially to himself, or any other superior of the order, the words of the heavenly bridegroom in the Canticles had been addressed : ' I charge you, by the roes and by the hinds of the fields that ye stir not up nor awake my beloved, till he please.' [1] It seemed to him that it was not only those who dared to disturb this holy and delicious repose [2] by their perverseness, who despised this exhortation, but even more so those who postponed the correction of the disturbance if they were already there, or did not take care to prevent those outside who would disturb it from entering. Andrew, as we have already related, having damaged his reputation and good name, retired to the home of his childhood.[3]

Chapter XIII

How he worked hard to obtain manuscripts of religious works, and concerning the Bible of the monks of Winchester which was given to the king and by him to Witham, which Hugh restored to its original owners, and the close friendship between these two religious communities.

It is right to relate briefly one of the deeds of this man who was filled with a double love for God and his neighbour, since it shows so strikingly the intense charity

---

[1] Cant. 2:7   [2] cf. Is. 58:13   [3] i.e. to Muchelney

consuetudine illius ordinis integro fratrum numero edificiis quoque regularibus decenter consummatis,[1] edificandis indesinenter in sancto proposito sibi commissarum ouium animabus boni huius pastoris inuigilabat sollertia. In cuius negotii non mediocre adiutorium, sacris codicibus conficiendis, comparandis, et quibus posset modis adquirendis, haut segnem operam impendebat. Hiis enim [a] pro deliciis et pro diuitiis tempore tranquillo, hiis bellico sub procinctu pro telis uel armis, hiis in fame pro alimonia et in languore pro medela, religiosis quibusque, maxime uero solitariam gerentibus uitam, utendum esse memorabat.

Hinc contigit [b] ut cum rege familiarius quodam tempore agens, de penuria librorum intersereret mentionem. A quo admonitus ut conscribendis insisteret per conductitios scriptores libris, membranas sibi deesse respondit. Tum ille : ' Et quantum,' ait, ' pecunie tibi uis conferri ad hunc supplendum defectum ? ' ' Vna,' inquit, ' marca argenti diu sufficiet.' Rex ad hec subridens ' O,' ait, ' quam immoderate grauas nos.' Iussitque incontinenti decem marcas fratri qui cum eo erat numerari. Promisit etiam unam bibliothecam, utriusque testamenti corpus integre continentem, se transmissurum ei. Rediit prior domum. Rex [c] promissi sui non immemor inquirit sollicite bibliothecam optime confectam, quam ei conferre potuisset. Suggeritur demum studiosius querenti monachos sancti Swithuni [2] egregiam

---

[a] + et Q
[b] om B
[c] + autem X ; + igitur c
[1] Adam states below that some of the buildings were of wood (IV, xiv). The lay brothers' church, of stone and revaulted by St Hugh in Early English style, survives as the parish church. Entries in the Pipe Roll show that the choir-monks' church was not completed before St Hugh became bishop of Lincoln in 1186. See Introduction, p. xxv.

which burned so brightly in him. When the buildings required by the customs of the order were almost finished [1] and the number of brethren was complete, the good shepherd concentrated upon the training of the souls committed to his care in their holy profession. He devoted much labour to the making, purchase, and acquisition by every possible means of manuscripts of religious works, since these were a great assistance in this task. It was a favourite saying of his that these were useful to all monks, but especially to those leading an eremitical life, for they provided riches and delight in times of tranquillity, weapons and armour in times of temptation, food for the hungry and medicine for the sick.

Once in private converse with the king, the lack of books happened to be mentioned. When he was advised to do his best to get them copied by professional scribes, he replied that he had no parchment. The king then said ' How much money do you think I should give you to make up this defect ? ' He answered that a silver mark would be enough for a long time. At this the king smiled. ' What heavy demands you make on us,' he said, and immediately ordered ten marks to be given to the monk who was his companion. He also promised that he would send him a Bible containing the whole of both Testaments. The prior returned home, but the king did not forget his promise, and tried hard to find a really magnificent Bible for him. After an energetic search he was at last informed that the monks of St Swithun[2] had recently made a fine and beautifully written Bible which

---

[2] Winchester cathedral, dedicated to St Swithun, was given a monastic chapter by St Ethelwold in 964. Both in Saxon times and during the episcopate of Henry of Blois (1129-1171) it was one of the most important artistic centres in England.

recenti et decenti opere confecisse bibliothecam, in qua
ad mensam edentium fratrum legi debuisset. Quo ille
comperto opido gauisus est, accersitoque quamtocius
priore illius ecclesie, sub multe recompensationis pollici-
tatione donari sibi munus optatum petiit, citiusque
impetrauit. Itaque prior Withamie cum fratribus suis
bibliothecam regio munere susceptam et inspectam non
mediocriter et ipsi letati sunt, in eo potissimum gauisi
quod stili elegantiam, totiusque operis uenustatem,
operosior emendatio sublimius commendaret.¹

Contigit post hec quemdam ex monachis ecclesie
Wintoniensis edificationis gratia uenisse Withamiam.
Quem prior more suo summa cum affabilitate optato *a*
reficiens sancte discretionis sue colloquio, didicit repente
ab eo cum quanta supplicatione dominus rex bibliothecam ipsam dignatus fuerit a priore suo postulare.
' Et nos quidem in eo,' ait, ' etiam gratulamur impensius
quod uestre illam contulit sanctitati. Que si uobis per
omnia placet, bene res processit ; sin alias, et si a uestra
consuetudine dissidet aliqua sui parte, nos ista pro libitu
uestro longe meliorem citius conficiemus, pro uestra in
omnibus dispositione ordinandam. Hanc enim nostro
usui nostreque consuetudini, nec sine magni sudoris
impensa, fecimus consonare.' Ad hec prior admirans,
nescierat *b* enim prius quonam ordine rex optinuisset
illam, fratri continuo ita affatus est : ' Itane dominus rex
ecclesiam uestram fraudauit adeo necessario labore
uestro ? Crede michi, frater amantissime, restituetur
uobis incontinenti bibliotheca uestra. Set et *c* uestrorum
fratrum deuote per uos supplicamus uniuersitati quatinus

---

a optate Xc   *b* nesciebat Q   *c* om B

¹ This was formerly believed to be the famous Winchester Bible in that
Cathedral's library. But it now seems certain that St Hugh's Bible is MS
Auct. E. Inf. 1-2 in the Bodleian Library at Oxford. This was probably
produced at St Albans but brought to Winchester with its decoration half
completed, presumably by bishop Henry of Blois (d. 1171), to improve the

was to be used for reading in the refectory. He was greatly delighted by this discovery, and immediately summoned their prior, and asked that the gift he desired to make should be handed over to him, promising a handsome reward. His request was speedily granted. When the prior of Witham and his monks received and examined the Bible given to them by the king they were not a little delighted with it. The correctness of the text pleased them especially, even more than the delicacy of the penmanship and the general beauty of the manuscript.[1]

One of the monks of Winchester happened afterwards to come to Witham for the sake of edification. The prior, with his accustomed courtesy, entertained him, and gave him the spiritual counsels he had desired. His guest unexpectedly informed him how earnestly the lord king had deigned to ask his prior for the Bible. ' We are especially glad,' he said, ' that he shòuld have given it to you, venerable father. If you are completely satisfied with it, all is well ; but if not, and if it differs in any particular from your usage, we will, if you like, speedily make you a far finer one, corresponding to your requirements in every detail. We took considerable pains to make this correspond to our own use.' The prior was amazed, for he had not known before how the king had obtained it. He immediately said these words to the monk. ' Did the lord king indeed defraud your monastery of such an essential fruit of your labours ? My dearest brother, your book shall be restored at once. I beg you

---

text of his Bible. Later changes in the Auct. Bible were for public reading. The finer, unfinished Bible mentioned by the Winchester visitor was the Winchester Bible. See W. F. Oakeshott, 'St Albans and Winchester contributions to St Hugh's Bible' in A. C. de la Mare and B. C. Barker-Benfield (ed.), *Manuscripts at Oxford : R. W. Hunt Memorial Exhibition* (Bodleian Library, Oxford, 1980), but also R. M. Thomson, *Manuscripts from St Albans Abbey 1066-1235*, I (1982), 33-36.

nostre dignentur humilitati indulgere, quod occasione nostri, nobis tamen id *a* ignorantibus, defectum sustinuerunt codicis sui.' Hiis monachus auditis uehementer expauit, orans gemebundis uocibus ne talia cogitaret uel loqueretur, nullatenus expedire affirmans ecclesie sue, ut sibi utiliter conciliata tali exhennio regis gratia quauis occasione desciuisset.*b* Hinc *c* prior exultans, ' Estne,' inquit, ' hoc uerum quod de eius fauore solito plus presumitis, nec uobis triste est tali hunc munere negotiis uestris propitium esse effectum ? ' Cum ille *d* fratribus suis omnibus ex hoc gaudium prouenisse assereret, Hugo subiunxit : ' Vt hoc,' inquit, ' gaudium perpetuetur in longum, cunctos necesse est lateat facta uobis restitutio pretiosi reuera laboris uestri. Si uero bibliothecam hanc recipere clanculo minime adquiescitis, ego illam ei restituo qui huc ipsam destinauit. Si uero modo eam reportaueritis,*e* hoc illi per nos nullatenus innotescet.' Quid multa ? Recipiunt monachi codicem suum quasi recenti dono acquisitum, multum de codice, set multo plus de transmittentis *f* dulcedine et caritatis ipsius plenitudine exhilarati.

Quo facto, ut premissum est, euidentius innotuit, quanto gemine caritatis ardore mens uiri beati flagrauerit, qui, gratia sui commodi, uiris noluit religiosis opus ad honorem Dei elaboratum deperire, ne uel in modico *g* eidem derogaretur diuino honori uel honorem exhibentium detraheretur utilitati. Proximos ergo et beneficio iuuit et exemplo, quatinus et *h* per lectionem proficerent codicis, et uirtutem emularentur impense sibi fraterne dilectionis, ex utroque uero in amorem

---

a om B
c Hic B
e reportaueris B
g momento X

b desiisset B² destitisset c ; destituisset t
d Tunc ille cum Xc
f + ac restituentis Xc
h om B

most earnestly and humbly to ask your brethren to forgive us, that, although we knew nothing about it, you lost your book through us.' The monk, terrified at what he heard, implored him in horrified tones that he would not think of doing what he said. It would be fatal to his own church that Hugh should on any pretext decline a royal gift which had so fortunately won for them the king's favour. This amused the prior, who answered : ' Is it true that you think that you are much more in his favour than usual, and do not regret that his goodwill towards you was purchased by this magnificent gift ? ' As he asserted that all his fellow monks were well content with the transaction, Hugh added, ' To make your satisfaction lasting the restitution of your precious masterpiece shall be kept secret by all of us. If you do not agree to receive this Bible secretly, I shall restore it to the man who sent it here, but if you take it away now, I shall never tell him.' There was no more argument. The monks received their book, as if it had been a newly acquired gift. They were delighted with the present, but still more with the courtesy and great generosity of the sender.

This action, as I have already said, demonstrated clearly the fervour of the twin loves which consumed the heart of this saintly man, since for his own advantage he would not deprive the monks of a masterpiece created for the glory of God, lest this might injure the divine honour even a little, or defraud those who had worked for it of what was profitable to them. His kindness and example were alike beneficial to his neighbours. From the reading of the book they received instruction, and were also inspired to imitate his brotherly charity, and both these things increased their devotion to their Creator. All his deeds, words and thoughts were

crescerent *a* sui conditoris. In hunc sane finem omnis eius actio, sermo et cogitatio dirigi consueuit ut prestaret proximo, et tam ipse quam proximus ex eo *b* placeret Deo. Set neque fraudari nouerat intentio eius pia et recta a spe sua. Conualuit siquidem ex illo presertim tempore inter utriusque loci accolas, Wintonienses uidelicet cenobitas et Withamenses heremitas, eximie dilectionis prerogatiua, prestante Dei gratia in euum duratura.

Capitvlvm XIV

Quod ad instantiam maxime uenerabilium uirorum, domini Roberti prioris Sancti Swithuni et solitarii Withamensis necnon et domini Radulfi sacriste, hec posteris de Hugone cognoscenda scripto mandata sunt.

Vidimus postea uirum omni laude attollendum quia omni uirtutum gratia decoratum, dominum Robertum, eiusdem cathedralis ecclesie Wintoniensis priorem, ut liberius uacaret Deo sancteque illius institutionis proficeret magisterio, relictis turmis obsequentium, Withamensem effectum solitarium.[1] De cuius uirtutibus uel moribus silere potius quam pauca dicere preelegimus, cum placide et sanctissime illius uite insignia recolenti ueniat plerumque in dubium, quid primum quidue precipuum in tot eius preconiis fuerit commendandum. Qui in suprema iam constitutus etate, iccirco asperum se dicebat heremitice conuersationis

---

a transirent Xc   *b* inde X ; ex hoc c

[1] Robert FitzHenry, prior of Winchester, 1187-1191, became a Carthusian under prior Albert at Witham where he died *c.* 1206. cf. *Witham chronicle*, 207-232. At least one of the Winchester community was much less favourable to Witham than might be inferred from the last sentence of Adam's preceding chapter : Richard of Devizes came to see his former prior there and dedicated his *De Gestis Richardi primi* to him in a very sarcastic preface. Another Winchester Benedictine who became a

directed to this very end, to assist his neighbour, and thus both of them should please God. From this time onwards there grew up an especially warm friendship between both communities, the monks of Winchester and the hermits of Witham, which with God's help should long endure.

CHAPTER XIV

How it was owing to the persuasions of two revered men, Dom Robert, prior of St Swithun's and a hermit at Witham and Dom Ralph the sacrist, that we have written these things about Hugh as a record for future generations.

We afterwards met Dom Robert, prior of the cathedral church of Winchester, a man endowed with every good quality and therefore deserving of the highest praise, who left his numerous subjects to become a hermit at Witham, in order that he might through the discipline of that holy community give himself more completely to God.[1] I shall not, however, even give a short character sketch of him, for when I considered his tranquil and saintly life I found it impossible to decide which of his many excellencies should be commemorated first, or deserved special mention. He used to say when he was a very old man, that the asceticism of the eremitical life was

Carthusian at Witham was Walter, formerly subprior of Hyde and afterwards prior of Bath ; but he was compelled by his bishop to return, and he died in 1198. For Richard's accusations of lack of hospitality, excessive interest in secular affairs and irresponsibility, cf. *Chronicles of the reigns of Stephen, Henry II and Richard I*, III, 381 and 403 ; and *Winchester Annals, Annales Monastici*, II, 68.

arripuisse institutum, quatinus moreretur tutius qui citius uidebatur moriturus, cum accelerandam quoque iam imminentem estimaret mortem, eo quod in tanto nature defectu tam insuetum subiret uiuendi rigorem. Verum superante in eo naturam Christi gratia, creuerunt ei etiam presentis uite spatia ad promerenda uberius perhennis uite premia. Audiuimus eum, postquam in celle solitudine, in cibi ariditate et in cilicii squalore tertium iam exegerat lustrum, cum spirituali iocunditate protestari ademptam sibi deliciarum preteritarum afflu-entiam, quam mensa pridem lautior cumulare solebat, optimam sibi ualetudinem et iuuenilium quodammodo annorum reparasse uigorem. Erat uultu placidus, corde serenissimus, canitie niueus, ore facundus, spiritu mitis, affectu suauis.[a]

Istius sane et uiri eque prestantissimi domini Radulfi, quondam sacriste illius ecclesie, monitis pre-cipue animatus, precibusque importunis compulsus sum aliqua posterorum notitie de presenti materia scribendo transmittere. Quorum iam uterque ex hac, ut accepimus, luce ad illam migrauit felicitatis eterne,[1] pro cuius desiderabili expectatione diutius flendo, ieiunando et uigilando, corporee lucis aliquamdiu priuati sunt uisione, instante iam beata corporis huius quod corrumpitur resolutione.[2] Hec uero de hiis paulo quam sperabamus diffusius prosecuti sumus, ut lectori claresceret euidentius ad quantam pietatis frugem bonitatis germina in Hugone pullulare consueuerint, quem [b] ad edificandum et plan-tandum super gentes et super regna [3] celestis clementia decreuit constituendum.

---

[a] sermone facundus . . . affatu suauis X   [b] quam B
[1] Therefore Adam wrote these words after 1206. See pp. x-xii
[2] cf. 2 Tim. 4:6   [3] cf. Jer. 1:10

what had attracted him, because he felt he would die with full assurance of salvation, if he were to die soon. His death was already approaching, and he hoped to hasten its coming, if, when his powers were already failing, he submitted to unaccustomed privations. The grace of Christ, however, triumphed over nature, and his life was prolonged, so that he might deserve more fully the reward of eternal life. When he had endured for fifteen years the solitude of his cell, the meagre fare and the irritation of his hair shirt, I heard him declare with great exultation that he had acquired a much greater abundance of consolations than he had been able to when his meals were larger and more varied, that his health was excellent, and that he had recovered his youthful vigour. He was a white-haired man with a placid face, a ready wit, an unruffled temper, and a sweet and equable disposition.

It was he and an equally admirable man, Dom Ralph, formerly sacrist of Winchester, who encouraged, entreated and finally compelled me to write this present work for the benefit of future generations. We have heard that both of them have departed from this present world to the life of eternal bliss.[1] Since they had prepared themselves for this desirable state for a long time by weeping, fasting and watching, and had even for some time been deprived of the sight of this earthly light, the beatific vision would follow immediately upon the dissolution of this corrupt body.[2] I have dealt with them rather more fully than I intended, to prove conclusively to my readers what an abundant crop of holiness was harvested from the seeds of Hugh's goodness. The divine mercy had indeed destined him to be placed over peoples and kingdoms,[3] to build and to plant.

LIBER TERTIVS

PROLOGVS

QUIA, prestante Domino, beati uiri gesta quibus ab ipso pueritie sue tempore omnipotenti Deo meruit placere *a* qualicumque stilo summatim exarauimus, nunc qualiter ad episcopatum, celesti prosequente gratia conscenderit, qualiter in eo uixerit et docuerit, succinctus sermo percurrat. Nec enim singula set neque precipua gestorum *b* eius atque uerborum a nobis modo recensenda promittimus, set ea sola nec tamen ea omnia que nobis sunt ex eiusdem actibus et memorabilibus dictis certius comperta et memoriter retenta. In quibus non admirationem superfluam legentium siue audientium captamus, set ea potius que sancta sunt et salubria nosse et imitari cupientium edificationem. Nam et in hoc etiam, traditam *c* a sanctis ordinis Cartusiensis auctoribus [1] grauitatem pariter et humilitatem altius *d* et perfectius mente tota imbiberat, ut nichil minus quam miraculorum prodigia mirari aut emulari uideretur, cum hec tamen de uiris sanctis lecta aut cognita suauiter referret et sublimius ueneraretur. Referebat, inquam, hec ad commendationem ea exhibentium et ad excitationem *e* talia admirantium, cum illi *f* sola esset sanctorum sanctitas pro miraculo, sola sufficeret pro exemplo. Vnico autem et uniuersali sibi erat *g* miraculo conditoris sui, que numquam ei deerat, precordialis recordatio, magnalium quoque illius stupenda et inexplicabilis multitudo. Plurima uero ad suam ipsius quandoque releuationem, necnon et aliorum sepius opitulationem,

---

a + usque ad episcopationem sui Q *b* gesta Xc
c hoc traditum ita Xc *d* arctius Xc
e exercitationem X *f* illa Xc *g* + pro Xc

BOOK THREE

PROLOGUE

We have now with God's help dealt briefly and baldly with the acts of this saintly man, which gained for him Almighty God's favour from his childhood onwards. Now, if heavenly grace assists us, we will go on to his elevation to the episcopate, his life as a bishop and his pastoral activities. We do not promise to set down all his deeds and words, or even the most notable of them, but only those which we have learned on unimpeachable authority, or remember for ourselves, and not even all of these. Our motive in making our selection was not to win the empty admiration of our readers or audience, but to edify those who want to learn what things are good and holy in order to imitate them. Hugh himself had so wholeheartedly, completely and perfectly absorbed the reserve and humility of the holy founders of the Carthusian order[1] that he thought miracles were the last thing to admire or wish to emulate, although he used to describe very attractively those worked by holy men which he had read or heard about, and had a great veneration for them himself. His object was to praise those who had performed them and to arouse the interest of those who were impressed by such occurrences, but to him the holiness of the saints was better than any miracle and alone provided an example to be imitated. The thought of his Creator, which was never absent

---

[1] cf. Guigo, *Vita S. Hugonis Gratianopolitani*, c. iv (P.L. 153, 773)

per eum dum aduiueret *a* seu scientem seu nescientem,
Dominum exhibuisse miracula, nemini qui familiarius
illi adhesit incertum fuit.   Set nec ista que utcumque
fidelibus communicanda scribemus pie lecturis rei huius
certitudo, superna opitulante gratia, denegabitur.   Hec
uero de prohemio libelli *b* huius tertii in uitam beati uiri
prelibasse sufficiat.   Iam hystorie seriem incultus licet
stilus euoluat.

a adhuc uiueret X
b libri Xc

from his inmost heart, and the mysterious and wonderful works of creation were for him the one universal miracle, for which he never failed to render heartfelt thanks. None of his household doubted that the Lord worked many miracles through him during his lifetime, whether he himself knew it or not, sometimes for his own needs, but more often for the benefit of other people, and any devout reader of the things which I propose to set down for publication among the faithful will by divine grace not fail to be convinced of this truth. This introduction will suffice for the third book of the life of this holy man. We will therefore now proceed with our homely narrative.

CAPITVLVM I

De Hugonis electione in episcopum. Et de amplitudine episcopatus Lincolniensis.*

Promoto in archiepiscopalem Rothomagensis sedem
ecclesie uiro uenerabili Waltero Lincolniensi episcopo,[1]
rex Anglorum Henricus secundus apud Egnesham [2] octo
ferme continuatim diebus tractatum habuit super uariis
regni negotiis cum episcopis et magnatibus terre. In
eodem siquidem monasterio tempore illo, pie memorie
Baldewinus Cantuariensis archiepiscopus [3] et suffraga-
neorum eius *b* quidam, hospitii gratia sese contulerant.
Rex singulis diebus illuc mane aduentabat ; indeque ad
palatium suum quod apud Wudestoke habetur,*c* post
actitatum cum predictis colloquium, denuo redibat.
Celebrate sunt tunc temporis ibidem episcoporum et
abbatum quorumdam electiones.[4] Huc et Lincolniensis
ecclesie canonici aduenerant, electuri seu potius suscep-
turi episcopum celitus electum.

Fuerunt eo tempore preminentiores ipsius ecclesie
persone non pauce, consiliis aut obsequiis etiam palatinis
ascripte uel addicte. Erant in secularibus famosi,

---

a diocesis Lincolniensis, et de commendatione morum Hugonis X
b eorum B
c habebatur Xc
[1] Walter of Coutances was a royal clerk who became canon of Rouen
and Vice-Chancellor of England in 1173 and seal-bearer in 1180. He was
freely elected bishop of Lincoln in 1183, and was translated to Rouen
the following year. In 1191 he became Justiciar and helped to raise
Richard I's ransom in 1193. He died in 1207.
[2] 25 May-2 June 1186
[3] Baldwin, archdeacon of Totnes, became a Cistercian monk at Ford
c. 1170, and was elected abbot there *c.* 1175. He became bishop of
Worcester in 1180 and archbishop of Canterbury in 1185. His conflict
with his monks lasted from 1186 till 1189. He went on the Crusade

CHAPTER I

Concerning Hugh's election as a bishop. The size of the diocese of Lincoln.

After that venerable man, Walter, bishop of Lincoln, had been raised to the archbishopric of Rouen,[1] Henry II king of the English, held a council at Eynsham.[2] There he discussed for almost eight days continuously various matters of state with the bishops and nobles of his kingdom. On this occasion the monastery gave hospitality to Baldwin, archbishop of Canterbury of blessed memory,[3] and to certain of his suffragans. The king used to come there each day early in the morning, and when the conference ended returned to his palace at Woodstock. Elections to various bishoprics and abbeys took place at this time,[4] and the canons of Lincoln arrived there to elect, or rather to receive the bishop designed for them by God.

Many of the dignitaries of that church were also members of the king's council and household, and were distinguished politicians and scholars and also men of considerable fortune. Most of them felt that no bishopric,

---

in March 1190, and died at Acre in November that year. Some of his theological and devotional works were still copied at Canterbury in the fifteenth century ; they are printed in P.L. 204, 402 *et seq.* For comparison of his character by Giraldus with St Hugh's, see Introduction, p. xxxii and M. D. Knowles, *The Monastic Order in England*, 316 *et seq.*

[4] Other vacancies filled at this council included Worcester and Hereford, to which William de Northall, archdeacon of Gloucester, and William de Vere were elected. Godfrey de Lucy, who was one of the unsuccessful candidates for Lincoln, was elected to Exeter but declined. The other two unsuccessful candidates for Lincoln were Richard Fitz-Neal the dean, later bishop of London, and Herbert le Poer, later bishop of Salisbury. Godfrey de Lucy later became bishop of Winchester.

litterarum sicut et diuitiarum mundanarum copia prepollentes. Plerique ex hiis nullum quamlibet amplum episcopatum magnitudine sua reputabant maiorem ; nimirum cum ipsi amplioribus cumularentur redditibus quam ingens quilibet episcopatus. Eorum tamen aliqui, siue ob bonum iuxta apostolum opus,[1] siue iuxta secularem ambitum ob honoris et potestatis decus, minime renuissent episcopari si affuisset qui coegisset. Verum Domino cor regis in manu habente et quo uellet illud inclinante,[2] annuentibus sibi memorato metropolitano aliisque nonnullis religiosis personis, maxime uero, de quo superius mentio habita *a* est, Bathoniensi episcopo Reginaldo instante, ad tot Dominicarum ouium custodiam rex ipse utiliorem prouideri satagebat pastorem. Illa namque diocesis, bis quaternos continens archidiaconatus, per nouem et eo amplius distenditur comitatus, urbes pregrandes, plebes uero complectitur innumeras, nec facile inuenitur alter eo uastior aut populosior episcopatus.[3] Vacauerat uero paulo ante sedes tam egregia annis circiter decem et octo : duobus uidelicet et semis post translationem prefati episcopi, quindecim uero ante illius consecrationem.[4] Tot annorum curriculis ager ille Dominicus cultoris industria destitutus, haut mirum si uitiorum sentibus multisque abusionum germinibus *b* squalebat opertus.

Discrimen tanti mali sibi rex sentiens imputari, quem uidelicet uacationis tam inconsulte auctorem extitisse patebat, omnimodis nititur per cultoris electissimi

---

a facta Xc
b graminibus X

however large, was beyond their deserts, since they had managed to acquire wealth in excess of that of the most extensive bishopric. Some of them would certainly not have refused a bishopric if pressed to accept it, either because according to the apostle it was a good work,[1] or from motives of secular ambition, because of the distinction and authority it conferred. God, however, had the heart of the king in his hand and inclined it to his will.[2] He therefore was determined, with the goodwill of the above-mentioned archbishop, and certain other devout persons, especially Reginald, bishop of Bath, who has already appeared in this narrative, to provide the Lord's flock with a better shepherd. The diocese contains eight archdeaconries and extends over more than nine counties, with many large cities and a big population, indeed it would be difficult to find a larger or more populous one.[3] A little time before, this important see had been vacant for nearly eighteen years, that is for two and a half after the translation of archbishop Walter, and for fifteen before his consecration.[4] As the field of the Lord had been left without the services of a husbandman for so many years, it is no wonder that it was foul and choked with the weeds of sin and the thorns of unrighteousness.

The king realized his culpability for its neglected condition, since the deplorable vacancy was patently due to him. He therefore did his utmost to make amends for

---

[1] cf. 1 Tim. 3:1   [2] cf. Prov. 21:1
[3] The diocese of Lincoln extended from the Humber to the Thames and included the counties of Lincs, Northants, Leics, Rutland, Hunts, Beds, Oxon, Bucks, and parts of Herts. It was the largest diocese in England.
[4] Robert de Chesney, bishop of Lincoln, had died in 1166. In 1173 Geoffrey Plantagenet, illegitimate son of Henry II, was nominated but never consecrated; he resigned in 1181. The long vacancy had seemed quasi-perpetual, and a monk of Thame had prophesied that there would never again be a bishop of Lincoln; cf. William of Newburgh, *Historia Rerum Anglicarum* (R.S.), bk. II, c. xxii; bk. III, c. viii and xxvi, and in *E.H.D.* II, 335, 361 *et seq.*

strenuitatem   omisse   diutius   culture   dispendia
compensare.

Clericis *a* itaque illis in uota disparia frustra studen-
tibus, nullius uero nisi propriam quisque suam ipsius
promotionem ex animo ut dicebatur expetentibus,*b*
insistunt plurimi, consulentes eis obnixius *c* ut uirum
incomparande bonitatis, priorem uidelicet Withamie,
studeant in pastorem optinere. Commendatur a multis
eius sanctitas, eius discretio ; affabilitas eius et religio in
immensum attollitur. Omnis denique morum elegantia,
omnis uirtutum quadratura in solo homine isto con-
uenisse predicatur. Nullus eo summo dignior sacerdotio
consona multorum uoce acclamatur.

Ad hec primum uelud horrore quodam perfundi
cerneres homines prefatos, homines nimirum que carnis
sunt sentientes *d* ; homines, inquam, etiam in causa Dei,
que hominum potius quam que Dei sunt querentes.[1]
Denique cultum religionis ipsius, ritus et loquelam illius,
sibi prorsus aut contraria aut ignota preferre *e* non sine
derisionis cachinno proferebant. Verum hec illorum
derisio a sanum sapientibus, magno eorum commodo,
salubriter derisa est ; ipsi quoque ad immensum non
modo sue, immo et totius ecclesie sancte decus, quem
pueriliter primo despexerant, mutato repente consilio,
unanimiter demum elegerunt. Ita quem ab eterno in
hoc ipsum elegerat Dominus, tempore diuinitus prefinito
eligitur ab hominibus. Gratulantur qui nouerant eum ;
qui notitie eius expertes erant mirantur ; in commune
uero ab omnibus Deus et Dominus uoce altissona col-
laudatur.

a Celeriter X
b expectabat c ; expectantibus X
c obnoxius Bc
d sapientes X
e proferre B ; *om* c

the havoc caused by the long neglect, through the energy of a carefully chosen husbandman.

As the clergy were hopelessly divided, since each of them, it is said, at heart desired the election of no one but himself, many persons urged and advised them to try to obtain as their bishop the prior of Witham, a man of exceptional goodness. Many commended his sanctity and wisdom, and lauded his charm and piety to the skies. All agreed that he was the only person who combined all the virtues with good breeding, and it was almost universally agreed that no more suitable bishop could be found.

The first reaction of these exceedingly worldly men, who even in God's business thought more of the things of man than those of God,[1] was one of utter horror. They declared, not without some scornful amusement, that they were strongly prejudiced against this unknown foreigner, and that his accent and even his order and its customs were abhorrent to them. Fortunately for them their scorn was treated with equal contempt by men of true discernment, and they themselves to their great honour, and indeed that of the universal church, suddenly changed their minds, and at last elected unanimously the man whom they had at first childishly rejected. Thus he whom God had appointed from all eternity, was chosen by men at the time ordained by Him, to the joy of those who knew him, and the amazement of those who knew him not. All, however, together loudly praised the Lord God.

[1] cf. Matt. 16:23

CAPITVLVM II

De locis in quibus uel debet uel non debet pontificalis celebrari electio Hugonis diffinitio, et quia repudiauerit electionem habitam de se non in capitulo Lincolniensi.

Clero igitur petente, rege approbante, proceribus cum episcopis acclamantibus, a metropolitano eius mox confirmatur electio ; ipso interim in sua heremo latente et quid de se ab illis longe a se positis ageretur prorsus nesciente. A loco autem ipso ubi celebrata est electio ipsa directi sunt quidam ad eum ex primis electoribus illis, iam in spe filiis et clericis suis, qui domini archiepiscopi mandatum cum litteris quoque regiis deferentes ut ad eum perueniunt, ei uocationis sue ordinem ad superiorem gradum exponunt. Quo ille audito, litteris etiam quas attulerant inspectis, quibus post alia denuntiabatur ei quatinus sub celeritate regi et archiepiscopo sese presentaret de consecrationis sue negotio tractaturus, tale incontinenti ad audita et inspecta responsum dedit :

' Non, inquit, uidetur mirandum si dominus archiepiscopus aut etiam dominus rex personam meam, quamuis tali honore indignam, licet tanto oneri *a* longe imparem, ad gradum libenter uideant prouehi altiorem. Nam et domino regi quis ambigat placiturum, si uiros a se religionis optentu de partibus ascitos remotis, prosperis in regno suo uideat florere successibus ? Nichilominus et domino Cantuariensi, qui religionis habitum iam pene solus inter episcopos terre huius preferre *b* uidetur,[1] quis nesciat esse uotiuum ut in suscepto *c* cure pastoralis officio coadiutores accipiat et comministros regularis

---

a onere Bct   *b* preferri Xc   *c* suscepte Xc

[1] The only other monk-bishop in England at this time was Gilbert Foliot of London, now old and going blind.

CHAPTER II

Hugh's verdict on where episcopal elections ought,
or ought not, to be held, and how he regarded his
election as invalid, because not made in the chapter
house at Lincoln.

At the request of the clergy, and with the king's
consent and the full approval of the nobles and bishops,
his metropolitan immediately confirmed his election.
Meanwhile he, in the seclusion of his hermitage, was
unaware of the decision taken in regard to him by
persons far away. Some of the chief electors were
dispatched to him from the place where the election had
taken place. These in the expectation of becoming his
sons and clergy, came to him bringing with them the
mandates of the archbishop and the king, and explained
to him the circumstances connected with his elevation
to a higher office. Having heard them and examined
the letters they had brought, which, after giving the other
information, ordered him to come as soon as possible to
the king and archbishop to discuss the business of his
consecration, he immediately gave the following answer.

'Although I am quite unfit for so great an honour,
and unequal to such heavy responsibilities, I am not
surprised that the lord archbishop and even the lord
king see fit to raise me to a higher office. Undoubtedly
it would please the lord king to see the members of an
order brought by him from distant regions flourish and
prosper in his kingdom. Undeniably the lord archbishop of Canterbury, who seems to be almost the only
monk amongst the bishops of this land,[1] must desire to
have assistants and fellow-workers in the pastoral duties
committed to him who have experience of and share

discipline experientia institutos ? ^a Verum hec istorum uota uel studia uobis ^b preiudicare non ualent. Vestrum est rectorem libere eligere, cuius de cetero moderamina ^c oporteat necessario moresque tolerare. Denique non in regali palatio set neque in pontificali concilio, dummodo schismatis uel alterius non interueniat noxa discriminis, quin potius in suo cuiusque ^d ecclesie capitulo rectoris ecclesiastici est celebranda electio.[1] Itaque ut mee uobis paruitatis sententia intimetur, noueritis me quicquid de eius ^e electione actum est irritum habere et prorsus inane. Vos quoque, pro infecto habentes quecumque super hoc pars quedam cetus uestri noscitur attemptasse, ad propriam cum Dei benedictione ecclesiam remeate. Ibi,^f Sancti Spiritus consilio pariter et adiutorio freti,^g canonicam pastoris uestri sollempniter celebrate electionem. Quod ut digne efficiatis, non regis non presulis, non denique cuiusque ^h hominis, set solius Dei omnipotentis uoluntatem, gratiam et fauorem pre oculis habeatis. Aliud a mea paruitate minime reportabitis. Abite igitur, et angelus Domini bonus comitetur uobiscum.' [2]

Eo itaque in ⁱ sententia persistente, cum nulla posset ratione induci ut uel regi seu archipresuli suam pro tali negotio presentiam exhiberet, illi ad eos qui se miserant quamtocius redierunt, miro modo in omnibus que ab eo audierant et que circa eum uiderant edificati. Nec solum ipsi set et omnes qui audierunt, mirati sunt et uehementer iocundati, collaudantibus in eo cunctis ac magnificantibus sinceritatem animi, uirtutem eximie discretionis, uiuacitatem consilii, zelum ecclesiastice libertatis.

---

^a experientie institutos B ; experientia instructos Q
^b hoc isto uota uel studia uestra Xc   ^c + uos Xc
^d cuiuscumque Q   ^e huiusmodi X ; huius c   ^f Ibique ocd
^g om c ; + iterum Xc, + inuocato X
^h cuiuscumque QX   ⁱ + hac Xc

the traditions of the monastic life. But their wishes and aims ought not to govern your choice. You have the right to elect your own bishop, since you will have to put up with his personality and authority. Also, provided that there are no serious divisions or other dangers the election of prelates should not be held either in a royal palace or an episcopal synod, but in the chapter house of the church concerned.[1] In my humble opinion, therefore, my election is null and void. You can thus assume that the proceedings of part of your community in this matter are uncanonical and return to your own church with God's blessing. There, trusting in the guidance and help of the holy Spirit, solemnly hold a canonical election of your bishop. To do this conscientiously, you must take no account of the wishes, goodwill and favour of king or archbishop or of any man, but only what is the will of Almighty God. This is the only advice I can give you. Go now and may God's good angel be with you.' [2]

As he was absolutely determined and nothing would persuade him to go to the king or the archbishop in connection with the business, they returned as quickly as they could to those who had sent them, greatly impressed in every way by their meeting with him and by his words. All whom they told were equally surprised and pleased. All commended and praised his integrity of mind, his remarkable prudence, his spirited advice and his zeal for the freedom of the church.

---

[1] St Hugh's protest was in accord with that of pope Alexander III to Richard of Canterbury, whom the Pope forbade to confirm elections held in the royal chapel. cf. Friedberg, *Decretalium Collectiones*, 417-8

[2] cf. Tob. 5: 21

Capitvlvm III

Quod citra iussionem prioris Cartusie noluerit electioni adquiescere, etiam in Lincolniensi postmodum capitulo satis fauorabiliter celebrate.

Talibus igitur ad notitiam Lincolniensis capituli perlatis, uniuersitas illius collegii iam quasi arram future strenuitatis et quasdam uirtutum primitias de suo se electo percepisse impensius gratulatur. Quique prius se male inductos et circumuentos querebantur ut hominem natura barbarum, moribus ut formidabant agrestem et asperum, sibi in rectorem et dominum elegissent, nunc uice uersa bonitatis et sapientie illius uirtute comperta, accelerant denuo ac de nouo illum eligere, utque super se pastoralis cure ministerium dignetur suscipere deuotissime supplicare. Mittuntur iterum cum litteris capituli, regis quoque et archiepiscopi, nuntii plures prioribus. Omnibus itaque existimantibus consummatum iam esse negotium, nec ullum de cetero ei superesse procrastinandi suffragium,[a] legati tam plene instructi, hylares et leti perueniunt ad eum. Presciuerat quidem ab olim uir beatus ad pontificatus officium se quandoque diuinitus perducendum ; unde, quod uitari[b] non posse dolebat ne demum fieret, quantum in se fuit ne citius fieret differri cupiebat.

Auditis ergo post inspectas litteras prefatas uerbis nuntiorum, sic eos alloquitur : ' Mirum est,' inquit, ' quod uiri adeo sapientes adeoque ciuiles me hominem incultum et ydiotam tantopere solicitatis, ut familiarem et michi amicam ab adholescentia mea quietem solitudinis auferre curetis, publicisque conuentibus et negotiorum implicamentis, michi prorsus insuetis et inexpertis,

---

^a subterfugium Xc   ^b uitare se X

CHAPTER III

How he refused to consent to his election, even after it had been made canonically in the chapter house at Lincoln, unless ordered to do so by his prior.

When his attitude was made known to the Lincoln chapter, all the canons were exceedingly pleased at this proof of the vigour and quality to be expected from their bishop elect. They had previously complained of being unjustly forced and cheated into electing as their head and ruler a man of no natural refinement, whose harshness and austerity they dreaded. Now, having discovered his goodness and wisdom, they speedily elected him once more, and earnestly begged him to accept the episcopal office. A much larger delegation than before was sent with letters from the chapter, the king and the archbishop. All believed that the business was now settled, and that even he could find no pretext for further delay. The envoys therefore came with full powers, confident and assured of success. The holy man had already been forewarned that God would at some time call him to the bishop's office, but, since it grieved him that he could not prevent it finally happening, he was determined to do his best to postpone it for as long as possible.

Having examined the letters and heard what the delegates had to say, he addressed them thus : ' I am very amazed that such intelligent and well-bred people should want a rough and stupid person like myself so much, that you put yourselves to such trouble to drag me from the peace and solitude to which I have been accustomed and enjoyed since my youth, in order to thrust me into public life and difficult problems about

ingerere laboretis. Verum quia, ut uideo,[a] id uobis
dissuaderi prolatis a me rationibus non potest, hoc
sciatis indubitanter quia uestri laboris meta in arbitrio
meo non est constituta. Latere uos non potest [b] quia
homo sum sub aliena potestate constitutus : monachum
me nostis, prioris [1] mei nutibus subiectum, seruande usque
ad mortem obedientie addictum, precepto illius qui in
has terras misit me usquequaque substratum. A meo
michi preposito domus huius custodia credita est,
nec admittit ratio ut ea neglecta alterius cuiuscumque
domus uel ecclesie suscipiam gubernacula. Dominus
quidem Cantuariensis primas et princeps ecclesie Angli-
cane sub pontifice summo est ; attamen in huiusmodi
alius inter nos medius est.[c] A uestre igitur petitionis
huiuscemodi intentione desistendum est, aut itineris
onerosi usque ad Cartusiam fatigatio [d] subeunda. Nam
citra prioris nostri iussionem, oneris tanti sarcinam
humeris meis nullus imponet.' [e]

Capitvlvm IV

Quod legati Cartusiam destinati sunt, ut peterent
concedi Hugonem ecclesie que uocauerat eum ; et
quibus interim exercitiis uacauerit ipse.

Hoc illius accepto responso, cum uerbum eius
cernerent penitus non posse mutari, redeunt illi tam de
infecto pro quo uenerant negotio mesti quam de futuri
pastoris sui [f] uirtutibus insignique constantia, unde non

---

[a] ut uideo / in Deo B
[b] hoc sciatis . . . non potest / om B
[c] in huiusmodi . . . est om X
[d] flagitio B
[e] + Vestre igitur petitionis huius arbiter ille inter nos medius est Xc
[f] om B

which I know absolutely nothing. As, however, I see
that nothing I say can dissuade you, I must tell you that
it does not rest with me to end your labours. You
cannot help knowing that I am not my own master,
and must realize that as a monk I am subject to the
will of my prior,[1] and bound to obey him till I die.
Being subject to him I came to this land by his order.
He committed this house to my charge and it stands to
reason that I cannot desert it in order to rule any other
monastery or church. The lord archbishop of Canterbury is certainly primate and head of the church in
England under the lord pope, but in my case I am not
immediately subject to him but to another. Therefore
you must either give up your intention and petition, or
undertake the long and strenuous journey to Chartreuse,
for no one shall lay this heavy burden upon my shoulders
except my own prior.

Chapter IV

How envoys were sent to Chartreuse, to beg that
Hugh should be surrendered to the church which had
elected him, and in what practices he occupied himself
during the interval.

Having received the answer, and perceiving that
nothing would make him go back on what he had said,
they went away saddened by their failure in the
business they had come about, but greatly pleased at

---

[1] This was Jancelin, prior of the Grande Chartreuse 1180-1233. His
rule was a time of great expansion for the Carthusian Order, which
numbered 47 houses at his death.

exigua iam ceperant documenta, hylares effecti. Verum, ne in *a* multis immoremur, honorabiles sub festinatione diriguntur Cartusiam legati. Quo peruenientes, petitionem Lincolniensis ecclesie, regias preces, monitionem archipresulis scriptis uerbisque allegant. Qui etiam, ut dignum fuit, honorifice sucepti, gratifice exauditi, reditum accelerant, mandatum prioris et fratrum ad Hugonem reportantes quatinus canonicam de cetero domino Cantuariensi obedientiam exhibiturus, in eo quoque ad presens suppliciter obediat ei ; ut, hesitatione omni seu dilatione postposita, suscipiat humiliter quod ei diuinitus constabat imponi iugum Domini.

Dum uero hec agerentur ab illis, Hugo minime indulgebat otiis. Omni namque instantia die noctuque compunctioni cordis ac puritati incumbens *b* assidue orationis, preparabat non cultum pretiosarum uestium ad iactantiam seu uasorum splendorem ad inanem gloriam, set animam suam ad temptationem. Imminentem enim non *c* aliter expectabat status sui mutationem quam nubibus conglobatis suspectam nauta tempestatem aut in longum feriatus miles olim formidatam agminum hostilium congressionem. Cum familiari uero prouisore et nutritore suo Deo de sumptibus sollicite tractabat necessariis ad diem festum quo erat ungendus oleo letitie[1]; de sumptibus, inquam, non quibus uentres reficeret destruendos escis eque destruendis[2] set quibus ingentem sensuum internorum et affectionum *d* multitudinem uirtutibus roboraret non defecturis. Nichil sane ducebat *e* miserabilius quam in die tante sollempnitatis exterius quidem madescere *f* sacramentalis olei

---

a *om* QXc   *b* intendens X
c temptationem imminentem. Non X   *d* affectuum X
e dicebat Xc   *f* madere Xc

the striking proofs they had been given of the firmness of mind and virtues of their future bishop. To cut a long story short, they hurriedly dispatched a distinguished embassy to Chartreuse. These, on their arrival explained the letters containing the petitions and requests of the chapter of Lincoln, the king and the archbishop. As was only right they were honourably entertained and got a favourable answer. They speedily returned, bringing with them an order to Hugh from the prior and brethren, that, as he must in future be bound to render canonical obedience to the Lord Archbishop of Canterbury, so he should humbly obey him in the present instance. He was therefore without further hesitation or delay to accept humbly the yoke which had certainly been laid on him by Christ.

Whilst they were thus employed, Hugh certainly was not idle. With immense concentration, humility and sorrow of heart he prayed assiduously day and night. He prepared no display of costly vestments or of plate from motives of ostentation and vain glory, but steeled his soul against temptation. He foresaw and dreaded the change in his way of life, just as a sailor when he sees heavy clouds gather foretells a storm, or a knight, after a long absence from the battlefield, a new encounter with formidable enemies. With God whose care and providence he had always experienced, he held earnest converse about the expenditure required on the feast-day on which he would be anointed with the oil of gladness.[1] This expenditure was not for perishable food to fill the belly, which is also doomed to destruction,[2] but for the strengthening of the numerous internal faculties and affections with power that lasts for ever. He believed

[1] Ps. 44:8
[2] I Cor. 6:13

pinguedine, interius uero tabescere squalore arentis conscientie. Quam ille *a* miserie immanitatem precauere satagens, ita se agebat in comparandis preparandisque copiis in hoc ipsum necessariis ac si nichil esset quicquid ab ineunte etate studii et laboris circa id negotii expendisset. Versabantur preterea indesinenter ei ante mentis oculos non imminentia deliciarum aut diuitiarum plerisque optata lenocinia, non dignitatis aut potestatis excellentia, non demum obsequentium sedulitas officiosa set amara uite contemplatiue dispendia, quiete et serene meditationis orationisque detrimenta. Nemo, ut plerumque ipse nobis secretius non sine gemitu fatebatur, cotidianam cordis eius exponere sufficeret agoniam qua medullitus angebatur, cum mox perdenda ymaginabatur fructuosa cellule sue otia, pro quibus succederent dispendiosa palatiorum negotia. Metuebat quoque ne inter hec, cedente psalmodia litibus, lectione sacra superfluis rumoribus, cederet pariter uel intima contemplatio tetris fantasmatibus uel interna puritas externis uanitatibus.

Denique cum redisse iam nuntios accepisset, quos certe maluisset tunc primum iter illud arripere, non cessabat fratres in sacro proposito paternis exhortationibus corroborare suumque timorem eorum suffragiis attentius *b* commendare. Viderint iam qui episcopatum tantopere *c* desiderant, qui ad prelationum culmina tot deuiis callium anfractibus aspirant, quonam uirtutum genere, quibus morum diuitiis, quibus stipendiis meritorum uirum istum antecedant. Iste et semetipsum *d* a uulneribus indempnem conseruare et aliena uulnera curare tam perfecte edoctus, pabulo quoque doctrine

---

a + huius X
b corroborare . . . attentius *om* Xc
c tanto tempore Bo
d seipsum QXc

that the most wretched thing which could happen would be to be decayed within with the dryness of an arid heart on the memorable day on which externally he would be wet with the richness of the sacramental oil. He laboured as hard to procure the virtues required to avoid such a terrible plight, as if whatever energy and toil he had devoted to this business from his youth upwards was of no avail. What absorbed him was neither the prospect of luxury and wealth so attractive to most people, nor the advantages of a position of rank and authority, nor even the ready obedience of his servants, but the bitter loss of the contemplative life and of quiet and tranquillity for meditation and prayer. He often told us sadly in private that no one could express the daily agony of heart which assailed him, when he pictured how soon he would lose the fruitful leisure of his cell, and exchange this for the time-wasting occupations of a man of affairs. In the midst of these, he dreaded that litigation would take the place of psalmody and idle gossip that of holy reading, and thus dark imaginations and worldly vanities would destroy his contemplation and purity of soul.

When he learned that the envoys whom he heartily wished had just begun their journey, had in fact returned, he continued to strengthen the vocation of his brethren by his paternal exhortations, and earnestly and fearfully to beg for their prayers. Those who desire to be bishops so much and who try to obtain high ecclesiastical office by underhand and unscrupulous means should consider whether they excel him in goodness, character and the other qualities which deserve such a reward. He who knew so well how to preserve himself from sin and how to cure the sins of others, who was so full of the food of sound doctrine, showed by his behaviour that he

salutaris adeo copiosus, intimo cordis affectu, euidentis-
simo etiam operis *a* effectu loquebatur, 'Non sum medicus et in domo mea non est panis, nolite constituere me
principem populi.'¹ Verum quo altius proprium in
omnibus attendebat uir beatus defectum, eo cumulatius
diuine plenitudinis percipere meruit supplementum,
illud doctoris gentium ex sententia decantans, 'Non
quod sufficientes simus cogitare aliquid ex *b* nobis quasi
ex nobis, set sufficientia nostra ex Deo est.'² Quia uero
non a se set a Deo sibi hanc sufficientiam esse sciebat,
noluit de alieno commodato *c* aut etiam dato insolescere
neque in magnis *d* ambulare, set sese attendens in se,
dona uero Dei que percipiebat supra se, ultimum tota
mentis affectione in ecclesiasticis studebat nuptiis locum
tenere. Is autem qui eum segregauit ex utero matris sue
et uocauit per gratiam suam,³ ut per eum glorificaret
nomen suum in multis gentibus, inuitatione amicabili
eum cogebat superius ascendere,⁴ quo de sufficientia
celitus sibi collata conseruis suis daret cibum in
tempore.⁵

Capitvlvm V

De profectione ipsius ad locum consecrationis sue, et
de regali munificentia ei in sua consecratione prerogata.

Trium itaque mensium elapso tempore a die electionis
sue prime, legatis sepedictis *e* regressis a Cartusia,
uocatione iam tertia compellitur exire de domo sua,

---

a corporis B
b a Xp (*and Vulg.*)
c commodo B ; commendato Xc
d + ac mirabilibus super se Xc
e supradictis Xc

was saying with the deepest sincerity, ' I am no physician, and in my house there is no bread, do not make me ruler over the people.'[1] His deep sense of his own complete unworthiness caused him to merit an immense increase of the divine fullness. Like St Paul he could say, ' Not that we are sufficient of ourselves to think anything of ourselves, but our sufficiency is of God.'[2] Since he realized this sufficiency was not of himself but was given him by God, he refused to take for granted or be presumptuous about what had been lent and indeed bestowed on him by another, but knowing himself and God's supernatural gifts for what they were his whole inclination was to take the lowest place amongst the guests at the marriage feast of the Church. God, however, who had set him apart whilst still in his mother's womb and had called him by His grace that His name might be glorified amongst many peoples,[3] with friendly insistence compelled him to go up higher,[4] so that from the plenitude conferred on him by God he might in due season give meat to his fellow servants.[5]

CHAPTER V

Concerning his journey to the place where he was consecrated and the king's great and unprecedented munificence towards him at his consecration.

When three full months had passed since his election and the envoys so often mentioned before had returned from Chartreuse, he, who had long ago left his country

---

[1] Isa. 3:7   [2] 2 Cor. 3:5
[3] cf. Gal. 1:15   [4] cf. Luke 14:8
[5] cf. Matt. 24:45

qui dudum egressus fuerat de terra et de cognatione sua.[1]
Egreditur ergo ad pontificalis percipiendam consecrationis benedictionem, inde prouenturus [a] ad montem
quem ei Dominus erat monstraturus [b] ; montem utique
egregium, non Libanum set Lincolniensium, ipsum
tamen et Lincolniensium et reuera Libanum ; Libanum,
inquam, non prouincie Fenicis set mistice candidationis,[2]
quem super niuem candidare ueniebat uir indutus
candidis.   Realiter enim niueus habitu, aspectu et uultu,
misterialiter uero uirtutum effectu candidus et nitidis-
simus, Lincolniam dealbauit exemplis, monitis et meritis;
dealbauit et niueis uirorum illustrium cateruis.   In hoc
quoque monte tamquam magnificus pacificusque
Salomon templum gloriosissimum edificaturus, in hoc
sacrificium acceptissimum excelso Domino frequenter
immolaturus tamquam fidelis et obediens Abraham,
in eo tamquam manu fortis uultuque desiderabilis
Dauid sepulchrum tandem famosissimum cunctisque
fideliter [c] uenerantibus saluberrimum erat [d] accepturus.

Pergens uero ad suscipiendum tantorum successuum
culmina humilitatis ima minime deserebat.   Complens
enim opere quod semper uoluebat in corde, uiri consilium sapientis, quanto maior erat,[e] quanto ad maiora
conscendebat, tanto se in omnibus humiliabat.[3]   Solitam
animi grauitatem cum exterioris abiectione cultus
retentans, sedebat equum non faleris adornatum set post
sellam [f] oneratum quibus diurno uteretur tempore seu
nocturno pellium et sagorum inuolucro.   Ita cum suis
clericis, equos sedentibus aureis decoratos sagmatibus,
electus Domini equitabat, illis uaria certantibus arte ei

^a peruenturus Xc   ^b ostensurus X
^c + illud Xc   ^d *om* Xc
^e quanto . . . erat / *om* Xc   ^f postela Xc

and kindred was forced by this third summons to depart from his home.[1] He set out to be consecrated as a bishop, after which he would come to the mountain the Lord would show him, a lofty mountain indeed, not Lebanon but Lincoln, nay rather both Lebanon and Lincoln, not the Lebanon in the land of the Phoenicians, but the Lebanon of mystical whiteness, which the man clad in white raiment had come to cleanse whiter than snow.[2] Outwardly, he was white in habit, appearance and countenance, inwardly he was much more so by his virtue, and he cleansed Lincoln by his teaching, example and holiness, by the fame of a group of illustrious men. On this mount like the magnificent and peace-loving Solomon he was to build a splendid temple, where like the faithful and obedient Abraham he would often offer sacrifice most acceptable to almighty God. There too like the valiant and comely David, he was to find a tomb which would finally be renowned and bring benefits to all the faithful who visited it.

Although he was on his way to receive the highest of the ecclesiastical orders, his utter humility remained unchanged. He acted on the advice of the sage, which was always in his thoughts, that the greater a man was and the higher he rose, the greater should be his humility.[3] Maintaining his usual seriousness and the external signs of the poverty of his order, his horse had no ornamental bridle or breastplate and had on its back behind the saddle, the roll of skins and rough blankets which he used during the day and night. Thus, the elect of God rode accompanied by his clerks whose

[1] cf. Gen. 12:1
[2] *Glossa Ordinaria* in Ps. 91:13 : *Libanus candidatio interpretatur.*
[3] cf. Ecclus. 3:20

suam sarcinulam auferre et ferendam suis sagmariis imponere. Verum cum ab eo neque seriis, ut hoc permitteret, neque ioco extorqueri potuisset, cauebat namque ante gradus sublimioris conscensum obseruationis pristine usum omittere quantulumcumque uel mutare, illi animo seculari confundebantur rubore uehementi in humilitate spiritualis uiri.[a]

Cum uero Wintoniensium appropinquaret[b] ciuitati, ubi et regia ei familia et ciuium occursura erat frequentia, quidam ex ipsis clericis, uerecundiam non ferens cordis sui uani, amputatis clam loris quibus selle astringebatur sarcinula memorata, predo efficitur improuisus, spolians nescientem onere quod ferebat. Perueniens tandem Londonias,[c] in festo die beati Euangeliste Matthei benedictione consecratus pontificali,[1] ordini apostolico ad euangelizandum pauperibus dignissime sociatur. Rex autem congratulans uoti sui circa illius promotionem se compotem effectum, gaudio gestiebat infinito. Contulit quoque ei liberalitate munificentissima uasa quedam aurea multaque argentea, uaria etiam in usus quoque[d] necessarios utensilia, adiciens in sumptus celebrande sollempnitatis uniuersa copiose impendia.

CAPITVLVM VI

De ipsius incathedratione.[e] Et de olore[f] quasi in prognosticalis euentus indicium ei mirabiliter datum[g] Meneuensis archidiaconi relatio.

---

[a] illi . . . uiri / om X
[b] appropinquarent Xc
[c] Londoniis Q
[d] quosque Q ; om Xc
[e] + apud Lincolniam X
[f] + seu cigno X
[g] dato X

horses had gold-embroidered saddle bags, and who tried to invent pretexts to transfer his bundle to one of their sumpter horses. Permission could not be extorted from him, either by serious requests or jests, for he had scruples about neglecting or making the least change in his former way of life before his elevation to a higher order. The humility of this spiritual man put their wordliness to the blush.

When they were approaching the city of Winchester, where they would be met by the king's household and a great throng of citizens, one of the clerks, whose vanity made him bold, secretly cut the strap by which the bundle I have already mentioned was fastened to the saddle, and thus robbed him without his knowledge of the burden which he had been carrying. At length they reached London, and there on St Matthew's day,[1] he was consecrated bishop, and most fittingly raised to the apostolic order to preach the gospel to the poor. The king displayed great joy and satisfaction at having fulfilled his vow in regard to his promotion. He gave him out of his royal bounty vessels of gold, and many different silver ones of which he stood in need. In addition he defrayed the immense cost of the consecration ceremony.

CHAPTER VI

Concerning his enthronement, and the archdeacon of St Davids' account of the swan which had apparently received by some wonderful means a prophetic awareness of his coming.

---

[1] On 21 September, 1186, in the Infirmary chapel of St Katherine at Westminster Abbey. As bishop-elect St Hugh had taken part in the Council of Marlborough on 14 September.

Incathedratus autem in ecclesia sua, Cantuariensi archidiacono sollempne ex more donarium postulanti, ita respondisse dinoscitur : ' Quantum,' inquit, ' dedi pro mitra, tantum nec amplius pro cathedra dabo.' [1] Suggerente uero procuratore domus sue quem sibi rex prouiderat oportere ex dammulis in saltu suo inclusis aliquantas capi ad sollempne conuiuium instaurandum, nec fas esse plures quam iussisset ipse comprehendi ; ' Trecente,' inquit, ' capiantur ; nec, si uideritis expedire, numero huic adicere dubitetis.' Quod ab eo, iuxta cordis sui magnificentiam simpliciter prolatum, regi et curialibus quibus sermo innotuit in iocundum uersum est prouerbium. Celebrantibus igitur cunctis apud Lincolniam in summa cordis letitia diem festum pro aduentu celitus sibi destinati rectoris,[a] Christi benignitas, haut longe a ciuitate ipsa, signo euidenti ualdeque memorabili ipsius uisa est primitiis allusisse. Quod a Meneuense archidiacono Girardo, inter alia quedam uiri Dei preconia litteris exaratum, ipsius uerbis uidetur exprimendum. Scribit itaque [b] de hoc in hec uerba : [2]

'Vt autem ad Lincolniensem reuertamur, illud de ipso, quod quasi in signum aliquod et pronosticalis euentus indicium absque dubio datum uidetur, sub silentio quidem pretereundum [c] non putaui. Eo namque die uel circiter illum proximo quo apud Lincolniam primo susceptus fuit Hugo episcopus et incathedratus, apud manerium ipsius, quasi per octo milliaria ab urbe Lincolniensi distans, iuxta Stowam, siluis et stagnis delectabiliter obsitum, olor nouus et numquam antea ibi uisus aduolauit. Qui infra paucos dies, cignos quos ibidem repperit plures mole sue magnitudinis omnes oppressit

---

[a] X add episode from Canonization Report : Egressus es in salutem populi tui, etc.

[b] scribitur supra Xc   [c] pretermittendum Xc

After his enthronement in his cathedral, the arch-deacon of Canterbury demanded the usual gift for the ceremony, to which he is reported to have replied, ' I will give for my enthronement only what I gave for my mitre, and no more.'[1]   When the major-domo whom the king had furnished him with suggested that some of the does in his park should be taken for the great banquet, but that it would be wrong to kill more than he had ordered, he answered ' Take 300 and don't scruple to increase the number if it seems good to you.'   The king and courtiers having heard of what his natural generosity and simplicity of heart had prompted him to say, it became a stock joke.   The feast day was kept at Lincoln by every-one with heart-felt joy at the arrival of the pastor sent to them by God.   Just after his coming, a manifest and very remarkable proof of Christ's favour towards him was given in the neighbourhood of the city.   As this has already been described by Gerald, archdeacon of St Davids', amongst certain other outstanding events connected with the saint, it seems best to quote his words. Here is his account.[2]

' To return to the bishop of Lincoln, I do not think I should omit an incident which undoubtedly was intended to be a sign and portent of what his coming implied. On the very day of Hugh's enthronement, or thereabouts, as bishop of Lincoln, at his manor near Stow, which is about 8 miles from the city of Lincoln, a delightful spot

---

[1] The enthronement took place on 29 September. The customary present was a horse or a cow (Higden, *Polychronicon*, VIII, 183) ; but the 3rd Lateran Council (1179) had forbidden that presents should be exacted on these occasions. This ruling was repeated by the Council of Westminster in 1200.

[2] This citation is from Giraldus, *Vita S. Remigii* (VII, 73-76), written during St Hugh's lifetime. The account is slightly modified in his *Vita S. Hugonis* (*ibid.*, 109).

et interemit, uno tantum feminei sexus ad societatis solatium, non fecunditatis augmentum, reseruato. Erat enim tanto fere digno robustior quanto cignus ansere maior, cigno tamen in omnibus et precipue in colore et candore simillimus, preter quantitatem etiam *a* hoc distante, quod tumorem in rostro atque nigredinem more cignorum non preferebat ; quinimmo locum eumdem rostri planum, croceoque decenter colore, una cum capite et colli parte superiore distinctum habebat.

'Auis autem hec regia, et tam qualitate quam quantitate perspicua, in primo ad locum illum presulis aduentu quasi sponte et absque difficultate domestica facta, ad ipsum in camera sua propter admirationem est adducta. Que statim a manu eius panem sumens et comedens eique *b* familiariter adherens, omnem ut uidebatur siluestrem interim exuta naturam, nec eius attactus *c* nec adstantium undique turbarum et intuentium accessus siue tumultus abhorrebat. Consueuerat etiam interdum, cum ab episcopo pascebatur,*d* capud cum colli longitudine tota in manicam ipsius largam et peramplam inque sinum interiorem auis extendere, ibique aliquamdiu, cum sollicitudine quodammodo *e* domino suo congratulans atque preludens, tamquam aliquid queritando musitare. Item, sicut asserebant ministri et custodes manerii, contra presulis aduentum ad locum illum, cum de more aliquamdiu abfuisset, tribus diebus uel quatuor solebat se solito alacrius auis agitare, uolitando uidelicet *f* in amnis superficie et aquas alis uerberando altaque uoce clamando ; interdum etiam a stagno exeundo, nunc ad aulam nunc etiam ad portam ulteriorem, tamquam aduenienti *g*

---

a + in X *b* + quam cg (*i.e. Giraldus*) *c* attractus g
d pasceretur X *e* quadam modo g ; quadam *only* X
f uolando scilicet Xc *g* uenienti QXc

surrounded by woods and lakes, a swan suddenly
arrived which had never been seen there before. In a
few days, by reason of its weight and size, it had fought
and killed all the other swans there, except for one female
which it spared for company and not for breeding
purposes. It was about as much larger than a swan as a
swan is than a goose, but in everything else, especially in
its colour and whiteness, it closely resembled a swan,
except that in addition to its size it did not have the
usual swelling and black streak on its beak. Instead,
that part of its beak was flat and bright yellow in colour,
as were also its head and the upper part of its neck.
This royal bird of unusual appearance and size, the first
time the bishop came to the place, suddenly became
completely tame. It let itself be captured without any
difficulty and was brought to the bishop for him to
admire. It immediately let him feed it, and remained
with him as a pet, and for the time being apparently lost
its wildness, and did not shun his attentions. It even
seemed indifferent to the noise made by the crowds
everywhere and the mob of spectators who constantly
came and went. When the bishop fed it, the bird
used to thrust its long neck up his wide and ample
sleeve, so that its head lay on its inner fold, and for a little
while would remain there, hissing gently, as if it were
talking fondly and happily to its master, and seeking
something from him. The officials and bailiffs in charge
of the manor, moreover, declared that whenever the
bishop returned after one of his usual absences, for three
or four days beforehand, the bird displayed more excite-
ment than was customary with it. It flew over the
surface of the river, beating the water with its wings, and
giving vent to loud cries. From time to time it left the
pond, and hastily strode either to the hall or to the gate,

domino obuiam pergens, magnis passibus deambulabat.
Credibile satis est quod imminente apparatu et instante
seruorum frequentia maiore atque discursu,*a* cum
subtilis sint et aeree uolucres nature, a quarum etiam
gestibus pronostica temporum multa sumuntur,*b*
etiam *c* is ex eadem forsitan natura auis hec perpendere
potuit. Mirum hoc etiam quod nemini preterquam
episcopo soli se familiarem uel ex toto tractabilem
exhibebat, quin potius, astans domino, ab aliorum
eumdem accessu, sicut aliquotiens cum admiratione
conspexi,*d* clamando, alis et rostro *e* minando uoceque
altissona iuxta nature sue modulos crocitando, defendere
solet, *f* tamquam se propriam eius *g* demonstrans
eique soli in signum fuisse transmissam manifeste
declarans.

' Non enim misterio carere potuit quod auis candida,
imminentis interitus *h* cantu nuntia, uiro innocenti, pio
ac puro mortisque minas, quia sancti mortem habent in
desiderio et uitam in patientia, nil formidanti, diuino
tamquam oraculo destinata transmittitur.*j* Quemadmodum enim auis ista candore spectabilis, mortis
discrimina docet non dolenda, et imminente letali *k*
articulo, tamquam de necessitate uirtutem faciens,
funebria fata canendo contempnit ; sic uiri uirtutum
meritis candidati, ab erumpnis huius seculi leti discedunt,
solumque Deum fontem *l* uiuum sitientes, a corpore
mortis huius liberari dissoluique cupiunt et esse cum
Christo. ' [1]

---

a decursu B   *b* noscuntur X
c et g   *d* conspeximus X
e rostris X   *f* solebat Xcp
g esse c ; eius esse gvp
h exterius c ; imminentis interitus / imminens mortis periculum X
j transmissa est Xc   *k* mortis Xc
l fortem v (*and Vulg.*)

as if going to meet its master on his arrival. It is quite conceivable that, as the fowls of the air are so sensitive because their natures contain so large an element of air and future events have frequently been predicted owing to their behaviour, that this bird may have known this instinctively from the preparations and bustle of the servants. Curiously enough, however, it was friendly and tame with no one but the bishop, and indeed, as I have sometimes seen myself, kept everyone else away from its master when it was with him, by hissing at them and threatening them with its wings and beak and emitting loud croaks as is the habit with swans. It seemed determined to make it completely clear that it belonged only to him, and was a symbol imparted to the saint alone.

'It must have had some hidden meaning that the white bird whose song heralds its own approaching death should have been sent as a messenger from God, to announce the death of this pure and holy man who did not fear its approach, for the saints desire death and merely endure life. Thus, this bird of brilliant whiteness teaches us that the pangs of death should be no cause for grief, and at the time of its death, as if making a virtue of necessity, shows its contempt for death by singing. In the same way, men whose virtues are of a crystalline purity, are happy to leave the toils of this world. Thirsting only for God, the fountain of living waters, they desire to be freed from the body of this death, and to be dissolved and to be with Christ.' [1]

[1] cf. Ps. 41:3 ; Rom. 7:24 ; Phil. 1:23

Capitvlvm VII

De ipsa aue plenior narratio.

Hec sane prefatus uir, in hac adhuc luce posito uiro Dei, ueraci de hiis stilo exarauit. Et [a] eo quidem tempore satis innotuerat isto Hugonem spiritu duci, istis eum [b] affectibus agi, ut esset ei mors in desiderio et uita in patientia pre amore fontis uite. Hoc tota ipsius uita quadam operum lingua fatebatur ; hoc tandem, imminente iam letali articulo, etiam corporis lingua solito ipse manifestius quasi cigneo quodam modulamine testabatur ; hoc etiam subiecta eius gestorum series, ab ipso exordio usque ad terminum executionis credite sibi ecclesiastice sollicitudinis, si recte perpendatur, continua inuenitur assertione preconari. Verum antequam ulterius progrediatur oratio, opere pretium uidetur de premissa plenius aue quedam referre ; ex quibus liqueat euidentius, non solum in solatium uite presentis seu in testimonium intime puritatis, set etiam diuinitus eam sibi fuisse transmissam in presagium quoddam tandem imminentis leti temporalis.

Experti quidem nouimus hominem [c] prorsus neminem set neque canem uel aliud quodlibet animal sub ipsius auis presentia, episcopo uigilanti siue dormienti, absque uehementi et inexorabili [d] eius impugnatione, propius assistere uel iuxta eum incedere [e] potuisse. Erat nobis frequenter,[f] quiescente episcopo, illius non parum molesta infestatio. Cum enim rei cuiuscumque ratio secus lectum dormientis transitum suaderet, illius ex-

---

[a] *om* B
[b] istis eum / istisque Xc
[c] hominum Xc
[d] intolerabili X
[e] accedere X
[f] sepius Xc

Chapter VII

A fuller account of this bird.

Whilst the holy man was still on earth the author I
have already cited gave a veracious account of this
matter. It was even then common knowledge that Hugh
under the guidance of the spirit of God, and because of
his devotion to the fountain of life already longed for
death and looked on life merely as something to be
endured. During his lifetime he confessed this by deeds
that spoke clearer than words, and finally at the approach
of death, manifested it even more clearly than had been
customary with him by singing as swans do. Indeed,
all his actions from the beginning until the termination
of the pastoral office committed to him, are a continuous
and eloquent proclamation of this. Before I go on, however, it seems to me well worth while to give a fuller
account of this bird, from which it will become abundantly clear that God sent it to him not merely for his
consolation in this present life, and as a proof of his
absolute purity of heart, but also that it might in the
end prophesy that his departure from this life would
shortly take place.

We know from experience that no man, dog or any
other animal could walk beside or be near the bishop,
whether he was asleep or awake, when this bird was
there, without being fiercely attacked by it. I myself
was often violently assaulted by it when the bishop was
resting. When anyone was obliged for any reason to pass
by his bed when he was sleeping, he could not pass
unnoticed, for it immediately got up to prevent him from
passing by its vigorous attacks. If it was afraid that it
might itself be overcome, it immediately emitted such

cubias nullus poterat eludere quin mox insurgens pugnaci insultu obsisteret transeunti. Que, si uiribus se opprimi forte timebat, uocibus immensi clamoris protinus indulgebat. Ita, cum tumultum fieri pausantis reuerentia prohiberet, utilitas omittebatur destinati itineris. Nec obsequiis uero, ut ita loquar, nec blanditiis cuiusquam aliquatenus flectebatur, quin zelo unius hominis ceteros hoc modo uniuersaliter insequeretur.

Quandoque, absente episcopo, ad ripam stagni cui innatabat consueuerat accedere, ibique, ministrante loci ipsius edituo, annonam percipere. Ad eum itaque, fame aliquotiens stimulante, familiarius ultroque cibanda accedebat ; cibata uero et satiata confestim abscedebat. Res mira ! Quem anno plerumque integro uel etiam prolixiori tempore, quasi bene cognitum sepius adierat, a domini tandem presentis accessu [a] seruientem suumque alumpnum non mitius [b] ceteris quos antea numquam uiderat, propellebat. Si quando episcopus per biennium ferme suum, ut interdum contingebat, ad locum illum distulisset accessum, domino tandem aduenienti [c] cum tanta congratulatione occurrebat, ut ex dilato eius aspectu non illius oblitam set ipsius potius desiderio fatigatam se fuisse miris quibusdam gestibus et sonoris uocibus indicaret. Asserebant non tantum custodes illius loci set etiam uicini quidam quia frequenter, nemine in partibus illis episcopi suspicante aduentum, ex auis huius plausu gestuque insolito illum citius affuturum presciuerunt. Cuius iam redas et preambulos dum foribus cerneret imminere, mox gurgite derelicto quem incolebat, aule penetralia citato gressu subintrabat. Cum uero introgressa spectantium turmis cingeretur, notata

[a] ad domini accessum Xc
[b] minus X
[c] aduentanti Xc

loud sounds, and thus, since the visitor's consideration for
the sleeper forbade noise, he generally abandoned his
journey no matter how necessary it was. No attentions,
I might say, or caresses ever shook its allegiance in the
least from this one particular person ; rather its
exclusive devotion made it attack everyone else in-
discriminately.

Whenever the bishop was away, it used to come to
the bank of the pond on which it was swimming and
there receive its food from a servant of the manor.
Hunger sometimes drove it to come quite near to him
to be fed, but immediately it had eaten enough it went
away. What was remarkable was that it prevented the
servant, whom it knew well and had gone to for a full
year or more, from approaching the bishop just as
fiercely as it did the others whom it had never seen. If,
as sometimes happened, the bishop did not visit that spot
for nearly two years, it met its master when he did arrive
with such great manifestations of joy, and showed by its
actions and the sounds it made, not only that it had not
forgotten him during his long absence, but had been sick
for his home-coming. The keepers of the manor and the
people of the neighbourhood used often to say that, when
no one in the district expected the bishop, they realised
from the unusual behaviour of the bird and the noise it
made that he would soon be arriving. When it saw that
the waggons and servants he had sent in advance were
almost at the door, it immediately left the water where it
lived and hurried into the hall. Although on entering
it was surrounded by crowds of onlookers, when at last
it heard the voice of its master as he entered, it gave a
very loud cry, and went to meet and greet him. It
accompanied him along the cloister to the threshold of
his private room, walking up the steps, and by the

demum uoce introeuntis patroni, mox et ipsa in clamorem
altissime uocis insurgebat ; occurrensque et quasi
salutans uenientem, usque in solarium camere ulterioris
prosequebatur, per claustrum quod interiacet, per gradus
etiam sublimes progredientem, alarum plausu ac modu-
late uocis sonitu gaudium insinuans quo nimium gestiebat. Perueniens autem cum eo ad locum sessioni eius
paratum, inde nusquam nisi uiolenter eiecta recedebat.
Pascebatur a manu ipsius pane copioso, in digiti unius
longitudinem grossitiemque inciso. Annis igitur ter-
quinis modico minus hanc uniformiter consuetudinem
retentabat.

Cum uero ad locum ipsum, circa Pascha proximum
ante suum *a* ex hac luce transitum, aduentu scilicet
postremo episcopus accessisset, non solum ei solitum non
exhibuit occursum set neque ad illum minari aut a
uiuario cui innatabat educi adquieuit. In ipsis autem
aquis uelud mestum gerens aut morbidum aspectum,
nichil quolibet gestu alacritatis preferebat. Mirantibus
ad hoc omnibus qui aderant, tandem, precipiente
episcopo ut introduceretur *b* uel inuita, triduo a
plurimis frustra insudatur. Capitur uero ad postremum
in carecto remotiori ubi fugiens insequentes latitabat.
Perducta uero ad episcopum, capite pendulo ac uelud
egris per omnia gestibus, mestam pretendebat ymaginem.
Cuius rei nouitas tunc quidem stupori fuit intuentibus.
Verum a loco ipso celerius abscedente episcopo, et post
sexti mensis a tempore illo excursum uiam uniuerse
carnis ingresso nec ab amica sibi uolucre ulterius uiso,
satis rei euentum considerantibus patuit quid gestus hic
lugubris protenderit, *c* quo adeo mesta illud uale ultimum
domino suo fecit. Permansit autem ibidem multis
temporibus postea.

---

a ante suum; *om* B   *b* introducetur B ; educeretur Xc
c pretenderit X ; protenderet c

beating of its wings, and by the gentle sounds it made, showed the excessive joy it felt. Having come with him to the place which had been made ready for him to rest, it never left him unless it was forcibly removed. He fed it from his hand with big fingers of bread. For almost fifteen years it acted habitually in this way.

When the bishop visited that place the last Easter before his departure from this earth, not only did it not come to meet him as usual, but it refused to be chased from the pond on which it was swimming in order to be brought to him. To the surprise of everyone, there it remained on the water looking depressed and ill, and its movements were languid. Finally, the bishop ordered that it should be brought to him, whether it wished it or not. For three days, a large number of people tried hard to do so, but their efforts were fruitless. It was at last captured amongst the rushes in a very remote part of the pond where it had taken refuge from its would-be captors. When it was brought to the bishop, with its hanging head and general air of wretchedness it seemed the very picture of grief, which strange occurrence amazed all who saw it. The bishop's visit was exceedingly short, and just six months afterwards he had gone the way of all flesh, and so was never seen again by his friend the bird. Those who thought about the matter, then realized that its melancholy air meant that it was very sadly taking leave of its master for the last time. It survived him however for a long time.

CAPITVLVM VIII

De sollicita eius diligentia super uirorum proborum
adquisitione quibus suam ornaret ecclesiam ; et de
magistris Roberto Bedefordense et Rogero Roluestonense
quos ei archiepiscopus legauit.ᵃ

Hiis in hunc modum prelibatis de signo quod uniuersi
mirantur uiro Domini exhibito per auem famosissimam,
ad alia quoque meritorum insignia, fidelibus uel ex parte
prout possumus intimanda, opitulante gratia Domini
nostri Ihesu Christi accedamus. Ac inprimis quantum
studii quantumque impenderit sollicitudinis ut ecclesiam
sibi commissam uiris adornaret illustribus uideretur ᵇ
commemoratione dignissimum.   Perpendens quippe
altiusque considerans quia absque uirorum proborum
adiutorio nec populo nec clero quem regebat conuenienter prodesse, nec quibusque ᶜ iustitiam ecclesiastice
iurisdictionis expetentibus ᵈ sufficeret competenter adesse,
uiros sapientia et scientia preditos et, quod pluris est, in
timore Domini probatissimos, suo instantius satagebat
lateri sociare.   Horum siquidem et consiliis fretus et
comitatus auxiliis, munus ᵉ suscepti regiminis strenuissime
adimplebat.   Hiis denique Lincolniensem ecclesiam
cunctis per orbem uniuersum ecclesiis gloriosius copio-
siusque illustrabat.   Hiis enim,ᶠ cum uacare cepissent,
prebendas seu et alia beneficia conferebat, hos uariis
dignitatibus, singulis quoque ecclesiasticis functionibus
preficiebat ; huiusmodi homines, non solum in toto orbe
Anglicano, immo et in ceteris ᵍ nationibus scholisque
transmarinis omni studio inuestigatos, ecclesie sue gremio
inserebat.

ᵃ delegauit X   ᵇ uidetur Qc   ᶜ cuilibet Xc
ᵈ expetenti sufficiebat X   ᵉ minus B   ᶠ etiam Q ; uero X ; *om* c
ᵍ exteris Qc ; extraneis X

Chapter VIII

His anxiety to acquire distinguished men for the honour of his church, and how the archbishop made over to him Master Robert of Bedford and Master Roger de Rolleston.

Having now described the affection displayed to the saint by the wondrous bird which so much impressed everyone, we must now with the assistance of our Lord Jesus Christ proceed to the best of our ability to impart to the faithful other manifestations of his holiness. Firstly, it seems most important to record the great zeal and anxiety he showed to secure distinguished men to raise the reputation of the church committed to his care. He thought, and indeed was completely convinced that without the assistance of highly trained men, he could not really be of much use to the clergy and people under his authority, and would be unable to do justice to any litigants in the ecclesiastical courts. He therefore worked hard to have as his assistants men well known for their wisdom and learning, and most essential of all, renowned for their fear of God, and with the advice and help of such companions he carried out the exacting duties of his office. Such men gave the church of Lincoln a greater fame and reputation than that of any other in the whole world, and on them he conferred prebends and benefices whenever they fell vacant, and promoted to different ecclesiastical dignities and offices. He sought for them throughout England and even in other countries and the schools on the continent, and made them members of his cathedral chapter.

Ad uenerabilem quoque metropolitanum suum superius *a* nominatum accedens, hiis eum *b* alloquitur, ' Nouit,' inquiens, ' pater uenerande, discretio uestra quantum expediat *c* non solum anime mee, non solum commisse indigno michi ecclesie, quin potius precipue uobis, deinde uniuerse pariter religioni sancte quatinus in officio michi credito non prorsus me inutilem studeam exhibere. Gratias ago bonorum omnium auctori Deo quia *d* in hoc ipsum ex munere suo uelle quidem adiacet michi ; ceterum implere *e* quod uelle merui, quam non sciam, quam non sufficiam per meipsum, ipse *f* melius nostis. Nec solum quidem ad hoc michi et scire et posse minus suppetit, uerum etiam a quibus suppleri congruentius possit meus in hac parte defectus non satis agnoui. Aduena quidem *g* homo sum : indigenas terre huius quo minus noui, eo imperfectius quibus meritorum suffragiis, quibus studiorum prepolleant experimentis, compertum habeo. Vobis ulteriorem *h* istius rei notitiam multiplex comparauit experientia. Vos inter eos nutriti, uos eis tempore longo prelati, eos, ut uulgo dicitur, ' intus et in cute' nouistis. Non igitur meo tantum quin uestro potius discrimini prospicientes, qui tam inscium promouere non timuistis ad opus hoc arduum, tales michi ex hiis qui uestro diutius lateri adherendo probabiles se in omnibus, uestro adprime informati exemplo demonstrarunt, committite *j* adiutores quos in partem sollicitudinis iniuncte securus *k* ualeam admittere, qui mecum onus cure pastoralis laudabiliter ualeant supportare.'

a sepius Xc	*b* + uerbis Xo
c expediebat B	*d* qui B
e om B	*f* per meipsum/*om* X ; ipse / ipsi o
g quippe QXc	*h* uberiorem Xc
j donate Xc	*k* inite securius Xc

Going to his archbishop whom I have already mentioned, he spoke to him as follows : ' A man of your experience must be well aware how important it is for the welfare not only of my own soul and that of the church committed to my charge in spite of my lack of fitness, but most of all for your own and that of holy Church that I should show myself not altogether unprofitable in my present office.   I thank God the author of all good things that he has given me this desire ; but you yourself know that I have neither the knowledge nor the ability to do what I wish.   Not only is it beyond my skill and experience, but I do not know who are the best men to remedy my deficiencies.   Being a foreigner, I do not know the inhabitants of this country sufficiently well to select those who have the qualities and gifts to assist me.   Long experience should enable you to deal with this problem.   You have grown up among them and been their superior for a considerable period and, to quote the proverb, ' know them through and through '. Consider therefore not so much myself but the risk you have incurred in daring to promote a completely inexperienced person to a very responsible post, and give me as my assistants some of the men who have been with you for a long period and have been influenced by your example, and been tested and found wanting in nothing. With such men I could confidently share my burdens, since they would be admirably fitted to assist me in my episcopal duties.'

Hiis archiepiscopus auditis non modice gratulatur. Ex una quippe uiri sancti petitione multa in eo [a] animi bona euidentius perspiciebat. Videbat primo quante istud humilitatis esset ut uir tantus tam de se infima sentiret, ut solus ipse eo se honore censeret indignum, quo diuino simul et humano probaretur iudicio esse dignissimus. Mirabatur contra usum humane infelicitatis hominem ex humili ad summa repente prouectum, plus humilitate quam dignitate, plus mansuetudine quam dominatione creuisse. Videbat quantum zelaret subditorum salutem, ad cuius procurationem tantopere expetebat bonorum opitulationem. Intuebatur quante sibi puritatis conscius, quanta beniuolentia in primatem suum plenus, quanta etiam prudentia per cuncta esset preditus qui eos sibi domesticos collaterales primosque fieri [b] consiliarios optasset quos hiisdem locis suus [c] habuisset metropolitanus.

Duos igitur ex hiis qui sibi adheserant ei delegauit, magistros [d] Robertum Bedefordensem [1] et Rogerum Roluestonensem,[2] quorum uterque in toto totius clero Anglie distinctis gratiarum prerogatiuis insignissime uisus est enituisse. Equidem de priore Roberto una erat omnium indubitata [e] sententia : quod in numero clericorum nullus eum zelo iustitie aut ingenii uiuacis acumine uidebatur anteire. Certabat in eius pectore cum puritate conscientie inundantis torrens doctrine, ut in gemino bono hoc emulari potius crederetur discipulum quem diligebat Ihesus quam magistrorum

---

[a] + signa X
[b] sibi Xc
[c] suis QXc
[d] magistrum scilicet Xc
[e] *om* Xc

On hearing this, the archbishop was exceedingly pleased, for this one request enabled him to see the great holiness of the saint. He realized first of all the utter humility which caused such a man to think so meanly of himself that he alone regarded himself as unfit for a position for which by God's judgment and any human estimation he was pre-eminently fitted. He was amazed that he showed none of the usual human weakness in men raised from a humble to a great position, and was neither arrogant or presumptuous, but more humble and diffident than ever. He saw how much he cared for the welfare of his flock, for whose benefit he was seeking able assistants. He realized his transparent sincerity, his obvious goodwill towards his archbishop, and the great discretion he showed in everything, but especially in the wish to have as members of his household, assistants and chief councillors, those who held the same position with his metropolitan.

Baldwin therefore assigned to him two of his own clerks, master Robert of Bedford [1] and master Roger of Rolleston,[2] both of whom were conspicuous amongst all the English clergy for their outstanding qualities. There was indeed only one opinion about the former, Robert, and this was that amongst the whole clerical order none excelled him in his passion for righteousness or in his acuteness of intelligence. His immense theological knowledge was equalled by his purity of conscience, and in these twin virtues he deserved comparison with

---

[1] He became precentor of Lincoln in 1188 ; acting for St Hugh he settled a dispute between Harrold Priory and Missenden Abbey (cf. *Bedford Hist. Rec. Soc.* xvii, 57).

[2] Roger of Rolleston, archdeacon of Leicester *c.* 1189, was dean of Lincoln from *c.* 1195 till his death in 1223. He was greatly trusted by St Hugh (see *infra* V, xvi) and was employed by popes as a judge delegate. On St Hugh's deathbed he took his place as arbitrator in the final settlement of the Canterbury case.

quempiam temporis istius. Cuius reuera diutius uita mundus iste immundus frui indignus fuit. Vnde ab eius ceno citius preripitur, et tamquam lilium fragrantissimum, cum illibato uirginei floris candore morte beatus immatura, in celestis amenitatem feliciter paradisi transplantatur.

Posterioris, uidelicet Rogeri, eo interim parcius laudes presens loquitur stilus quo eas immensius et clerus attollit et populus. Est enim adhuc, et extet utinam in euum longissimum, ecclesie Lincolniensis decanus, uir incomparande moderationis, liberalitatis et prudentie secularis.[a] Elemosinarum saltem illius et deuotionis preconium lectori minime furaremur [b] nisi Scripture precipienti contraire timeremus : 'Ne laudaueris' inquit, 'hominem in uita sua.'[1]

Capitvlvm IX

Quod Hugo nouus adhuc pontifex nulli contra iustitiam detulerit potestati ; et quod summum regis forestarium excommunicauerit, primamque post episcopatum regis petitionem super collatione cuiusdam prebende minime exaudierit.

Hiis aliisque lateri suo uiris eximiis sollicite adherentibus, pontifex nouus totius subito terre sibi subdite faciem uisus est innouasse. Loquebatur cum fiducia uerbum Dei,[2] operabatur cum instantia que legis erant Domini,[c] adimplens illud beati Iacobi : 'Sic loquimini et sic facite quasi per legem libertatis incipientes iudicari.'[3] Quia uero iuxta Scripturam alterius loci, 'Vbi

---

[a] singularis Xc
[b] + eximius c ; eximius intimaremus X
[c] que legis Dei erant X

the disciple whom Jesus loved rather than with any master of this age. He was snatched away early from the snares of a world unworthy to have him for long and by a happy and early death, like a fragrant lily with the whiteness of its virgin bloom still intact, was trans- planted into the delights of the celestial paradise.

Of the latter, Roger, my pen is now not lavish in its praises because of the general commendation of both clergy and people. He is at present, and I hope will be for a very long time, dean of Lincoln, a man of unusual tact, generosity and worldly wisdom. I would not defraud my reader of a eulogy on his almsgiving and piety, if I were not afraid of disobeying the scriptural precept ' Do not praise a man during his lifetime '.[1]

CHAPTER IX

How Hugh, still in the early days of his episcopate, would obey no authority against his conscience, and how he excommunicated the king's chief forester, and refused the first request made to him by the king after his consecration in regard to the collation of a prebend.

With these and other gifted men as his counsellors and members of his household the new bishop immedi- ately transformed his diocese. He preached the word of God with vigour,[2] and zealously carried out his command- ments in accordance with the words of St James : ' So speak ye and so do as they which shall be judged by the law of liberty.' [3]   Indeed following another text from the scriptures ' Where the spirit of the Lord is there is

---

[1] Ecclus. 11:30   [2] cf. Acts 4:31   [3] Jas. 2:12

Spiritus Dei, ibi et libertas,'[1] peccantes libere increpabat, nullis contra iustitiam potestatibus deferebat.

Vnde contigit ut in ipsis promotionis sue auspiciis, dum in sublimes quasdam regni potestates ecclesiasticam districtius exequitur *a* cohercionem, ipsum quoque non mediocriter uisus sit *b* offendisse regem. Est enim inter alias abusionum pestes prima in regno Anglorum tyrannidis forestariorum, pestis uidelicet prouinciales depopulans. Huic uiolentia pro lege est, rapina in laude, equitas execrabilis, innocentia reatus. Huius immanitatem mali nulla conditio, gradus nullus, nec quisquam, ut totum breuiter exprimamus, rege inferior euasit indempnis, quem illius iniuriosa iurisdictio non sepe temptasset elidere. Hac cum pernicie primus Hugoni congressus fuit ; hec illi prima et prelii causa et materia fuit *c* triumphi. Hec eum ancipitem gladium Spiritus exerere *d* primitus coegit. Cum enim more solito ut in ceteros, ita et in suos homines contra ecclesie sue libertates *e* forestarii debachari cepissent, eo usque res tandem processit ut summum regis forestarium nomine Galfridum[2] excommunicationis uinculo innodaret. Quo rex comperto uehementem *f* exarsit in iram.

Contigit interea unam ex prebendis ecclesie Lincolniensis, decessu canonici qui eam possederat uacantem, nouum expectare dispensatorem. Hoc aulici audito regem concito exorant quatinus uni eorum ipsam ab episcopo conferri litteratorie deprecetur. Arbitrantur se obsequium etiam in hoc prestare uiro[3] cui dedissent occasionem motam aduersus se indignationem regiam utcunque mitigandi. Nec cunctatur rex petitioni eorum fauere, quippe et in hac parte pontificis animum libenter

a exequeretur Xc   *b* est Xc
c om Qc   *d* exercere Xcp
e libertatem Xcmp   *f* uehementer Xc

liberty '[1] he rebuked sinners sternly, with no undue consideration for persons of importance.

Whence it came to pass that at the beginning of his episcopate when he was more lavish in his punishment of some of the most powerful persons in the kingdom, he greatly annoyed the king. The worst abuse in the kingdom of England, under which the countryfolk groaned, was the tyranny of the foresters. For them violence took the place of law, extortion was praiseworthy, justice was an abomination and innocence a crime. No rank or profession, indeed, to sum up, no one but the king himself was secure from their barbarity, or free from the interference of their tyrannical authority. When Hugh first came up against this scourge, it brought about his first conflict and victory. It was what first forced him to use the two-edged sword of the spirit. When in their usual way the foresters maltreated his men as they did other people, in defiance of the liberties of the church, he finally excommunicated the chief-forester, a man named Geoffrey.[2] The news roused the king to great indignation.

Meanwhile a prebend in the church of Lincoln became vacant on the death of the canon who held it, and it fell to the new bishop to collate. The courtiers, when this became known, begged the king to write to the bishop and ask him to give it to one of themselves. They believed that they would help him by doing so,[3] since it gave him a chance of appeasing the king's anger. The king readily granted their request, as he was

---

[1] 2 Cor. 3:17

[2] Probably Geoffrey, warden or chief forester of Windsor forest. cf. Pipe Roll, 30-34 Henry II. *Publications of the Pipe Roll Society* (1912-1915, 1925), XXXIII-IV, XXXVI-VIII, 58, 26, 115, 149, 194

[3] cf. John 16:2

cupiebat propositumque explorare. Consistebat eo
tempore rex quidem ^a apud Wudestocham, episcopus
apud Dorkecestram, que ab inuicem mansiones tredecim
creduntur millibus ^b disparate. Lectis ^c uero episcopus
petitoriis sibi destinatis, ' Non,' inquit, ' aulicis set potius
ecclesiasticis ecclesiastica oportet beneficia conferri
personis, quorum possessores ^d non palatio aut
fisco siue scaccario set, ut docet Scriptura, altario ^{e,}
conuenit deseruire.[1] Habet dominus rex unde exhibeat
obsequentes ^f negotiis suis, habet unde compenset in
temporalibus pro temporalibus sibi militantium laborem.
Bonum est ei ut summo Regi militaturos deputatis
eorum necessitatibus permittat gaudere prouentibus,
nec debitis eos priuari stipendiis adquiescat.' Hec
dicens, regios a se nuntios inanes et uacuos redire non
expauit.

CAPITVLVM X

Qualiter Hugo, a rege accersitus sibi irato, eius non
modo simultatem paruipenderit set etiam ipsum comiter
deriserit. Et de beniuolentia predicti forestarii post
absolutionem erga episcopum habita.

Talibus uero in curia declaratis de Lincolniense
adhuc nouo ac quasi recenti ^g episcopo, non defuerunt
qui regem, ut iam uidebatur satis commotum aduersus
eum, in uehementiorem niterentur furorem sermonibus
incitare uenenatis. ' Iam,' inquiunt, ' domine, in mani-
festo est quam ingratus sit tantis homo iste beneficiis
uestris; iam patet quo loci operam locaueritis ^h et

^a quidam B² ; *om* c	^b *om* B ; millibus disparari X
^c Letis B	^d possessiones Xc
^e altari Q	^f obsequentibus Xco
^g recenter X	^h locaveris B

very anxious to find out how the bishop would act in this matter. The king was then at Woodstock and the bishop at Dorchester, places which are about thirteen miles apart. After reading the letters he had received containing this request, the bishop answered ' Ecclesiastical benefices should not be conferred on royal officials, but on ecclesiastics, since their holders should not serve at court, at the treasury or the exchequer, but as the Scripture enjoins, at the altar.[1] The lord king has the wherewithal to pay his own servants, he has possessions with which to reward those who transact secular business for him. It is only right for him to let those who are serving the king of Heaven enjoy the provision made for their needs, and not allow them to be deprived of the salary due to them.' Having spoken these words, he had the courage to send the royal messengers away with a curt refusal.

CHAPTER X

How Hugh, when summoned by the angry king, showed no fear at his wrath but pleasantly teased him. And the affection of the above-mentioned forester for the bishop after his absolution.

When the behaviour of the new bishop of Lincoln became public property at court, many people did their best to fan the already strong indignation of the king against him by poisoned words. ' Sire,' they said, ' the black ingratitude of the man for your unusual favours is now obvious, the reward you have received for taking so

---

[1] cf. 1 Cor. 9: 13

impensam, dum eius tantopere promotioni inuigilastis.
Et utinam tantummodo gratiam non referre contentus
sit homo animi inhumani, non autem et iniuriam
rependere *a* insistat pro tanto honore. Ceterum quid
pro uobis eum speremus subsequenti tempore esse
facturum aut uestris in *b* quantum delaturum confidamus,
quem iam cernimus post tot adhucque recentia beneficia in tantilla re uestram adeo irreuerenter excellentiam
contempsisse, quem et proceres intimosque balliuos
uestros tam proterua *c* dolemus sententia confudisse ? '

Ad hec princeps ille, quamuis plurimum turbaretur,*d*
modestie tamen cancellos non excedens, misit protinus
et episcopum ad se accersiuit. Quem foribus iam
imminere prenoscens, cum uniuersa nobilium qui tunc
ibi aderant frequentia, in saltum contiguum ascensis
equis secedit. Vbi in loco residens ameno consulibus
ceterisque magnatibus in modum corone consedentibus
precepit ut nullus accedenti episcopo assurgeret, nullus
aduenientem salutaret. Nec mora : adest ille, assistit,
salutat regem et consedentes, set nullus eum resalutat.
Quos ut uidit incurios sui tacitosque sedere, accedit
propius, manuque leniter scapulis imposita magni
cuiusdam consulis qui proximus assederat lateri regio,*e*
locum sibi iuxta regem ipse facit. Obstinato quoque
silentio cunctis diutius insistentibus, ut liceret presentibus
illud Virgilianum reminisci,

Consedere duces, intentique ora tenebant,[1]

rex tandem uultum erigens demissum, dari a quodam
assistentium acum sibi precepit cum filo. Quo facto,
suere cepit manu propria lesum panniculoque inuolutum

---

a respondere o ; impendere Xc   *b* *om* Xc
c proteruius X   *d* conturbaretur X
e regis X

much pains for his advancement is notorious. Well would it have been if this ill-bred man had stopped short at failing to be grateful, instead of doing his best to recompense such great promotion with injury. What indeed can we hope that he will do for you in future, or how much can we trust that he will further your interests, when already we see that, after so many recent favours, he bluntly refuses your highness such a little thing, and to our grief has so insolently excommunicated your nobles and trusted officials.'

In spite of his great anger, the king behaved with restraint. He sent a summons to the bishop, and when he knew that he was about to arrive, mounted his horse, and withdrew with all his nobles, who were there in considerable numbers, to the neighbouring forest. He sat down in a pleasant spot and the earls and other magnates formed a circle round him. These he commanded not to rise or greet the bishop when he arrived. To make a long story short, he came and approached, he greeted the king and the company, but no one returned his greeting. When he saw them sitting there silent and indifferent, he came up and put his hand lightly on the shoulder of the earl who was sitting next to the king, and made him give him his seat by the king. A heavy silence ensued, and all of them waited for a long time. Virgil's lines are apt,

' The chieftains sat, with intent faces.' [1]

Finally, the king raised his head and ordered one of the attendants to give him a needle and thread. Having received it, he began himself to put stitches into a membrane bandaged round an injured finger on his left

---

[1] Virgil, *Aeneid*, bk. II, l. 1 ; *Conticuere omnes, intentique ora tenebant.*

leue sue digitum. Agebat hoc ne nil ageretur *a* aliquamdiu, nichil interim loquens. Ita uero se gerebat ut
solent nimium irati, cum *b* in eis animi rancor uocis
absorbet officium, meatu spirituum intercluso.

Hec episcopus intuens ac sui causa omnem huius
simultatis pompam exhiberi cognoscens, apud se, uelud
a sublimiori quadam intime rationis specula, cogita-
tionum carnalium molimina longe despexit. Ac demum
conuersus ad regem, hiis uerbis paucissimis totam cordis
eius erectionem tumidam elisit, ipsumque uerborum uim
non ferentem corpore etiam resupino solotenus deiecit.
Verba ipsa exprimemus, nil eis demendo uel adiciendo.
Ait ergo : ' Quam similis es modo cognatis tuis de
Falesia.'[1] Hoc quasi telo, blando quidem et leui set
mirum in modum penetrabili et preacuto, rex precordia-
liter traiectus conserit digitos, soluitur in cacchinum,*c*
ore supino in terram deponens ceruicem. Sub tali
diutius schemate risibus frena laxabat. Ex consedentibus
qui uerbum intellexerant miro tenebantur stupore ;
mirantur *d* enim supra modum sub tali articulo tale
improperium tanto *e* principi ab homine tali fuisse
intortum. Subridere tamen et ipsi, se cohibere non
ualentes, ceperunt, animis expectantes attonitis quidnam
ad audita rex tandem esset responsurus. Plures, sensum
nescientes prolati sermonis, amplius stupebant ob
repentinam gestus regii permutationem.

Quorum demum ignorantiam rex ipse intelligens,
proprie, ut eos instruat, efficitur interpres iniurie.
Preuentus namque tam urbane inuectionis nouitate,
medullitus commouebatur, hominisque confidentiam
et ipse admirans, sic orsus *f* est loqui. ' Num,' inquit,

---

a ageret Xc
c chaminum B
e tali Xc

b *om* Xc
d mirabantur Xcp
f exorsus X

hand. There was silence, whilst he did this for some time to avoid the embarrassment of doing nothing. Angry people are accustomed to behave in this way, since their rage has rendered them speechless and they cannot give vent to it.

The bishop looked on and realized that this display of anger was for his benefit. He contemplated this conflict of human passions as though from some lofty watchtower of inward reason. At last he turned to the king and with these few words lanced his swollen and inflamed heart, and when he would listen to no reasonable arguments, flung him flat on the ground. We will quote his very words without omission or addition. He said ‘ How you resemble your cousins at Falaise.’ ¹ This shaft, said lightly and in a low tone, pierced the king to the heart. He pressed his fingers together, and, dissolved in helpless laughter, rolled on the ground. For a long time he could not restrain his merriment. The people present who understood the gibe were absolutely amazed that a man in Hugh’s position had dared to make fun of so mighty a king at such a moment. They were not, however, able to refrain from smiling, and waited in suspense to hear the king’s reply. Most of them, however, not understanding the meaning of what the bishop had said, were absolutely at a loss to account for the king’s sudden change of attitude.

At last, the king became aware of their confusion and informed them himself about the jest at his expense. He was overcome by the novelty of this courteous mockery, and his good humour was restored, and he was impressed

---

¹ St Hugh’s impudent joke referred not only to the humble origin of William the Conqueror, but also to his illegitimate birth. His mother was Arlette, a tanner’s daughter of Falaise.

'intelligitis cuiusmodi nobis contumeliam barbarus iste intulerit? Ego uobis dictum ipsius explanabo. Constat genetricem proaui nostri Willelmi, triumphatoris huius terre, de stirpe mediocri traxisse originem ac de opido famoso Normanorum quod Falesia nuncupatur fuisse oriundam. Municipium hoc arte pelliparia celebrius excolitur. Quia uero me suere digitum meum derisor iste conspexit, iccirco similem Falesiensibus et eorum me cognatum esse improperauit.'

'Attamen age,' inquit ad episcopum, 'uir bone, quidnam tibi uisum fuit ut nobis inconsultis principalem forestarium nostrum anathemati subiceres, nostram insuper petitiunculam ita floccipenderes ut neque per teipsum ad nos uenires huius repulse expositurus rationem, neque uerbum per nostros nobis nuntios placabile remandares?' Talia expostulanti mox ita respondet episcopus: 'Noui,' inquit, 'uos ut episcopus efficerer studiosius insudasse. Vt igitur uestram a discrimine animam expedirem, quo illam periclitari contingeret, si quod mei noscitur esse officii circa ecclesie michi commisse utilitatem exequi non curarem, necesse fuit et oppressorem illius *a* ecclesie per censuram ecclesiasticam cohercere, et indebite prebendam sibi in eadem ecclesia cupientem extorquere nullatenus exaudire. Excellentie autem uestre presentiam pro utrolibet adire negotio, non modo superfluum esse, immo et ineptum sentiebam; cum uestre discretioni pronum sit quod rite geritur prudenter aduertere, et uoluntati uestre nichilominus sedeat quod rectum esse cognoscitis fauorabiliter approbare.'

Huiusmodi rationibus rex quod contradici posset non inueniens, postposito temere concepto simultatis nubilo, amplectitur iam ore sereno pontificem, eiusque orationi-

---

a ipsius QXc

by the savoir-faire of the man. He spoke thus ' You cannot understand the way this barbarian has insulted us, so I will explain. The mother of our great-grandfather William, the Conqueror of this land, is reputed to have been of humble birth, and to have come from the important Norman town of Falaise, which is celebrated for its dressing of hides. This joker saw me sewing my finger, and so complimented me on my resemblance to my cousins at Falaise.'

' Now, tell me,' he said to the bishop, ' my good friend, why without informing me have you thought fit to excommunicate my chief forester, and to treat my trifling request to you with such contempt, that you neither came yourself to explain why you had refused it, nor sent any excuse by our messengers ? ' The bishop at once answered these remonstrances in these words : ' I know that you worked hard to make me a bishop. I am therefore bound to save your soul from the perils which would befall it, if I was not careful to do my clear duty to the church entrusted to my charge. It is essential to excommunicate the oppressor of my church, and still more to refuse those who try to obtain prebends in that church illegally. I deemed it unnecessary and inadvisable to approach your highness on either matter, since you are quite wise enough to recognise what is right, and would certainly wish to show your approval of what you know to be so.'

The king found nothing to take exception to in this explanation, and the last traces of his hasty resentment being now dissipated, he embraced the bishop with a beaming face and commended himself urgently to his prayers. He left to his decision the question of the absolution of the excommunicated man, who, being thoroughly contrite and humbled, took the oath in the

bus sese commendans obnixius, illius per omnia reliquit
dispensationi qualiter hominem sententia innodatum
absolutionis beneficio redonaret.[a] Quem ualde con-
tritum animo et humiliatum, prestito iuxta formam
ecclesie sacramento, publice cum suis complicibus
uirgis cesum absoluit ; dataque benedictione, in omne
reliquum uite sue tempus speciali quadam beniuolentia
familiarius eum sibi deuotum sensit et suis negotiis
prouisorem. Sic in rege, sic in satellite ueridicam esse
Scripture sententiam uir iustus experitur qua dicitur,
'Qui corripit hominem, gratiam postmodum inueniet
apud eum magis quam ille qui per lingue blandimenta
decipit.'[1] A prebendarum quoque uiolentis postula-
tionibus quibus uelud importunis miluorum unguibus
uniuersas passim infestabant ecclesias et diripiebant eas,
hac una[b] interim repulsa curiales uehementer repressit
et eorum a se importunitatem[c] procul auertit. Eius
tamen uenerationi et ipsi certatim inseruiebant adeo ut
deuotionis eorum et industrie experientiam plurimum
ipse sepius commendaret, familiaribus suis asserens,
quibusdam eorum se libentius beneficia largiturum am-
pliora, si non curie tenerentur nexibus irretiti.

Capitvlvm XI

Quod non modo curiales set etiam aliarum ecclesiarum cathedralium personas prebendabat rarissime ; et
qualiter respondit cuidam magistro litteratissimo am-
bienti in ecclesia Lincolniensi prebendari.

Nec tantum curiales, immo et quarumlibet ecclesiarum cathedralium clericos, sue canonicos ecclesie rarius
efficiebat, residentiam precipue in ecclesia Lincolniensi

---

[a] renodaret c ; denodaret X   [b] om Xc   [c] ingluuiem Xc

form prescribed by the church and, after being publicly flogged with his accomplices, was absolved. The bishop gave him his blessing, and all the rest of his life he was devoted to him and became his especial friend and benefactor, taking pains to promote his interests. Thus the saint found both king and servant examples of the text ' He that rebuketh a man shall afterwards find more favour with him than he that flattereth with his tongue.' [1] Moreover, by this one refusal he firmly put a stop to the inordinate demands for prebends by royal clerks, who devastate and plunder all the churches like rapacious birds of prey, and freed himself from their persistent requests. They revered him, and they vied with each other to do him service. He was well aware of their loyalty and assistance and often commented on it, telling his clerks that he would gladly have collated some of them to rich benefices, if they had not been completely absorbed in government work.

Chapter XI

How he very seldom gave prebends either to royal clerks or the canons of other cathedrals, and his answer to a certain master with a great reputation who sought for a prebend at Lincoln.

It was exceptional for him to make either royal clerks or the clergy of any other cathedral canons of his church, because he expected those on whom he conferred the

[1] Prov. 28:23

ab illis expetens, quibus illius ecclesie canonica stipendia
conferebat. Nimirum sicut qui *a* altario deseruiunt
altario iure participantur,[1] ita minime deseruientibus
altaris commoda dicebat incongrua ratione prouenire ;
cum et ecclesias debitis seruientium excubiis ex eo
fraudari contingeret et speciem uideretur habere rapine,
cum militaturis deputata militie spiritualis stipendia non
militaturi presumerent occupare. Nam et illam quoque
Apostoli sententiam in hac potissimum causa intelligi
et teneri debere sentiebat, ut qui in sanctuario nequaquam laborant *b* in eo etiam non manducent [2] que
sanctuario consecrantur. Si enim gloriatur doctor
gentium quod sine sumptu posuit euangelium,[3] quam
ignominiosi, aiebat, reputandi sunt qui, sine euangeli-
zandi studio, sine ministrandi obsequio, sumptus
euangelizantibus aut ministrantibus assignatos usurpare
presumunt.

Meminimus autem quendam eo temporis *c* summi
fere inter theologos canonicosque Parisienses nominis,
dixisse quadam uice Hugoni : ' Gloriosam, domine
episcope, pre cunctis totius orbis ecclesiis uestram
exhibuistis ecclesiam insignium multitudine clericorum ;
essetque michi, nec enim id celandum uobis duxi, satis
optabile eorum numero quolibet uel perexili titulo
sociari.' Cui statim episcopus : ' Et nos,*d* ' ait, ' eorum
uos numero libenti animo iungeremus si etiam inter eos
residere uelletis,*e* si quoque ad scientiam mores uobis
equis passibus responderent.' Preerat enim scholis
Parisiensibus, regens et ipse scholas, celebrior tamen eo
tempore scientia quam disciplina. Qui, responso tali

---

a Nec mirum. Sicut enim Xc   *b* laborarent X
c tempore QXc   *d* + etiam Xc
e uelitis Q

revenues of the canonries of his church to reside at Lincoln. He said emphatically that, as they who served at the altar were rightly partakers with the altar,[1] it was unjust that the endowments of the altar should go to those who never served there. This seemed to him a species of robbery, since it meant that the churches were deprived of their ministers because non-combatants were not ashamed to take possession of the emoluments set aside for the army of holy Church. He felt that the instructions of the apostle that ' he who did not minister in any way in the temple, should not live of the things consecrated for the temple '[2] applied especially to this particular case, and should be observed. If, he said, the apostle of the Gentiles gloried that he preached the gospel without charge,[3] how base must those be who, with no intention of preaching, or of any kind of pastoral work, dared to seize the revenues intended for preachers and pastors.

I remember how at about that time one of the most renowned theologians and canons of Paris said on one occasion to Hugh, ' My lord bishop, you have made your church more famous than any other church in the world owing to its innumerable distinguished canons, I will not conceal from you that I greatly desire to be one of them, however modest the prebend.' The bishop immediately answered ' I would very willingly have you amongst them, if you were ready to reside and your virtue were equal to your learning.' He presided over the schools at Paris and ruled the scholars there, but was at that period more renowned for his scholarship than for his conduct. This rebuke caused him to blush that he had expressed too freely, although not with complete candour, what he

---

[1] cf. I Cor. 9:13   [2] cf. 2 Thess. 3:10   [3] cf. I Cor. 9:18

accepto, erubuit se nimis libere protulisse quod minus sincere uoluebat in pectore ; expertus in se uerissimum esse quod de sincerissima libertate huius uiri non semel in patria sua se meminit audiuisse. Recedens autem ab eo, castigatioribus *a* de cetero moribus fertur institisse.

Homines uero quieti spiritus et pudici artius diligebat, nec alios suo de certa conscientia gregi aliquatenus sociabat, quantalibet industrie cuiuscumque aut literature prerogatiua eminerent. Nouerat enim sapientiam que de sursum est, primum quidem pudicam, deinde pacificam ore apostolico diffiniri.[1] Itemque illud uiri sapientis memoriter recolebat quia illaudabilis est scientia quam uita maculat impudica. Nichil autem pacis bono in hac uita dicebat preferendum, nichil seditionis et turbationis peste amplius fugiendum, ideoque uitandam omnimodis societatem alio spiritu ad schismata anhelantium et discordias inter fratres seminantium admonebat.

Capitvlvm XII

Quod primum Baldewino Cantuariensium archi-episcopo et deinde illius successori Huberto nisus sit dissuadere contentiose cuiusdam capelle constructionem ; et quid mali eius inchoationem sequeretur predixit. Et de unitatis constanti perseuerantia episcopi cum suis canonicis.

Pie recordationis Baldewino Cantuariorum archi-presuli, quorumdam instinctu ecclesiam seu capellam in honore pretiosi prothomartiris Stephani et incliti neo-martiris Anglorum Thome in territorio ciuitatis sue

---

a + se Xc

had in mind, and found from his own experience that what he had often heard in his own country about the devastating frankness of Hugh was absolutely true. I believe that he reformed somewhat after his departure.

He very much appreciated even-tempered men, not full of their own importance and seldom, purposely, included those of a different disposition in his chapter however great their usefulness or their reputation for learning, for he knew that the apostle had said that the wisdom which is from above is first pure and then peaceable.[1] He also remembered the words of the wise man that learning contaminated by loose-living is contemptible. He used to declare that nothing in this world was preferable to the blessing of peace, and nothing more to be avoided than the evils of strife and dissension. Therefore he advised people to avoid association with those of another spirit who maliciously ferment divisions and stir up enmity amongst their brethren.

CHAPTER XII

How he tried hard to dissuade first Baldwin, archbishop of Canterbury and afterwards his successor, Hubert, from the construction of a certain church because of the quarrel it occasioned, and the evils he predicted would ensue from its foundation. Also concerning the unbroken harmony between bishop Hugh and his canons.

At the instigation of certain personages, Baldwin, archbishop of Canterbury, of pious memory, was eager to erect at Canterbury a church or chapel, dedicated to

---

[1] Jas. 3:17

construere festinanti, cum *a* monachi cathedralis ecclesie uehementius obsisterent, opus *b* in sui asserentes preiudicium attemptari Lincolniensis Hugo, quod rei probauit euentus, super eodem ab illo consultus negotio, certissimo *c* predixit oraculo : 'Si inter uos,' inquit, 'domine archiepiscope, et capitulum uestrum huius operis causa schisma quod non expedit contingat suboriri, et discipline uigor in conuentu uestro emarcescet et ordinis censura imminuetur. Hinc quanta successura sint pericula animarum nullius estimatio sufficiet premetiri. Vos preterea regie uestram oportebit auctoriatem substernere seruituti ; curie insuper Romane, necnon et plurimorum in sublimitate consistentium uariamque habentium potestatem, subiacebis *d* fastui ac timori ; ipsius quoque summi pontificis, hora omni et tempore omni, motus necesse erit animosque uereri. Ipse, tam consummato quam opere isto inchoato, demoliri precipiet quicquid demum cognouerit preiudicialiter actitatum.' *e*

Cum diceret archiepiscopus sanctum Thomam huiusmodi *f* fabrice in honorem sancti leuite Stephani instituende gessisse propositum, satis ad hoc eleganter respondit episcopus, 'Sufficiat,' inquiens, 'uos simili iam proposito martiri adequatum ; si meam uultis *g* audire imperitiam, ulterius eo minime procedetis.' Verum illo aliorum potius consiliis innitente mentisque propositum in operis effectum perurgente, tandem expertus didicit quam uerum sit quod Scriptura dicit, 'Anima uiri sancti magis *h* enuntiat aliquando uera quam septem circumspectores sedentes in excelsum *i* ad speculandum.'[1] Nam malorum que iustus predixerat ne unum quidem

---

a festinabat, cui X   *b* + illud Q   *c* peritissimo B²
d subiacebitis QXc   *e* attemptatum Xc   *f* huius Qc
g uolueritis X   *h* om Xo (*and Vulg.*)   *i* excelso Xcp (*and Vulg.*)

the most holy protomartyr Stephen and the venerable martyr of England, Thomas. The monks of his cathedral chapter hotly opposed him, alleging that its erection would greatly injure them. When he consulted Hugh, bishop of Lincoln, about the matter, Hugh had the foresight to tell him exactly what would happen. 'If,' he said, 'because of this foundation, an unfortunate quarrel should arise, my lord archbishop, between you and your chapter, the discipline of the community will be badly affected, and the reputation of the whole monastic order will suffer. No one can estimate the immense danger to souls which will result. You yourself, moreover, will be forced to make use of the royal authority to the detriment of your own, and expose yourself to the greed and political manoeuvres of the Roman Curia, and of various highly placed individuals in Church and State. All the time, indeed at every moment, you will have to dread the intervention and reactions of the pope. Whether the buildings have been completed or merely begun, he will command them to be demolished, if he believes that they infringe other people's rights.'

The archbishop said that St Thomas had proposed to found a church dedicated to the holy deacon St Stephen, to which the bishop wittily replied, ' Be content with sharing the martyr's intention ; I venture to advise you to go no further.' He, however, preferred other advice, being eager to carry out his project, but at length learned from bitter experience the truth of the text ' The spirit of the righteous man makes known the truth more fully than seven watchmen seated on a high place to watch.'[1] For every single misfortune the saint had foretold came to pass: the buildings were demolished and

---

[1] Ecclus. 37:18

preteriit inexpletum. Structura uero illa iussu domini
Pape funditus eliminata est et demolita, auctore, cum
ruboris et peccati multiplicis questu, operam perdente
operisque impensam.

Idem quoque eiusdem successori *a* in opus simile
gestienti et uir fidelis predixit et rerum finis induxit.
Nam et ipse haut procul a Londoniis capellam conten-
tiosam, instar prioris que secus Cantuariam diruta fuit,
fretus regia potestate erexit ; clericos in ea prebendarios
sub decano, secularium more canonicorum, aut per
seipsos aut per interpositas personas ministraturos
instituit. A quibus iam circa locum pluribus constructis
edificiis, protractata in longum inter patrem et filios,
archipresulem et monachos, lite amara ; multis personis
electissimis, tam e monachis quam e clericis, Romanis
febribus in urbe obiterque *b* sub hoc intestino bello
extinctis ; uiri tandem magnanimi inconsulta molitio,
eodem ipso demoliente, in puluerem redacta est. Fecit
hoc quam inuitus, tam et confusus, apostolica nimirum
seueritate compulsus. Ad postremum uero, iam uiro
Dei Hugone per ultimam uite mortalis egritudinem ad
eternam properante felicioris uite incolumitatem, ipso
simul arbitro et coniudicibus suis a summo delegatis
pontifice, pax inter predictos reformata est : mirum in
modum exultante in hoc et diuine clementie gratias
referente eodem ueracissimo filio pacis. Gratulabatur
namque impensius quia instar beatissimi Martini,*c* cuius
semper et amator deuotus et strenuus imitator esse meru-
erat, 'hanc uirtutum suarum bonam fecisset *d* consumma-
tionem, qua pacem ecclesie Dei redditam reliquisset.' [1]

Verum hiis per excessum quemdam necessario anti-
cipatis, ea que cepimus directe narrationis serie pro-

---

a + Huberto X   *b* obitisque o ; ob iter Xc
c + Turonensis archiepiscopi X   *d* fecisse X

razed to the ground by order of the lord pope, and the founder, bewailing his disgrace and his many sins, lost his labours, and the money he had spent on them.

When Baldwin's successor embarked on a similar work, this loyal friend said the same and predicted what the end would be. With the king's full support, he built a church not far from London, on the model of the former one near Canterbury, which had been destroyed. This also caused litigation. The prebends he established there were held by clerks who, like secular canons under the rule of a dean, were to perform the offices, either personally or through their vicars. After extensive building operations on the site, and a long and bitter domestic lawsuit between the archbishop and his monks, and after many excellent persons, both monks and clerks, had died of fever at Rome or on the way there and back as a result of this domestic conflict, this haughty man had finally himself to demolish and level to the ground the edifice he had so rashly erected. He did this ignominiously and unwillingly under pressure from the pope. Finally, during the last mortal illness of Hugh, the man of God, when he was already on his way to the bliss and safety of eternal life, peace was made between the two parties by him and his fellow judges delegate appointed by the pope. This sincere lover of peace was greatly delighted and gave thanks to the merciful God. He rejoiced exceedingly, since like blessed Martin, for whom he always had a great devotion, and whose example he aspired to follow, his last good deed was to restore peace in the church of God.[1]

It has been necessary to make this digression and deal with these matters out of chronological order, but now I shall resume again the thread of my narrative.

[1] Sulpicius Severus, *Epistola III* (C.S.E.L. I, 147)

sequamur. Monebat indifferenter quoslibet et indesinenter prelatos unitatis et concordie uinculum cum
suis inuiolabiliter subiectis retinere, suimet illis exemplum
proponens. Aiebat namque : ' Quia noui me cum filiis
nostris bonum pacis et unitatis tenacius obseruare, non
regem, non quemlibet *a* timendum michi estimo
mortalem, set neque internam perdo securitatem que
sempiterne imitatrix et preparatrix *b* existit tranquillitatis.
Nec uero,' inquit, ' iccirco michi a dominis nostris '—sic
enim suos canonicos nuncupabat—' quies hec differtur *c*
totius ignara discidii, quia lenem me sentiunt et man-
suetum. Sum enim reuera pipere asperior atque morda-
cior, qui et eorum presidens capitulo, ex re frequenter
leuissima nimis inflammor ad iram. Illi uero scientes
quia oporteat *d* eos qualem susceperunt, talem et
sustinere me, faciunt de necessitate uirtutem deferentes
michi. Gratias illis habeo copiosas. Numquam ne uel
in uno quidem sermone restiterunt michi ex quo primum
inter eos residere cepi. Egredientibus autem uniuersis,
finito capitulo, nullus ut arbitror de nostra sibi estimat
dilectione diffidendum, nec ipse me existimo *e* a quouis
eorum non amari.' Talis uero ac tantus ei dilectionis
affectus, ad singulos uiritim *f* ecclesie sue filios, ab
exordio promotionis sue usque ad extremum uite ipsius
perseuerauit diem, ut illius euidenter se probaret
imitatorem esse, de quo Euangelista Iohannes uenerabili
profitetur assertione, ' Cum dilexisset suos qui erant in
mundo, in finem dilexit eos.'[1] Quorum etiam tuitioni se
obiciens, si quando ex eis quempiam grauandum quo-
cumque incursu agnouisset, non modo facto immo et
sermone dicere consueuerat, ' Qui tangit uos, tangit
pupillam oculi mei.'[2]

a + esse Xc   *b* imperatrix Xc   *c* defertur Xc
d oportet X   *e* estimo Xc   *f* nimirum Q

He besought people of every sort, but especially superiors, to maintain unbroken the bond of unity and peace between themselves and their subjects, citing himself as an example. Indeed, he used to say ' Since I know that I have strictly maintained the blessing of peace and union with my sons, I do not think that I need fear the king or any other man, nor do I lose the inner peace which is a reflection and preparation for the peace of heaven. This unruffled harmony between me and my lords (for this was his name for his canons) is not because they find me mild and gentle. On the contrary I am more astringent and biting than pepper, and when I am presiding at chapter the least thing often rouses me to anger. They realise that they must take me as they find me, and bear with me, making a virtue of necessity, for which I am most grateful to them. They have never opposed me on a single occasion since I came to live amongst them. When the chapter ends, and they go out, I do not think any of them has any doubt about my affection for him, and I believe that they too are all fond of me.' His devotion to each of his canons was so strong from the first days of his episcopate to the very end of his life, that he obviously followed the example of the Lord of whom the venerable evangelist John said 'Since he had loved his own who were in the world he loved them unto the end.' [1] He came to their defence if ever he saw that any of them was being oppressed or molested. Thus, his actions corresponded with one of his favourite sayings, ' Whoever injures you, touches the pupil of my eye.' [2]

---

[1] John 13:1   [2] Zach. 2:8

Capitvlvm XIII

De moderamine frugalitatis ipsius in cibo et potu.
De modestia et hilaritate eius inter prandendum. De
uirium eius magnitudine in officii sui executione. De
condescensione eius in aliorum infirmitate. Et quod
manus impositionem numquam equo sedens cuilibet
impertierit.[a]

Quoniam de uiri sancti moribus plura [b] in pre-
cedentibus libellis disserere curauimus, iccirco de hiis
nunc parcius dicendum estimamus. Hoc autem,
quamuis ob uitandum lectoris fastidium breuitati magn-
opere studeamus, nequaquam duximus reticendum quia
in uictus parsimonia, post susceptum pontificatus laborem, solito minorem uisus est tenuisse districtionem. A
carnis siquidem et sanguinis omnimoda perceptione et
sanus et egrotus abstinens, piscibus crebro uescebatur.
Vini quoque usum non respuens set eo moderate utens,
tam corporee fragilitati iuxta apostoli consilium [1]
prospiciebat quam iuxta eiusdem exemplum, ut omnibus
omnia fieret,[2] conuiuantibus et conuescentibus secum
honestissima se dispensatione conformabat. Erat quoque
in mensa hylaris et iocundus set non sine grauitate et
modestia, illud semper attendens et quandoque hortanti-
bus se ad letandum ore etiam proferens quod in libro
Hester legitur, 'Leti sumus secundum facies [c] sanctorum.'[3] Si quando histriones uel musici quauis occasione interessent sollempnibus conuiuiis, ubi ipse siue ad
propriam siue ad mensam resideret alienam, tunc quam
maxime grauitati studebat, uix umquam a mensa oculos

---

[a] imposuerit X. *In c this chapter is the first of book IV, to which the first
sentence forms a prefatiuncula*
[b] plus Xc   [c] faciem QXcm (*and Vulg.*)

CHAPTER XIII

Concerning his restraint and austerity in food and drink, and his courtesy and gaiety at table. How he was indefatigable in the performance of his duties, and yet considerate towards the weakness of other people. How he never confirmed anyone when on horseback.

As I have described the saint's general behaviour in detail in the preceding books, I think it is unnecessary now to say much about it. Yet, in spite of it being my great aim to avoid wearying my readers by long-windedness, I believe that I should mention that he was somewhat less abstemious in the matter of food after his assumption of the episcopal office than had been his wont before. He never touched flesh meat whether in sickness or health, but frequently ate fish. He did not abstain from wine altogether, but drank it in moderation, both on account of bodily weakness as the apostle advised [1] and also as following his example to be all things to all men,[2] and with the most exquisite courtesy to put those who ate with him at their ease. He was gay and lively at table, but at the same time dignified and restrained, always remembering, and sometimes even quoting to those who urged him to be merry, the text from the book of Esther ' The beauty of the saints has made us glad.' [3] If, as occasionally happened at the grandest banquets, either in his own household or when he was a guest elsewhere, there was music or acting, he displayed the greatest detachment, hardly ever raising his eyes from the board. Every word and gesture made it apparent to those present how completely withdrawn he was, as

---

[1] cf. 1 Tim. 5:23   [2] cf. 1 Cor. 9:22
[3] In reality : Judith 16:24 (*Vulg.*)

erigens, et ita se in omni gestu et sermone exibens ut
manifestum esset intuentibus quia tunc se ad interiora
artius constringeret, cum sensus exteriores huiusmodi
lenocinia blandius mulcerent. Sacras inter uescendum
lectiones tanta audiebat diligentia ut, preter non-
nullorum passiones martirum, preter gesta quorumdam
sanctorum et celebriores de precipuis sollempnitatibus
sermones doctorum, totum fere ex integro uetus nouum-
que instrumentum,^{a} exceptis quatuor euangelistarum
libris quos aliis, sicut inferius dicetur, temporibus legi
instituit, tum ad nocturnum coram se officium, tum ad
prandium faceret recitari.[1] Vt autem supra memora-
uimus, hoc ^{b} uniformi iugiter institutione et ipse seruabat
et quibusque rationabile Deo cupientibus obsequium [2]
prestare obseruandum inculcabat, ut omni scilicet et
tempore et loco, quod rerum exigeret presentium
instantia, conuenienter adimplerent. Ad quod etiam
dignius exequendum, seipsum habilem quantum potuit
et ydoneum studuit exhibere.

Sentiens autem, experientia docente, magni esse
laboris opus episcopalis officii nec sine uiribus etiam
corporeis id decenter posse impleri, ita iumento corporis ^{c}
alimenta prebebat ut necessariis usibus congrue sub-
ueniret.^{d} Quod eo securius eoque sufficientius faciebat
quo minus ^{e} ne contra suum recalcitraret sessorem,
castigatione diutissima iam satis edomitum metuendum ^{f}
erat. Nam et per continuum frigidioris diete usum eo
usque internas iam corporis uires attriuerat, ut fatiscente^g
naturali calore crebras ^{h} infrigidati stomachi perferret
molestias, yliacis insuper passionibus sepius amarissime

---

^{a} testamentum Q; instrumentum uel testamentum X
^{b} + ministerium Xc ^{c} corpori Xc
^{d} subseruiret QXc ^{e} om X
^{f} + non Xc ^{g} satisfaciente B
^{h} om B

if only his exterior senses were being charmed by these sweet delights. At mealtimes he had the scriptures read to him with such assiduity that at mattins and dinner he managed to cover practically all the Old and New Testaments with the exception of the four gospels, which, as I shall show later, he had read to him at other times, and in addition to this the passions of some of the martyrs, certain lives of the saints, and the best known sermons of the fathers for the great festivals.[1] As we have already mentioned, he made it a fixed rule, which he impressed on all those who desired to serve God conscientiously,[2] to do all the time and in every place whatever was essential at that particular moment. As far as it lay with himself, he made a point of being in a fit state to carry this out as competently as he could.

Finding by experience that his episcopal duties were very heavy and could not be properly discharged without a strong physique, he gave to his body, as to a baggage-animal, the food required to perform its necessary task adequately. He did this more readily and with less scruple because he knew that through his long mortifications it was so much under control that there was no cause to fear that it would rebel against its master. Indeed, by the continual use of a chilling diet he had so weakened the internal bodily organs that, the natural

---

[1] This list accords well with a marginal entry (*c.* 1200) in the earliest catalogue of Lincoln Cathedral library recording the books given by St Hugh :

> Duo magna volumina sermonum catholicorum doctorum per totum annum.
> Et libellum de vita patrum cum rubeo coopertorio.
> Et psalterium cum magna glosatura quod G. precentor habet.
> Et preterea Omelarius in corio cerulio, qui sic incipit *Erunt signa.*
> Et martilogium cum textu iiii evangeliorum quod cantor habet.

This last item was probably the book St Hugh used for his daily reading of the Gospel every day after the Martyrology at Prime. See II, p. 193.

[2] cf. Rom. 12:1

torqueretur. Nichilominus tamen inter hec affuit ei et affluxit gratia singularis, robur illi accumulans fortissimis quibusque admirandum. Videre quasi miraculum erat quemadmodum in dedicationibus ecclesiarum, in celebrationibus ordinum ceterorumque ecclesiasticorum officiorum seu quibuslibet pontificalis ministerii exercitiis, in quibus plurimum uideretur esse laboris, omnium sibi adherentium uires solus *a* ipse excederet ; quemadmodum non solum fessis set pene deficientibus cunctis, aliis ad resumendas uires paululum secedentibus, aliis ad obsequendum ei succedentibus, ipse indefessus et alacer de opere ad opus, de labore percurreret *b* ad laborem. Ad ista nonnumquam surgebat ante lucem et usque ad profundas sequentis noctis tenebras ieiunans, nec a labore cessans, diem medium transigebat. Plerumque, dum immodicus estatis feruor immineret, quosdam ministrorum altaris cogebat panis et uini modicum prelibare ; ne pregrauati estu, ieiunio et labore citra periculum, post totiens repetitos circuitus in ecclesiarum dedicationibus, astare demum et sumministrare missarum sollempnia celebranti nequiuissent. Cum, pregustatis iussu suo panibus, horrori quibusdam et formidini esse sensisset sacrum inter agenda uel calicem uel dominicam contingere sindonem, arguebat eos quasi pusille fidei et discretionis infirme, qui nec obedire iubenti sine hesitatione didicissent nec rationem perciperent circumspecte iussionis.

Quotienscumque iter agenti occurrissent, ut assolet, qui per manus sue impositionem confirmari expeterent aut qui paruulos ei ad illum percipiendum *c* sacramentum offerrent, mox loco oportuno in pedes ab equo descendens, quod illius erat officii sollicita deuotione

---

    a suas B   *b* currebat cd ; percurrebat X
    c participandum percipiendumque Xc

heat being lessened, he suffered discomfort from the coldness of the stomach and often also from distressing forms of colic. Yet, in spite of this, he possessed so unusual a measure of divine grace that his endurance amazed even the most robust people. It was almost miraculous to see how at church consecrations, or ordinations, or other ecclesiastical ceremonies, or in the execution of any of his pastoral duties which were particularly tiring, his staying power was greater than that of his assistants. When they were not merely tired but completely exhausted,· and some of them withdrew to recuperate whilst others took their places in order to assist him, he seemed fresh and ready for each new duty. To carry these out he frequently rose before it was light and worked without food until the evening when it was really dark, not even pausing at midday. Often in summer when it was very hot, he made his assistants at the altar take a little bread and wine, lest after so many repeated processions at the dedication of churches they should run the risk of being too much overcome by the heat, the long fast and their labours to be able to assist him when celebrating high mass. When, after obeying his orders and eating bread they were afraid and had scruples about touching the holy chalice or the corporal in the course of their ministrations, he rebuked them for their want of confidence and common sense, since they had not learned to obey him readily, and had not seen that his order was wise and sensible.

Frequently when he was travelling about, people flocked to him to ask him to confirm them, or brought their children to be confirmed. As soon as he reached a suitable place he dismounted, and did his part with earnest devotion in whatever diocese it was. Neither

adimplebat, in quacumque diocesi hoc accidisset. Nulla
umquam fatigatione aut infirmitate, nulla itineris
festinatione, nulla uie asperitate aut aeris intemperie ut
equum sedens *a* tantum exhiberet sacramentum potuit
induci.

Sicut non absque rubore et quodam mentis dolore
postea uidimus episcopum quemdam etate iuuenem,
uiribus prestantem, in loco etiam et *b* tempore satis
ameno, nec festinandi necessitate ulla preuentum, equo
sublimem chrismate sacratissimo paruulos imbuentem.
Eiulantibus uero paruulis et inter equos pugnaces et
recalcitrantes pauitantibus *c* simul et periclitantibus,
alape a curialibus dabantur ministris et insontes ab
insolentibus cedebantur, cum interim nichil horum
dolorum et periculorum episcopo cure esset. Non sic
Hugo noster, set diuerso satis modo se habere solebat.
Nam et etate iam grauis, cunctisque sepius que itineran-
tibus occurrere solent constrictus incommodis, equo
descendebat paruulosque et eorum baiulos ad se leniter
et successiue accersiebat ; ministros suos laicos uidelicet
si quippiam forte eis *d* intulissent molestie, terribiliter
increpando, nonnumquam etiam colaphizando seuerius
cohercebat. Hinc data benedictione optata circum-
stantibus, infirmis quoque qui affuissent,*e* oratione ad
Dominum pro eis fusa, in spem *f* adipiscende sospitatis
cum exultatione respirantibus, repletus et ipse benedictionibus cunctorum, ceptam repetebat uiam. Quam-
plurimos autem per huius modi ipsius orationem seu
benedictionem, speratam consecutos fuisse incolumitatem, indubitanter sepe agnouimus.

---

a equo insidens **X**   *b* *om* **B**
c pauentibus **X**   *d* *om* **Xc**
e accessissent **Xc**   *f* spe **B²** **QX**

fatigue nor sickness, nor the need for hastening on his journey, nor the roughness of the road, nor the bad weather could persuade him to administer the sacrament on horseback.

To my shame and sorrow, I afterwards saw a certain young bishop, of exceptional strength, when the spot and the weather were both admirable and he had no reason to be in a hurry, sprinkle children with the sacred chrism whilst on horseback. The children howled and were terror-stricken, and in actual danger amongst the fiery and kicking horses. The ruffianly retainers cuffed and struck these innocents, but the bishop took no notice of their danger and panic. Our Hugh used to behave in a very different way. Although already advanced in years, and subject to all the inconveniences which often afflict travellers, he used to dismount and gently summon the children and their godparents to him one after another. If by chance his lay attendants laid their hands on them, his anger was terrible and sometimes he even restrained them by blows. Having given the bystanders the blessing they hoped for, he prayed to God for any sick persons who were there, thus arousing their hope of recovering their health, and went on his way accompanied by the blessings of the crowd. I know for certain that many people often made the recovery they had hoped for as a result of his blessing and prayers.

Capitvlvm XIV

Quod ex multa puritatis et innocentie habundantia
paruulis, exemplo Saluatoris nostri, lenem se et accessi-
bilem prebebat. Et de duobus lactentibus qui supra
nature facultatem adiocari episcopo uisi sunt. Et de aliis
duobus paruulis, quorum unus in torrentem cecidit set
periculum euasit.

Ex multa quidem puritatis et innocentie habundantia
ut erat simplicitatis et munditie et *ᵃ* precipuus amator et
custos, infantilem*ᵇ* uir sanctus miro*ᶜ* excolebat affectu
non modo sinceritatem set etiam etatem. Emulabatur
namque in hoc totius auctorem munditie et innocentie,
qui discipulis loquebatur,*ᵈ* 'Sinite paruulos uenire ad me,
et ne prohibueritis eos ; talium est*ᵉ* regnum celorum.'[1]
Talibus, ubi eos repperisset, spirituali quadam suauitate
dulcius adiocabatur ; a talibus uix adhuc balbutientibus
miri cuiusdam leporis semiuerbia*ᶠ* eliciebat. Imprime-
bat subinde frontibus uel quibusque sensibus eorum
uiuificum sancte crucis signum, fausta eis imprecans
eosque iterata sepius benedictione communiens. Illi
quoque mira ei uicissim celeritate familiariter alludere
gaudebant, quique omnium pene uirorum aspectus
uereri solebant, ei potius quam suo parenti desideranter
adherebant.*ᵍ*

Vidimus paruulum quemdam, menses sex ab ortu
habentem, cum ei frontem consignaret chrismato sacro,
tantis illi omnium artuum motibus applausisse, ut
singulare illud precursoris Domini in utero exultantis
gaudium emulari crederetur.[2] Laxabat uero ita risibus

ᵃ om QXc
ᶜ + modo B
ᶠ + enim Xc (*and Vulg.*)
ei potius . . . adherebant *om* B
ᵇ infantulum o ; infantium Xc
ᵈ in Euangelio loquitur, dicens : Xc
ᶠ similia X

Chapter XIV

How his absolute purity and innocence made him like our Saviour, gentle with and attractive to children, and how two infants with quite exceptional precociousness responded to the bishop's advances. Also concerning two other children, one of whom fell into a stream with a strong current and had a miraculous escape.

Because of his unsullied innocence, which made him set great store by sincerity and simplicity, the saint had an unusual affection for children because of their complete naturalness. In this he resembled the Author of perfection, who said to his disciples ' Suffer the little children to come unto me and forbid them not, for of such is the kingdom of heaven.' [1] Wherever he found them, he caressed them lovingly with angelic tenderness, and even when they could hardly talk, they made affectionate noises. He used to make the sign of the cross on their foreheads and their mouths and eyes, and bless them again and again, praying for their welfare. They in their turn made friends with him surprisingly quickly, and even those who generally were terrified of almost everybody, came to him more readily than to their parents.

I saw a child of about six months, who, when he made the sign of the cross on its forehead with the holy oil, expressed such great delight by the movement of its limbs, that it reminded one of the joy of the Baptist, leaping up in the womb.[2] The tiny mouth and face

---

[1] Mark 10:14 ; Matt. 19:14   [2] cf. Luke 1:41

inexplebilibus oris labella exigui ut putaretur incredibile sic posse in tali etatula solis adhuc uagitibus assuetum ridere. Deinde brachiolis quasi ad subuolandum nunc contortis nunc *a* disiectis, ceruicem huc illucque iactando*b* quasi importabilem sibi esse monstrabat propter *c* letitie qua afficiebatur magnitudinem. Tunc manum *d* eius utrisque attrectans palmulis et distringens pro modulo suo, ori applicat *e* ; applicitam uero allambere potius quam osculari festinat *f* ; faciebat hec diutissime. Pontifice infanti et infante pontifici, inauditum de se inuicem spectaculum delectabiliter exhibente, stupebant qui aderant ; et de gemino istorum spectaculo quod forinsecus erat mirabile in oculis suis, ad quoddam sublimius mentis spectaculum ducebantur *g* intrinsecus. Videbant et considerabant illud de Euangelio exhiberi, tam in puero quam in episcopo, 'Beati mundo corde, quoniam ipsi Deum uidebunt.'[1] Quid enim uideret quo tantum gauderet infantulus in episcopo nisi Deum qui erat in ipso? Quid uero attenderet episcopus in infantulo, quo tantopere intenderet tantus tantillo, nisi sciret magnum quid esse quod latebat in tam pusillo? Miranda sunt hec et uehementer stupenda, presertim hiis qui spectaculum illud, quale illud tunc inspexerunt, tale adhuc animo altius impressum gerunt. Oblata sunt quidem puero ab ipso episcopo poma uel que talibus esse solent grata pleraque alia, que singula, ac si tedio sibi forent, repellebat. Que repellendo cum quasi uicisset, totus in episcopum inhiabat. Ipsius quoque nutricis que eum gestabat, cum quodam fastidio manus sibi admotas respuens,*h* oculis in episcopum intendebat, manibus illi applaudebat, ore indesinenter arridebat.

---

a tunc B   *b* directis certatim huc illucque, *om* iactando X
c *om* Xc   *d* manuum B   *e* applicabat Xco
f festinabat QXc   *g* ducebant X   *h* respiciens Q

relaxed in continuous chuckles, and it seemed incredible that at an age when babies generally yell it could laugh in this way. It then bent and stretched out its little arms, as if it were trying to fly, and moved its head to and fro, as if to show that its joy was almost too great to bear. Next, it took his hand in both its tiny ones and, exerting all its strength, raised it to its face. It then proceeded to lick it instead of kissing it. This it did for a long time. Those present were amazed at the unusual spectacle of the bishop and the infant absolutely happy in each other's company. The sight of the attractive scene between the two of them turned men's thoughts to higher things. As they watched the bishop and the child they realized the aptness of the words of the gospel ' Blessed are the pure in heart for they shall see God.' [1] What could the infant have seen in the bishop which gave it so much delight, unless it were God in him ? What drew the bishop to the baby and made so important a person pay such attention to so small a being except the knowledge of the greatness concealed in such a tiny frame ? This scene was so surprising and wonderful that the spectators remember it now even more vividly than when they saw it. The bishop gave the boy an apple and several other things which children usually like, but he refused to be amused by any of them. He rejected them all and seemed completely absorbed and fascinated by the bishop. Disdainfully pushing away the hands of the nurse who was holding him, he gazed hard at the bishop, and clapped his hands smiling all the time.

---

[1] Matt. 5:8

Asportato demum eo, cum mirarentur presentes super tali prodigio, asserentes numquam uisum *a* fuisse tripudium tam immensum in tam angusto corpusculo, episcopus semel alias tale quid se uidisse narrauit. ' Nam dudum,' inquit, 'cum prioratum gererem Withamie, contigit me tempore generalis capituli adire Cartusiam. Occasione autem itineris preteriens castrum de Aualun, cuius frater noster Willelmus [1] arcem noscitur optinere, declinaui in domum eius. Ibi nobis presentabatur puerulus,*b* necdum fandi potens, filius uidelicet eiusdem fratris nostri. Hic similibus per omnia nobis applaudebat motibus ; ita ut dimissus a nutrice et super lectum nostrum expositus,*c* inter gaudia que ducebat etiam cachinnari quodam modo super uires nature cerneretur.' Et hec quidem episcopus.

Ceterum uidetur recte considerantibus pie credendum in hiis paruulorum exhibitis supra rationis ordinem plausibus et gaudiis, non modo presentem uiri sancti admirandam gratiam, et eorum innocentiam piam mirabili diuinitatis nutu fuisse commendatam, set etiam futuram eorum innocentium *d* alicuius meriti prerogatiuam esse demonstratam. Quod de uno quidem illorum iam presentia nobisque certius agnita uirtutum illius studia hodieque *e* testantur. De altero *f* etsi nichil postmodum innotuerit nobis, bona tamen et tantis auspiciis non deteriora speramus, fauente qua per tantum pontificem illustrari plenius et confirmari meruit gratia Spiritus Sancti. Oblatus autem fuit *g* in aula que habetur in castello insigni de Niwerch, et est quidem iuris *h* ecclesie Lincolniensis set diocesis

---

a tale uisum Xc   *b* paruulus X
c appositus X   *d* eorumdem innocentiam Xc
e hodie Xc   *f* secundo X
g + ei infantulus quem ei adiocari conspeximus X
h iurisdictionis X

When finally he was taken away, the company expressed surprise at such an unusual spectacle, and declared that they had never seen such a tiny being express such immense joy. The bishop described how he had once seen the same thing before. ' Some time ago,' he said, ' when I was prior of Witham, I went to Chartreuse for the general chapter. As the castle of Avalon which belongs to my brother William [1] lay on my route, as you know, I stopped with him, and was presented to his son. The little boy could not yet speak, but showed his delight at seeing me by exactly the same gestures. When his nurse left him lying on my bed, he was observed to show his pleasure by chuckling in a way which seemed quite amazing for his age.' These were the bishop's very words.

Those who ponder over this carefully must believe that the divine purpose was not merely through the exceptional delight and joy manifested by these children to testify in a marvellous way to the wonderful holiness of the saint and their angelic innocence, but also to show that those innocents possessed the advantage of some special merits. One of these children is still with us, and I know him well and can vouch for his unusual goodness. I never heard anything more about the other, but such auspices lead me to hope that he is equally good, through the grace of the Holy Spirit, whose light and consolation he received from so holy a bishop. He was brought to him in the hall of the fine castle at Newark, which belongs to the church of Lincoln, although in the diocese

---

[1] For St Hugh's brother William see *below* II, pp. 17, 164, 171. Another William of Avalon, probably a relative of St Hugh, was a canon of Lincoln from *c.* 1193 ; he gave four books to the Chapter library.

Eboracensis.[1]   Oriundus uero a uicino fuit uico, ultra
flumen quod Trenta nuncupatur, de genere plebeio.

Et ista quidem paulo de hiis latius prosecuti sumus,
non solum quia lectori non penitus ingrata ea fore
credebamus, set etiam ut qualem se ad omnem uir
piissimus exhibuerit [a] etatem hominum summatim doce-
remus.   Quatinus sicut per etatum momenta ab ipsis
pene cunabulis usque ad annos iam canescentis etatis,
adiuuante Domino, ipsius gradatim prouectus moresque
uel actus explicare curauimus, ita consequenter etiam,
uti [b] singulas ipse in aliis tractauerit etates, seriatim
panderemus.   Sciendum igitur quia ipsos qui adhuc
paruuli ab eo indulgentius tractari solebant, mox ut
intelligibiles [c] annos cepissent attingere, a sua, ne forte in-
solescerent, arcebat ulteriori illa familiaritate.   Ex ipsis
uero quosdam litteris imbuendos tradens, ecclesiastica
postmodum bene proficientibus contulit subsidia.

Verum de hiis licet adhuc plurima que non inutiliter
scriberentur suppetant, ob uitandum lectoris tedium hec
interim de hiis dixisse sufficiat ; ut prolixitatis fastidium
declinemus,[d] hec interim lectori sufficiant.   De uobis
enim, O Cadomensis Benedicte, O et Nouomensis
Roberte,[e] plura referre supersedemus ; quorum uterque
in puerili quondam etate omnium pene non tantum
puerorum, immo et uirorum stupor fuit.   Quorum
posterior, tempore etiam posteriori, apud Siluanectum a
Cantuariense [f] archiepiscopo Huberto aere comparatus
exiguo, in Angliam cum ipso perlatus a Galliis est, ut
Lincolniensi episcopo singulari dicendi facetia delicias
exhiberet.   Cui mox ut apud Lameheiam de nauicula

---

[a] exhibuit X
[b] + quemadmodum X
[c] intelligentie X
[d] ut *and* declinemus; *om* B
[e] De duobus uero aliis, Cadomensi Benedicto et Nouomensi Roberto X
[f] Cantuariensi X

of York.[1] He was born of humble stock in the neighbourhood, on the other side of the river Trent.

I do not think my readers will be displeased that I
have dealt rather fully with this matter, since I wish to
inform them briefly about the impression made by the
saint on people of all ages. With God's help we have
taken pains to describe his progress, deeds and habits
at every stage in his life almost from the cradle to hoary
old age, and, as a corollary, ought to give descriptions
of his behaviour to other people of different ages. It
should however be known that as soon as they reached
the age of reason he kept the children he had treated
with such affection at a distance in order that they should
not become too forward. Some of them he educated,
and afterwards gave ecclesiastical preferment to those
who showed promise.

Although much might still be written with profit on
this subject, I will now leave it alone for fear of wearying
my readers. If I am to avoid giving offence by too long a
narrative, the reader must be content with this. I will
refrain from saying very much about Benedict of Caen
or Robert of Noyon, both of whom in their boyhood were
prodigies, not only in comparison with other boys but
even in comparison with men. The latter was bought
at a later date for a small sum by Hubert, archbishop of
Canterbury, at Senlis and came with him from France
to England, to delight the bishop of Lincoln by his
unusually witty remarks. When accompanied by the
Canterbury clerks Hugh met him at Lambeth, where

---

[1] The Soke of Newark, where bishop Alexander had built a castle and
where there was a hospital for lepers whom St Hugh tended (cf. Giraldus
VII, 107-8), was a jurisdictional peculiar of the bishops of Lincoln.

ad salutandum archipresulem descendenti[a] clericis comitatus Cantuariensibus occurrit, tamquam proprium
reperisset genitorem, neglecto archiepiscopo, letissimus
adhesit. Annorum uero quinque uidebatur esse aut
paululum maioris etatis. Hunc post aliquanti temporis
spatium   apud   Alnestoam   litteris   commendauit
informandum.[1]

Benedictum, si memoria non fallit, apud Cadomum
prius ipse inuenit, secumque diutius quousque scilicet
secundam attigisset etatem retentum scholisque tempore
demum congruo deputatum, beneficio etiam perpetui
redditus temporis processu donauit. Hunc ipsum Benedictum in torrentem quodam casu rapidissimum, ab
equo domini Rogeri tunc Leircestrensis archidiaconi
nunc autem Lincolniensis decani, cum quo simul
equitabat delapsum, non minori Dominus miraculo per
merita Hugonis conseruauit indempnem quam olim
eripuerat Placidum puerum magni optentu Benedicti
per discipulum eius Maurum in fluctibus ambulantem.[2]
Nam et hunc deorsum per integrum fere stadium fluctus
detulerat, sicut illum per unius fere sagitte iactum intror-
sum unda rapuerat. Verum euentus ipsius ordinem
eidem qui iam in studiis floret, aut eorum cuilibet qui
interfuerunt, plenius exponendum relinquimus, quia ad
alia explicanda festinamus.[b]

[a] discedenti B
[b] X *insert a 15th chapter about St Hugh's miracles during his life taken from the* Canonization *report.*

he had got off the wherry to greet the archbishop, the boy promptly deserted the latter and attached himself to the bishop as joyfully as if he had been restored to his father. He seemed to be about five or a little older. After a little while Hugh sent him to Elstow for his education.[1]

Benedict, if I remember rightly, he found for the first time at Caen, and kept him for a longer time until he was a youth. When he was old enough he sent him to the schools and eventually gave him a benefice as a permanent provision. This Benedict once had the misfortune to fall off the horse of lord Roger, then archdeacon of Leicester and now dean of Lincoln, with whom he was riding pillion, into a river in flood. Through the merits of blessed Hugh, God preserved him just as miraculously as he formerly saved the boy Placidus at the prayer of the great St Benedict, by means of his disciple Maurus, who walked upon the waters.[2] Benedict was carried for almost a mile down stream, just as the waters snatched away Placidus to the distance of an arrow's flight. He is now doing well at his studies, so I shall leave the incident to be described better by him or anyone else who was present, and at once resume my narrative.

[1] Medieval bishops generally forbade nuns to teach boys and girls. This action of St Hugh was unusual for his time.
[2] cf. St Gregory, *Dialogorum liber II*, c. 7 (P.L. 66, 146).

The Diocese of Lincoln

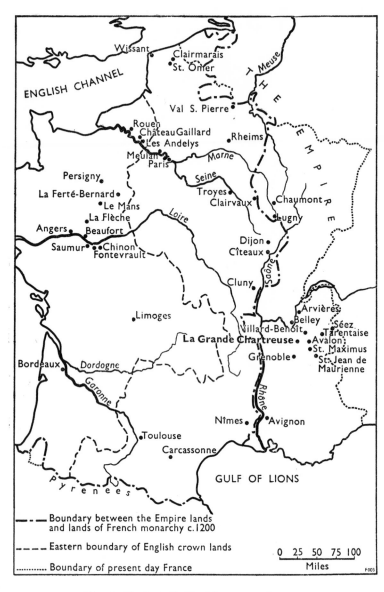

Map to illustrate St Hugh's overseas journey